Profane Angel

ALSO BY JERRY VERMILYE
AND FROM MCFARLAND

Buster Crabbe: A Biofilmography (2008; paperback 2014)
Ingmar Bergman: His Life and Films (2002; paperback 2006)

Profane Angel

The Life and Career of Carole Lombard

JERRY VERMILYE

McFarland & Company, Inc., Publishers
Jefferson, North Carolina

LIBRARY OF CONGRESS CATALOGUING-IN-PUBLICATION DATA

Names: Vermilye, Jerry, author.
Title: Profane angel : the life and career of Carole Lombard / Jerry Vermilye.
Description: Jefferson, North Carolina : McFarland & Company, Inc., Publishers, 2024 | Includes bibliographical references, filmography, and index.
Identifiers: LCCN 2023042896 | ISBN 9781476662671 (paperback : acid free paper) ∞
ISBN 9781476651606 (ebook)
Subjects: LCSH: Lombard, Carole, 1908-1942. | Motion picture actors and actresses—United States Biography. | Motion pictures—United States—History—20th century.
Classification: LCC PN2287.L625 V47 2023 | DDC 791.4302/809273 [B]—dc23/eng/20231002
LC record available at https://lccn.loc.gov/2023042896

BRITISH LIBRARY CATALOGUING DATA ARE AVAILABLE

ISBN (print) 978-1-4766-6267-1
ISBN (ebook) 978-1-4766-5160-6

© 2024 Jerry Vermilye. All rights reserved

No part of this book may be reproduced or transmitted in any form or by any means, electronic or mechanical, including photocopying or recording, or by any information storage and retrieval system, without permission in writing from the publisher.

Front cover: Publicity photograph of Carole Lombard, 1936 (author's collection)

Printed in the United States of America

*McFarland & Company, Inc., Publishers
Box 611, Jefferson, North Carolina 28640
www.mcfarlandpub.com*

To Jeffrey Carrier
For all his help

I was fond of Carole—it was impossible not to like her—but she used to love to shock me by using language that no nice girl should use, and every time she did, I would react just as she knew I would. I think she often threw in a four-letter word just to see the expression on my face.
—Patsy Ruth Miller in 1988

Table of Contents

Preface 1
The Biography 3

THE FILMS
(in Order of Release)

A Perfect Crime	69	Me, Gangster	84
Gold Heels	70	Show Folks	85
Dick Turpin	70	Hubby's Weekend Trip	86
Gold and the Girl	71	The Campus Carmen	86
Marriage in Transit	71	Ned McCobb's Daughter	87
Hearts and Spurs	72	Matchmaking Mamas	87
Durand of the Badlands	73	High Voltage	88
The Road to Glory	73	Don't Get Jealous	89
The Johnstown Flood	74	Big News	89
The Fighting Eagle	74	The Racketeer	91
Smith's Pony	75	Dynamite	91
A Gold Digger of Weepah	75	The Arizona Kid	92
The Girl from Everywhere	76	Safety in Numbers	94
Run, Girl, Run	77	Fast and Loose	94
The Beach Club	77	It Pays to Advertise	96
Smith's Army Life	77	Man of the World	97
The Best Man	78	Ladies' Man	99
The Swim Princess	78	Up Pops the Devil	100
The Bicycle Flirt	79	I Take This Woman	101
Half a Bride	79	The House That Shadows Built	103
The Divine Sinner	80	No One Man	103
The Girl from Nowhere	81	Sinners in the Sun	104
His Unlucky Night	82	Virtue	106
Smith's Restaurant	82	No More Orchids	108
Power	83	No Man of Her Own	109
The Campus Vamp	83	From Hell to Heaven	111
Motorboat Mamas	84		

Table of Contents

Supernatural	112	*The Princess Comes Across*	137
The Eagle and the Hawk	114	*My Man Godfrey*	139
Brief Moment	116	*Swing High, Swing Low*	141
White Woman	117	*Nothing Sacred*	144
Bolero	119	*True Confession*	146
We're Not Dressing	122	*Fools for Scandal*	148
Twentieth Century	123	*Made for Each Other*	150
Now and Forever	126	*In Name Only*	152
Lady by Choice	128	*Vigil in the Night*	154
The Gay Bride	130	*They Knew What*	
Rumba	131	*They Wanted*	156
Hands Across the Table	133	*Mr. & Mrs. Smith*	159
Love Before Breakfast	135	*To Be or Not to Be*	161

Carole Lombard on Radio 165

Bibliography 167

Index 169

Preface

Some seventy-odd years after the premature death of Carole Lombard, a mention of her name is inclined to draw the response, "Wasn't she married to Clark Gable?" Well, yes, but not before having lived some 30 years, co-starring with him in a film and appearing in 78 motion pictures of her own.

In the 21st century, via Turner Classic Movies, DVDs, Blu-rays and streaming services, most of Lombard's best work is preserved for the pleasure and edification of current and future generations interested in the history of classic cinema. Thus, it's possible that such inspired comedies as *Twentieth Century*, *My Man Godfrey* and *Nothing Sacred* will remain familiar, along with the more serious but equally worthwhile films *In Name Only*, *Vigil in the Night* and *Made for Each Other*. And then, in a class by itself, is her last and perhaps best film, the celebrated anti–Nazi satire *To Be or Not to Be*.

Some sources label Carole Lombard a screwball comedienne, and that's doing her an injustice. A closer study of the many available titles from her considerable *oeuvre* reveals this undeniably glamorous beauty to have also been a top-notch actress, proficient in all genres.

As famed in her day for her salty tongue as for her talent for zany humor, Lombard discovered that she faced an uphill battle when her fans declined to embrace their favorite screwball in anything but comedy. This image was undeniably intensified by her off-screen persona, fostered by the movie magazines and newspaper press, as an irrepressible madcap who loved practical jokes and held legendary Hollywood parties. Her late-career dramatic efforts, which she hoped might qualify her for an Academy Award, were ironically offset by the fact that her one and only nomination was for the landmark comedy *My Man Godfrey* in 1937.

And finally, of course, there was her indelible image as the third and best-remembered of movie "king" Clark Gable's five wives. To the public, theirs was an apparently idyllic union, tragically cut short by a

Preface

shocking airplane crash. At the age of 33, Lombard had already made 78 motion pictures—a lifetime's output in the filmography of many another movie star.

In the wake of her passing, a bereft Gable spent his final years seeking to replace her, a hopeless quest, for Carole Lombard was one of a kind.

The Biography

On October 6, 1908, Jane Alice Peters (the future Carole Lombard) arrived to increase the population of Fort Wayne, Indiana's second largest city. The third and last child born to Frederic Peters and Elizabeth ("Bess") Knight Peters, she joined brothers Frederic Jr., known as Fritz (born 1902), and Stuart (born 1906) in a comfortable, upper-middle-class household on Rockhill Street. Outwardly, the Peters family gave off the appearance of being happy and well-adjusted. But, prior to his marriage, Frederic been injured in an elevator accident that left him with a limp as well as irregular headaches of increasing severity. In an era when some disorders of the brain were a mystery to medical science, these "spells" bred tension and uncertainty among his wife and sons. Baby Jane Alice only knew that she adored her father.

As a little girl, she was very much a tomboy. Her best friends were her brothers, who were not only fiercely protective but also allowed her to join in their games. She enjoyed Saturday lessons at Trier's Dancing Academy as well as weekly visits to the Gaiety and Colonial movie theaters in downtown Fort Wayne, where she thrilled to the celluloid adventures of serial queens Pearl White and Kathlyn Williams. By the age of six, Jane knew that, like them, she wanted to be a movie star.

While Bess Peters made sure that little Jane maintained her feminine side with pretty dresses and hair ribbons, she made no effort to restrict her daughter's tomboyish participation in such male-oriented pursuits as boxing and baseball. Oddly enough, the child entered kindergarten with reserve, well-liked yet never mingling with the other girls.

In the autumn of 1914, after Jane began first grade, a big decision was made by Grandmother Knight, a widow with considerable means. She would sponsor an extended "vacation" for Bess and her three offspring, with the suggestion of destinations as exotic as Paris and London. Finally, it was decided that they would go to California, a state where some of their Hoosier friends had already relocated. Frederic

The Biography

Peters sanctioned this vacation-from-marriage, and there was no indication that his foursome might not return to Fort Wayne. All the Peters children knew at the time was that they would miss a school semester.

Their journey began with a four-day train trip to San Francisco, where the damp climate only worsened a head cold Jane Alice had contracted in Indiana. Then they proceeded to Los Angeles, where they were welcomed by the Charles Pigeon family. Old friends from Fort Wayne, the Pigeons had found the Southern California climate more congenial than the Midwest.

The first of several Los Angeles addresses for the Peterses was a two-bedroom apartment at 1435 Hoover Street. While Bess surveyed the job market for herself, Jane entered the first grade at Hoover Elementary School, and Stuart began third grade. Fritz settled into junior high. Bess briefly considered seeking employment in the motion picture industry, while remaining wary of its possibly negative influence on her children. Finally, she decided on remaining a homemaker for the time being, concentrating on her family. There was continued cross-country financial support from both Grandmother Knight and Frederic Peters, who maintained a regular correspondence during the separation.

The Peters children made the adjustment to their new environment, and Jane Alice did well enough in school. Pastime activities no longer included dancing lessons, but moviegoing continued to absorb all three children, with the inevitable acting-out of what they had earlier witnessed on-screen.

With the family's move to South Catalina Street in 1916, Jane now attended Cahuenga Elementary School. Many of the students there had parents working in the motion picture industry. In the absence of her father, Jane drew ever closer to Bess, who'd always remain her best friend. On the rare occasion of Fred's visits to Los Angeles, he bonded with his wife and children, and yet there was no indication of a permanent reunion, either in Fort Wayne or Los Angeles. He would always return to Indiana as scheduled, with no disruption of their unconventional marital arrangement. Neither spouse appeared to seek or require alternate romantic fulfillments.

Bess much enjoyed the Southern California lifestyle, developing a social network that thrived on dinner parties and an ever-growing circle of friends that included the Wises, the Lombards and the Platts. Through Mrs. Platt, Bess became intrigued by the "science" of numerology and developed an interest in the Bahá'í faith, which appealed to her indifference to organized religion. She was especially captivated by the idea of complete equality for men and women, an influential element in young Jane's upbringing.

With her blue eyes, blonde hair and perfect features, Jane Alice Peters had long been considered a beautiful child among Bess' circle of acquaintances. And more than one of her mother's friends urged Bess to consider trying to get Jane into the movies. Of course, it was an idea that had originally entered the child's impressionable mind back in Fort Wayne. But Bess had her reservations, based not only on the suspect morals of the industry, but also on her knowledge of the overwhelming number of girls and young woman attempting to break into motion pictures.

By 1918, young Jane had voiced her ambition to be a film star like her current favorites Mary Miles Minter and Constance Talmadge. Bess gave no serious thought to child exploitation. She had heard all about the negative aspects of stage mothers and movie mamas, and had no wish to join their ranks. However, dramatic training seemed like an advisable step. After a careful survey of the field, she enrolled Jane in the Miriam Nolkes Dramatic School for Girls.

For the next three years, Jane faithfully maintained a schedule of once-a-week classes at Mrs. Nolkes' school, where she learned all about body movement, vocal technique and the sort of demonstrative overacting characteristic of that era. Among her fellow students was the year-younger Betty Jane Young, then a close friend, who later gained a measure of fame as Sally Blane at about the same time that Jane became Carol (no -e yet) Lombard. Betty Jane's older sibling found lesser fame as Polly Ann Young; both were far surpassed by their kid sister Gretchen, destined for major film stardom as Loretta Young.

The adult Carole Lombard later recalled the "fun" experience of Mrs. Nolkes' academy, especially when the

Jane Alice Peters (the future Carole Lombard), circa 1919.

The Biography

opportunity arose to play male roles in wigs and mustaches. Although her comely appearance made young Jane a natural for princess roles, just being pretty could be boring. She much preferred the character challenges of male attire. In an all-girl school, someone had to take the boys' parts, so why not her?

During this period, the Peterses moved to Harvard Boulevard between Sixth and Wilshire, and then to the Bryson Apartments at Wilshire and Rampart. Because of these moves, Jane switched elementary schools several times, thus inhibiting her from establishing long-lasting alliances with other youngsters. At the same time, she drew closer to her brothers, especially Stuart, who was only two years older. The six-year age difference between Jane and Fritz now made him seem like an adult to the girl, especially when he quit school to help support the family.

Jane's young dream of being in the movies was realized by chance in the spring of 1921, when she was 12, and not because of her preadolescent beauty. As film director Allan Dwan described it to interviewer Peter Bogdanovich decades later:

> I saw a kid playing baseball on the street with some other kids. She was a cute-looking tomboy … a hoyden, out there knocking hell out of the other kids, playing better baseball than they were. And I needed someone of her type for this picture. She'd never acted, so we talked to her parents and they let her do it, and she was very good. Her name was Jane Peters, and she later changed it to Carole Lombard.

Dwan was already an established director, best known for his association with the athletic star Douglas Fairbanks, with whom he was then preparing the spectacular *Robin Hood* (1922). But first he would complete a less important assignment for Associated Producers, a standard melodrama called *A Perfect Crime*. In it, young Jane (unbilled) enjoyed two days of employment, portraying the little sister of its star, Monte Blue. The picture received limited distribution by the disinterested Fox Film Corp. in the summer of 1921, then was forgotten. Dwan was complimentary toward working with the girl, and intimated that there might be a somewhat larger role for her in his upcoming picture *A Broken Doll*. Instead, he cast another juvenile actress, affording Jane the first of many disappointments attendant on a professional movie career. Even more disappointed than her daughter, Bess Peters was thus inspired to reverse her previous aversion to movie mamas and become one herself, shepherding Jane on a succession of interviews that proved fruitless. The girl had enjoyed her initial filming experience, and had photographed well in *A Perfect Crime*. Filmmaking agreed with her, but her time had not yet come.

By the time she was 14, Jane and her family had moved again, this time to a roomy house on South Manhattan Street. Financial backing still came from Fort Wayne, but Bess now supplemented her income in small ways as a numerology counselor. More importantly, Fritz now helped support them with his salary from Bullock's, Southern California's most prestigious chain of department stores. Having started working with them on the lowest rung of the ladder, he was now well on his way to what would eventually become a 50-year association with Bullock's.

With her entry into the seventh grade at Virgil Junior High, Jane appeared to have outgrown her tomboy phase. Whereas her feminine grooming had previously been Bess' concern, now Jane took full charge of her new focus on makeup, hair styling and attire that might qualify her as a "flapper." While her female classmates seemed totally focused on boys, Jane found other pursuits of interest, including tennis, as taught to her by a Swedish-born seventh grader named Carol Peterson. She also found a new friend in Sally Eilers, one year her senior and already considered the school's best actress in their stage productions.

Jane's most lasting girl-to-girl friendship was with a Virgil student named Dixie Pantages. Originally, the two had enjoyed a preadolescent relationship when the Peters family lived at the Bryson Apartments and Dixie bore the surname of Nelson. But her mother had died, and the girls lost touch when Dixie was formally adopted by the wealthy Pantages family, of movie palace fame. Now, with their friendship renewed, Jane found herself traveling in a headier Jazz Age smart set, surrounded by affluent and attentive young people. As a teenaged beauty, Jane was readily accepted, yet she was able to maintain a certain inaccessibility, supported by the intimidating presence of two protective brothers. As Fritz Peters later described it to Lombard biographer Larry Swindell:

> Stuart and I couldn't trust ourselves with girls, so we weren't about to trust other boys with our sister. They were always around, like a swarm of hornets, but they just couldn't get anywhere. And she liked it that way—liked the attention, but wasn't boy crazy at all. Maybe living with Stuart and me sort of immunized her against falling for a boy, at least for a while.

Jane was eventually courted by Jack Hearst, scion of newspaper tycoon William Randolph Hearst, and Bill Ince, whose father was pioneer filmmaker Thomas Ince.

In school plays, she competed unsuccessfully with Sally Eilers for

The Biography

the female leads, and settled for character parts. More successful at athletics, she excelled at tennis and at a variety of track events. In the spring of 1924, Jane's striking looks made her the school's Queen of the May, which brought her to the attention of famed comedian Charlie Chaplin's general manager, Alfred Reeves. Reeves consulted with Bess Peters before setting up an interview for Jane with Chaplin, then seeking a leading lady for his upcoming vehicle *The Gold Rush*. Bess was warned about the newlywed Chaplin's reputed attraction to pretty young girls, and accompanied Jane to the appointment. The result was a screen test that produced no immediate results, although the Great Man was reported to have scrawled "too pretty" on a Jane Peters comment card. But her test was apparently seen by other industry executives, including J. Stuart Blackton of the venerable, but now-struggling Vitagraph Company. No contract ever evolved from their meetings, and yet Blackton's suggestion that "Jane" was too common a name inspired her to come up with "Carol," after her former schoolmate Carol Peterson. Jane now became "Carol Peters" to her friends, as well as at future auditions.

A growing circle of acquaintances with movie industry affiliations had by now made of Bess a virtual agent for her beautiful daughter, and so a casting call tip resulted in Jane-Carol styling her blonde hair in pigtails to apply for a child-extra bit in Mary Pickford's *Little Annie Rooney* at United Artists. It was a part she almost had—until Pickford got a look at the newcomer and decided Carol was too much competition for "America's Sweetheart." Perhaps as a measure of compensation, UA's Al Lichtman introduced Bess to the influential movie columnist Louella Parsons, who took an immediate interest in this beautiful teen who had been rejected by such Hollywood giants as Chaplin and Pickford. In years to come, Louella would take credit for "discovering" the girl.

Parsons arranged a meeting between Fox Films' production chief Winfield Sheehan and the Peterses. No pushover for talent-challenged young hopefuls, Sheehan was unexpectedly and utterly charmed to the extent that he offered to sign Carol to a Fox contract without so much as a screen test. Under their agreement, she would be paid $65 a week for the term of a year. Should Fox be pleased with her work, the contract might be extended to as much as five years. To the 16-year-old, this seemed like an excellent arrangement. As far as her schooling was concerned, Bess had agreed that her daughter might abandon classes, once she secured a position in the film industry.

There were objections to her surname. Family derivatives were considered, and "Carol Knight" was briefly selected, until Bess came up with "Lombard," after her old friends Harry and Etta Lombard. "Carol Lombard" appealed to Sheehan, and its newly dubbed recipient began practicing her new autograph.

Immediately, after signing her Fox contract in October 1924, Lombard was assigned to an unbilled one-scene bit in the minor-league Western *Gold and the Girl*, starring fellow Hoosier Buck Jones. Her second Fox picture was even less fortuitous: She enjoyed *Dick Turpin*'s eighteenth-century costuming, but all of her limited footage from that Tom Mix vehicle landed on the cutting room floor.

Despite her moviemaking activities, Carol found time to maintain friendships with her former classmates at Fairfax High, especially those as skilled at dancing as George Rosenberg and Tommy Lee. The Jazz Age was now in full swing, and everyone was performing the energetic Charleston. On Friday nights, the mandatory venue for Lombard and her fashionable friends was the Cocoanut Grove, a night spot located in the new Ambassador Hotel, with its virtual jungle of palm trees and live monkeys. When partnered with Lee, Lombard frequently won the Grove's Charleston contests. Then competition arrived in the form of Metro-Goldwyn-Mayer starlet Joan Crawford. From a later perspective, Lombard reflected:

> Joan had great body tension. She was better than I, but she seemed to be working at it, and for me it was all play. It was a thrill to beat her, and she liked to beat me, too. But that wasn't the big thing with her. She didn't just want to get a start in pictures, she kept talking about reaching the very top. She wouldn't be satisfied until she was a real star, and that didn't worry me. I never thought about it.

Among Lombard's flapper friends were future movie players Helen Twelvetrees, Dorothy Sebastian and Loretta Young's older sisters Sally and Polly Ann. Interviewed in later years, Dixie Pantages recalled the remarkable sexual innocence of Lombard and her crowd, especially in an era that scarcely catered to such outmoded behavior.

Winfield Sheehan now recommended Lombard as possible ingenue for *Lightnin'*, a major Fox production and the latest assignment for that studio's up-and-coming young director Jack (later "John") Ford. But Carol wasn't cast. Ford later reflected on the reasons why:

> She was a remarkably unaffected girl, very bright, and rather obviously virginal. All of these qualities were appropriate to the needs of my picture, but I saw that the poor child was frightened by the other actors. Now *Lightnin'* was basically a piece for character actors, and my principal players had been in pictures as long as there had *been* pictures, and with stage experience before

The Biography

that—people like Jay Hunt and Otis Harlan and Edythe Chapman. Well, Carol was afraid she couldn't hold her own in such company, and when I saw that it really bothered her, I told Sheehan it might be a better idea to put her in with less experienced people, perhaps more nearly her own age.

Lombard was inappropriately miscast as a mature woman in the domestic comedy-drama *Marriage in Transit*. Her thirtysomething leading man, Edmund Lowe, was sufficiently stage-trained and self-centered to effectively upstage 17-year-old Lombard's every scene, thus rendering her most promising screen appearance to date negligible. With her hair slightly darkened, studio makeup artists and costumers worked hard to bridge the two actors' age gap, but to little avail. The movie's critics were impressed with her physical appearance, if not her performance. Sheehan reasoned that she wasn't yet ready for leading parts. In the meantime, Lombard willingly posed for studio publicity stills, cheesecake photos and test shots.

Relegated once more to Westerns, she was cast opposite Buck Jones in *Hearts and Spurs* (1925) and, in a secondary role, in his subsequent programmer, *Durand of the Badlands* (1925). While such ineffectual casting might have discouraged an ambitious Crawford, Lombard didn't mind. For one thing, her Fox contract was extended to five years, with her weekly salary raised to $75. And she was popular among her fellow players and technicians. For the moment, she was enjoying life, and her career held promise.

Lombard's legendary reputation as an uninhibited potty-mouth stems from this period. Bess Peters had given her daughter a level head and the ability to handle challenging situations involving the opposite sex. While not appearing prudish, Lombard had nevertheless maintained her virtue. And her several years at the studios had given her the confidence to deal with offensive male behavior. But as she had to fend off the increasing passes and flirtations of her male co-workers, she sought help from her brothers, who knew all the era's so-called "bad language," while refraining from using it around either Carol or Bess. As Fred Peters recalled to Lombard biographer Larry Swindell:

> She said she wanted us to teach her all the dirty words we knew, when to say them and what they meant. She'd hit on the idea of discouraging her would-be seducers by swearing at them. She memorized all the terms and our definitions like she was studying for a test. And, from then on, if some guy made a pass at her or tried to, he'd hear such talk as he just wouldn't expect to come from such a beautiful girl, who was also a nice girl in every way. And she had the style to carry it off.

The Biography

As Lombard once stated: "If you're a young blonde around this man's town, you have to keep the wolf pack off somehow. If you know all those words, they figure you know your way around and they don't act quite so tough. It's better than having a blacksnake whip in your hand."

Lombard posed for studio portraits, modeled bathing suits and was pictured in fan magazines, alongside articles of sometimes questionable verity. She went on arranged dates with Fox's younger male contract players and was photographed at supermarket openings and football games. She also tested for, or was announced for, several pictures she never made. In short, she was being given the standard public exposure by a Hollywood studio sanguine about her future. This sort of publicity also brought her comely face and figure to the attention of executives at rival studios.

When the notorious 44-year-old womanizer John Barrymore summoned her to discuss the female lead in his independent romantic drama of the Russian Revolution, *The Tempest*, she did so with Sheehan's blessing. And although Bess no longer accompanied her daughter to such auditions, Lombard's private "schooling" was sufficient to deal with situations like this: "My mother believed that, in any civilized meeting between a man and woman, there was no such thing as seduction. The woman, she said, was the one who controlled the events." And control them Lombard did. Her meeting with Barrymore led to a screen test and the announcement that Fox would loan her out for the role. But problems over financing the costly production delayed its start. Instead she went on to a supporting part in *The Road to Glory*, the directorial debut of Howard Hawks, and then she was scheduled to appear in director Frank Borzage's romantic comedy *Early to Wed*.

Lombard's plans for the immediate future were suddenly derailed in October 1925 by an accident that nearly ended the 17-year-old's promising film career. Driving back from a basketball game in her wealthy buddy Harry Cooper's Bugatti roadster, they were involved in a minor collision that shattered the windshield and left a sliver of glass in Lombard's left cheek. The attending doctor warned her that employing an anesthetic would relax the facial muscles and might result in serious disfigurement.

Bess took charge of the crisis, locating a specialist who understood the importance of salvaging a pretty starlet's physical appearance. Lombard submitted to 18 stitches, followed by plastic surgery, all without the comfort of a painkiller. It took her surgeon four hours to perform, while leaving her no assurance of facial dexterity in the future. In the meantime, she was instructed to keep her head as motionless as possible for ten days while ingesting only liquid nourishment through a straw.

Her recovery took time and left her with a slight but undeniably visible facial scar that could easily be hidden with makeup. Fox paid her basic hospital bills, but not for the surgery. *Early to Wed* was filmed with Kathryn Perry replacing Lombard, and Dorothy Sebastian was announced to appear opposite Barrymore in *The Tempest*. (Further delays eventually led to *her* replacement by the German import Camilla Horn.) Lombard's brief appearance in several scenes of *The Johnstown Flood* may be attributed to script adjustments made in the wake of her accident. Worst of all, Fox suddenly canceled her contract without further compensations, their defense being that their agreement stipulated that she be held responsible for her physical being. In the wake of the accident, Fox executives had expressed concern for her future value to the studio.

The experience of her slow recovery made Lombard more introspective. Dixie Pantages reported that Lombard's response to her expression of sympathy was "Isn't it better to have a scar on your face than on your soul?"

For the remainder of 1926, Lombard faced no movie cameras. Instead, she returned to dancing at the Cocoanut Grove, albeit with an array of newcomers, for most of her old friends had graduated from high school and gone on to college elsewhere. For an artistic outlet, she joined an amateur Hollywood theater group called The Potboilers and took supporting parts in two of their productions. And she turned 18, which caused her to seriously consider her movieland prospects.

Among the Peters family's Hollywood circle was fellow Hoosier John Bowers, who had struggled for over a decade to become a leading man, if not a movie star. Bowers had long championed Lombard whenever the opportunity arose, and was able to set up an interview with producer Samuel Goldwyn, who asked why Fox had dropped her. She allowed that she might not have been what that studio wanted. This inspired Goldwyn to investigate further, leading to the conclusion that a facially scarred starlet, no matter how slight the blemish, was a waste of his time.

By now, Lombard's scar was barely noticeable, yet she had self-consciously adapted the partial solution of wearing her hair over her left cheek. Bowers suggested that she might consider changing her name and starting over, discarding her earlier credentials. It was an idea that she chose to reject, for she was already quite well-known about town, both socially and professionally.

The Biography

And then her luck changed. Former schoolmate Sally Eilers had found regular employment in the comedy shorts produced by Mack Sennett, and Sennett was seeking to add another pretty girl to his stable of "bathing beauties." Sennett was aware of Lombard's accident but harbored no misgivings since her figure was good and his close-ups were few. His two-reel situation farces were often improvised on location at California beaches, and the only question was whether Lombard could play comedy.

Sennett's vogue, which had enjoyed its greatest popularity with the Keystone Cops of an earlier film era, was by now on the wane, but he offered steady employment, and for Lombard, the work was great fun. At the weekly rate of $50, she willingly agreed to accept a beginner's position. Unfortunately, she tended to sunburn quickly, so was seen but briefly in her initial Sennett two-reelers. Until she acquired a filmable tan, she was assigned to studio-shot indoor pictures. In *Smith's Pony*, she played the wife of portly Billy Gilbert. Sennett shorts were customarily completed in a week, beginning on Mondays, so there was an incentive to get the work done by the end of Fridays.

For Lombard, the Sennett ensemble provided a valuable lesson in the art of comic timing and behavior, and she studiously watched, listened and absorbed. Especially helpful were the women of his troupe, including diminutive Daphne Pollard, sturdily built Dot Farley and hefty Madalynne Fields, whom Lombard dubbed "Fieldsie." She and "Fieldsie" forged a close and immediate friendship destined to last far beyond their Sennett years. While it was up to the likes of Vernon Dent, Billy Bevan and Andy Clyde to provide most of the laughs in these shorts, along with the distaff efforts of Pollard, Fields and Farley, Sennett enjoyed exploiting the eye-candy appeal of girls like Lombard, whether in bathing suits or in more stylish attire.

In the course of a year, Lombard enjoyed a pay raise to $500 a month and appeared in no less than 18 Sennett two-reelers. Several of them showcased scenes in the early Technicolor process; Lombard photographed as strikingly as she did in monochrome. She survived the pratfalls, the mud puddles and the custard pies in such titles as *A Gold Digger of Weepah*, *The Swim Princess*, *The Beach Club*, *The Bicycle Flirt* and *The Campus Vamp*.

In the spring of 1928, between Sennett assignments, Lombard accepted an offer from the Poverty Row company Rayart to play a secondary role in *The Divine Sinner*, a cheapie in which she got no help from its nominal director, Scott Pembroke, nor ever received full

The Biography

compensation for her efforts. Other than providing an item for her résumé, *The Divine Sinner* was a miserable experience. Its few Los Angeles engagements were brief, and Lombard advised her pals to avoid it.

Two years after the fact, Lombard's automobile accident was largely forgotten, although she continued to favor hair over her left cheek. She began to find occasional supporting roles, including a return to Fox for the crime drama *Me, Gangster*, in which she had an effective scene as a heavily made-up tramp named Blonde Rosie. There were other brief, freelance jobs, including at Paramount, where she enjoyed a scene with Gary Cooper in *Half a Bride* that was cut from the movie before its release.

An inside source informed Lombard that Mack Sennett's arrangement with his distributor Pathé was about to terminate. In the meantime, Sennett agreed to loan her to Pathé, which was now under the jurisdiction of ambitious Joseph P. Kennedy, as he saw fit. In *Power*, she and a novice blonde Joan Bennett were simply billed as "Dames," and

Lombard (left) with Eddie Quillen and Bessie Barriscale in *Show Folks*.

The Biography

they got to shake their stuff in a dance sequence. Far more rewarding was Lombard's assignment in the comedy-drama *Show Folks*, in which she was given third billing after Eddie Quillan and Lina Basquette. Its newly imported German director, Paul Stein, admired the blonde starlet and she was shown to advantage as the female heavy. Like all of Lombard's previous films, this was a silent, although *Show Folks* offered songs, synchronized sound effects and a short talking sequence. Interviewed in the mid–1970s, Quillan shared warm memories of Lombard, especially her popularity with the production crew.

In Hollywood, word was out that Pathé was in trouble and that Kennedy was working to turn things around with the addition of "new faces." With that in mind, Lombard secured a meeting in which she and the movie mogul dealt forthrightly with one another. He admitted that he was impressed with her work in *Show Folks* but told her that she should lose 20 pounds (Sennett had encouraged her to *gain* weight for his two-reelers). Also, Kennedy wondered, could she talk for talking pictures? Her cool response: "What do *you* think? Am I talking to you now?" She also let him know of her ambition to play leading roles. The result was a contract, signed on her twentieth birthday, making Lombard a featured Pathé player at the salary of $400 a week. What she didn't know until later was that her Pathé contract could revert to Mack Sennett without her consent.

Ned McCobb's Daughter, the last of her 1928 features, had the disadvantage of being a silent when talkies were the new rage. Lombard got some critical notice as a waitress pursued by a bootlegger (George Barraud) who tempts her with ill-gotten jewelry. The film was based on Sidney Howard's popular stage play, but because it was a silent, it received scant notice.

A Lombard glamour portrait from 1928.

The Biography

Warner Brothers had initiated talking pictures with 1927's Al Jolson vehicle *The Jazz Singer*, which boasted his singing and also dialogue sequences. That studio had also pioneered with the July 1928 release of Hollywood's first all-talkie, the incompetent melodrama *Lights of New York*. Movieland's other studios quickly began to follow, beginning with Fox and Paramount. Eventually, Pathé conceded as well.

With the sound revolution, the studios had to find writers who could turn out dialogue (and not merely intertitles) and actors with acceptable voices. Many a silent star's career crashed because of a badly pitched voice or one that resonated with inappropriate regional accents. Every studio now made vocal tests of their star players, striking fear into the hearts of one and all. Actors with stage backgrounds were favored, and there was a sudden influx of Broadway actors whose cultivated tones impressed Hollywood hotshots.

At Pathé, it was decided that contract players lacking theatrical experience would be let go, but then the company's new stage-trained director Edward H. Griffith came up with a better solution. Each of the dozen-odd young people in question would be given a talkie screen test that he would direct, using dialogue from Philip Barry's play *Paris Bound*—Griffith's next picture.

Lombard memorized a scene and performed it with an intimidated juvenile hopelessly trying to disguise his rural sounds with a high-society accent. Aware that final decisions would be made by Joe Kennedy, she was not encouraged. But before she knew her fate with Pathé, she returned to Mack Sennett for a final pair of two-reelers: *Matchmaking Mamas*, a domestic farce that reunited her with old pal Sally Eilers, and *Don't Get Jealous*, her last silent.

And then came Kennedy's decision: Lombard and blonde Diane Ellis would remain on the Pathé roster. In Lombard's case, her speaking voice was considered ordinary but pleasant, and sufficient to qualify her for leading roles.

At Pathé, without any immediate acting assignments, Lombard posed for publicity photos and worked with Dan McElwaine, an old friend from her Fox days, to promote her image around town. As a result, interest in her services was expressed by such important people as MGM's Irving Thalberg and Cecil B. DeMille. Howard Hughes, who had already spent two years working on his airborne epic *Hell's Angels*, was seeking a new American leading lady to replace the Swedish-accented Greta Nissen (a victim of the sound revolution). A meeting with Lombard led to a screen test and, in short order, a romantic liaison with the tall, handsome, 23-year-old millionaire. According to some reports, he was her first love. This affair, carried out in characteristic Hughesian secrecy, lasted several months. It ended when he encountered 18-year-old Jean Harlow, whom he eventually cast in *Hell's Angels*.

Pathé cast her in her first talkie, *High Voltage*, along with fellow survivor Diane Ellis. This was a routine program melodrama about a small group of people stranded in a snowstorm, with Lombard arousing the interest of both William Boyd and Owen Moore. On the set, she found it necessary to dampen the ardor of both the aging Moore and director Howard Higgin by making use of her now-habitual blue vocabulary. The tactic worked most effectively: Her would-be seducers backed off.

A striking scene portrait from *High Voltage*.

The Biography

Cecil B. DeMille approached Joe Kennedy about borrowing Lombard for MGM's *Dynamite*, to star Conrad Nagel and Charles Bickford. Her supporting role would pair her romantically with young up-and-comer Joel McCrea. With Kennedy's blessing, she worked several days on *Dynamite* before DeMille fired her for not taking her part seriously. An autocrat on his movie sets, DeMille was put off by her flubbing of lines and nervously joking about it; he reprimanded her, "This isn't a Keystone comedy." For a time, she was devastated by the dismissal.

Pathé cast her in a pair of program melodramas, *Big News* and *The Racketeer*, both opposite Robert Armstrong. In the former, she was reunited with Gregory La Cava, the director of her excised scene in *Half a Bride*. This time she was the stylishly dressed leading lady, the neglected spouse of investigative reporter Armstrong.

As La Cava confided to his *Big News* cast at the start of production: "I've read the script and I think it stinks. And when something stinks, you try to do anything that will distract people from the smell. So let's be very distracting about this. And even if it isn't very exciting, you can pitch your voices a little higher and they'll *think* it's exciting."

Pleased with the Lombard-Armstrong teaming, Pathé paired them again in *The Racketeer*, directed by *High Voltage*'s Howard Higgin. She played a girl torn between love (Roland Drew) and obligation (Armstrong) amid a gangland setting. The results were negligible in all departments.

For a while, Lombard had the studio's promise of a more prestigious film, as the very blonde Ann Harding's sister in the film version of Philip Barry's Broadway comedy hit *Holiday*. Lombard even agreed to go dark-haired for contrast to its star. But then that role went to Mary Astor. Lombard was informed that, with the completion of her year's contract, Pathé would not be renewing her option or that of her friend Diane Ellis.

Lombard was told that tough economic times were behind the studio's belt-tightening. And yet something didn't quite jibe. Ellis came up with the actual rationale, and the dismissals began to make sense: Pathé was negotiating for the services of glamorous, stage-trained Constance Bennett, who couldn't brook the possible competition of two pretty and equally blonde contract players on the same lot.

By this time, Lombard was sufficiently established to find freelance employment until such time as a major Hollywood studio might consider her as a prospect for stardom, for it was stardom that she now wanted. Through old acquaintance Winfield Sheehan at Fox, she obtained the second female lead in an A-Western, 1930's *The Arizona Kid,* starring Warner Baxter and Mona Maris. As the movie's scheming villainess, Lombard enjoyed playing a part for which some critics thought her ill-suited. However, she did find a champion in the film's director, Alfred Santell, who believed that her dramatic possibilities had yet to be fully explored. He and Fox screenwriter S.N. Behrman, who were preparing to collaborate on a production of Jack London's *The Sea Wolf,* appealed to Sheehan to cast her as that grim sea adventure's unglamorous female lead. At a time when *The Arizona Kid* was still in production, Sheehan chose to defer any such casting decision and/or the possibility of a term contract. Before that could occur, Lombard had accepted an offer from Paramount.

Despite her unfortunate experience with that company's *Half a Bride,* she continued to entertain the possibility of securing an eventual Paramount contract. But first there was the fun of sporting a flashy and revealing wardrobe in support of Charles "Buddy" Rogers in the studio's breezy musical comedy *Safety in Numbers.* Cast as one of three party girls assigned to "educate" naïve young millionaire Rogers, Lombard failed to get her man (that distinction went to the movie's briefly starred leading lady, Kathryn Crawford), but she did bring intelligence to Marion Dix's smart dialogue. Director Victor Schertzinger took note of Lombard's dancing skills, and he favored her natural beauty with numerous close-ups. *Safety in Numbers* was devised to please the young fans of "America's boy friend" Rogers, and most publications found it pleasant entertainment. But Mordaunt Hall of *The New York Times* termed the picture "so ridiculous that consideration of its merits can only be given to some charming musical interludes that are skillfully woven into the film."

For the first time in her career Lombard attracted favorable commentary from the moviegoing public, with some of Rogers' fan mail even protesting that he didn't "get" the right girl (Lombard) at the film's finale.

Her winning personality and outgoing nature attracted important allies at Paramount, including studio boss B.P. Schulberg's general manager, Sam Jaffe (not to be confused with the well-known character actor). She had also won the notice of publicist Arch Reeve, casting director Fred Datig and especially Schulberg's not-yet-famous new assistant, David O. Selznick. Based on their collective recommendation, Lombard was elated to find herself starting the spring of 1930 with a seven-year Paramount contract that paid $375 a week, with the possibility of considerable raises at the time of option renewals. And there was a relaxed atmosphere of congeniality, both before and behind the camera, that she had not found at other studios.

Among Lombard's close friends at Paramount were directors Ernst Lubitsch and Rouben Mamoulian and screenwriters Donald Ogden Stewart and Preston Sturges. The latter made a successful play for her affections that came to an abrupt halt when she discovered him talking to others about their "relationship." Meanwhile, she dated a variety of young men (some of these dates arranged by Paramount's publicity department) while generally discouraging anything serious. She accepted gossip column items about her "romances" as part of the business. Nor did she object to the titillating disclosures that she slept in the nude and didn't wear a bra, explaining with disarming frankness, "Maybe I would if I had anything worth covering up."

Perhaps Lombard was not considered easy to cast, because it wasn't until after *Safety in Numbers* was previewed that she was assigned to *The Best People*, adapted from Avery Hopwood's stage play by Doris Anderson and Preston Sturges, who tailored the secondary role of showgirl Alice O'Neil especially for Lombard. Paramount had filmed the Hopwood work five years earlier as a silent, with Esther Ralston in the part now played by Lombard. In predictable fashion, wealthy parents disapprove when their two offspring pair with a chorus girl and a mechanic. Eventually, the older couple discovers that these outsiders have more to offer than their own children, resulting in a double wedding.

The fact that much of the picture was shot at Paramount's Astoria, New York, studio afforded Carol and Bess Peters the opportunity to sojourn in Fort Wayne for four days. In Indiana, Lombard got to visit with her father, who no longer traveled to California, and reacquainted herself with friends and relatives. Fort Wayne was proud to welcome home a local girl who had made good, and Lombard managed to control her salty tongue and create only the best of impressions. And while she and her cousins revisited the memorable sites of her childhood, Bess and Fred sat down with lawyers to work out a divorce settlement that would allow Bess the freedom to remarry, if she so chose.

Introducing seasoned Broadway actress Miriam Hopkins to movie audiences, *The Best People* was retitled *Fast and Loose*, which did nothing to help its box office showing. The film is noteworthy for adding an "e" to "Carol," the result of a gaffe by Paramount's publicity department, which accidentally turned out display posters spelling her name

"Carole." Lombard's considered response: "What the hell, let's keep it with the 'e.' I don't think I've ever seen it spelled that way, and I sort of like it." And so, almost in mid-career, Carol Lombard became *Carole* Lombard. However, she advised studio publicists to come up with a valid explanation for her public. In the end, it was attributed to numerology: a 13-letter name was considered more favorable to her destiny.

Of the 62 features that Paramount turned out in 1931, Carole Lombard had leading roles in five. Female competition for parts was strong, for the studio now had under contract the likes of Jean Arthur, Tallulah Bankhead, Clara Bow, Nancy Carroll, Ruth Chatterton, Claudette Colbert, Frances Dee, Marlene Dietrich, Kay Francis, Wynne Gibson, Miriam Hopkins, Sylvia Sidney and Lilyan Tashman. Despite their range in age and type, most of the parts in which one actress was cast could easily be played by another. For a time, Lombard obediently played what she was assigned, leaving the complaining and the role-switching to others.

On the occasion of her twenty-second birthday, Lombard began work on her first leading part for Paramount: *It Pays to Advertise*, which the studio had filmed once before in 1919. A slight comedy about (what else?) the advertising business, it paired Carole with boy-next-door Norman Foster in what the studio hoped might be a new film team. In 1919, the Lombard and Foster roles had been enacted by Lois Wilson and Bryant Washburn.

Lombard completed the movie in time to enjoy Christmas with her mother and siblings at their luxurious rented home on Rexford Drive. Fritz Peters remained firmly established with Bullock's, while brother Stuart, then dealing with a drinking problem, worked at various brokerage associations.

While she appreciated her family's togetherness and financial comforts, Bess nevertheless expressed the hope of seeing her offspring happily wed. Numerologically, she could foresee 1931 as a favorable marriage year for Carole.

Paramount publicists decided to promote Lombard's naturally elegant appearance as a studied blend of the stylish glamour already exemplified by that studio's German import, Marlene Dietrich, and the fashionable Kay Francis. With an echo of the appellation that had earlier attached to silent star Corinne Griffith, Carole was dubbed her studio's "Orchid Lady" and accordingly photographed with appropriate floral adornment. In addition, she was swept into a succession of motion pictures in which her carefully photographed image took precedence over the substance of her roles.

The Biography

Man of the World cast her opposite William Powell in a movie that would prove a milestone in each player's résumé. For him, it marked Paramount's hope of moving him permanently from the character parts with which he'd long been associated (and away from the recurring role of amateur detective Philo Vance) and into romantic leading man status. For Lombard, it teamed her with an actor whom she'd long admired in her most prestigious casting to date. *Man of the World* was considered a grade-A production, for which Broadway import Miriam Hopkins had originally been set. Hopkins, in turn, was reassigned to a picture *Lombard* had hoped to make, the Maurice Chevalier vehicle *The Smiling Lieutenant*.

Carole's disappointment was soon mitigated by an immediate attraction to Powell that was noticeably mutual. In the aftermath of *Man of the World*'s release, she excused her rather listless acting by acknowledging that infatuation. Indeed, the picture very much belongs to her debonair and charismatic leading man, whose fadeout pairing with the more exciting Wynne Gibson is quite understandable.

Man of the World proved so popular that Paramount quickly reunited Powell with Lombard in the similarly named *Ladies' Man*, which billed her third, after Powell and Kay Francis. Hollywood gossip now implied that Lombard had become Powell's lover, while her "Orchid Lady" promotion had proven so successful that she was kept busy making one picture after another. Next, *Up Pops the Devil* reunited her with Norman Foster in a routine comedy-drama about young marrieds.

On June 26, 1931, Lombard put an end to the rumors by marrying William Powell. The ceremony was performed by a Congregationalist minister in the privacy of the Peterses' Rexford Drive home. Previously married, he was the father of a six-year-old son who lived with

A glamour portrait used to advertise *Man of the World* in 1931.

his mother. There was a 16-year age difference: She was 22 and he was approaching 40. And they were not similar in temperament: While Powell was intellectual, introverted and given to moods, Lombard was casual, outgoing and impulsive. He liked classical music; she responded more to popular tunes of the day. He was skilled at sophisticated ballroom dancing; she was still very much the Jazz Age flapper.

Not everyone in Powell's Hollywood circle was readily accepting of Lombard, and even the press implied that she was an ambitious gold-digger. Adding to their marital challenges were his presumptuous press comments to the effect that she'd be retiring from her career to become a full-time wife and, perhaps, mother. Although Carole wouldn't

Photographed with William Powell at the time of their marriage, with Edith Wilkerson, one of the six wives of *Hollywood Reporter* publisher Billy Wilkerson.

The Biography

rule out children, she emphatically made it known that, after her years of striving to succeed in films, she wasn't about to give it all up. In the possible event that the union didn't last, could she then hope to resume an abandoned career?

As Mrs. Powell, she was faced with a new and more luxurious style of living in his Tudor mansion on Havenhurst Drive, including chauffeured motorcars and servants, plural. And although they now appeared to embrace one another's differences, it soon became apparent that each seemed resolved to change the other to closer reflect his or her own self.

Careerwise, Lombard's fifth and final 1931 release was *I Take This Woman*, about a countrified cowboy (Gary Cooper) who falls for a ranch-visiting New Yorker, with rocky romantic results. Lombard looked glamorous but uninspired. The movie was not a success.

During the Powells' Hawaiian honeymoon, Lombard was doubly plagued by illness (first toxic poisoning, then malaria), which prevented her from appearing opposite Phillips Holmes in *The Beachcombers*, a picture that was postponed. Josef von Sternberg then tried to interest her in playing the society girl in *An American Tragedy*, again featuring Holmes. She turned him down because Powell, for some reason, disliked the director, despite having scored a career milestone under his tutelage in 1928's *The Last Command*. The role was given to Frances Dee.

Continuing to star in lackluster Paramount pictures, Carole seemed content to drift along on her "Orchid Lady" petals, especially in the costumes created for her by Paramount's chief designer Travis Banton. Edith Head, who was then just starting her fabled career as Banton's assistant, later assessed the secret of Lombard's look: "Her clothes always looked as though they belonged to her. Nine out of ten actresses thought in terms of costumes, but to Carole they were just clothes. Some girls never learn to wear elegance naturally, but it seemed that Carole had always known how."

Her wardrobe was the main attraction in her first 1932 release, *No One Man*, coincidentally one of three Lombard pictures that year whose titles began with *No*. *No One Man* afforded her top billing in a soap opera about yet another spoiled rich girl with man problems (Ricardo Cortez vs. Paul Lukas).

Love and marriage appeared to have taken the old ginger and vitality out of Lombard's screen persona. That, in addition to unexciting film assignments, did nothing for her career, perhaps accounting for Paramount's plan to loan her out to Warner Brothers for the James Cagney picture *Taxi!* Both Powell and Carole's agent, Myron Selznick, took a dim view of that idea, recommending that she refuse on the grounds that the role wasn't right for her. It was a ploy she might have later regretted. For, although studio boss Schulberg accepted her decision, *Taxi!* scored a box-office hit teaming Cagney with Loretta Young. Instead, Carole remained at Paramount, filming *Sinners in the Sun*, as *The Beachcombers* was now renamed. Its title promised much more than was delivered on-screen, save for those fans eager to see their "Orchid Lady" in yet another collection of stylish Banton couture. *Variety* termed it "[a] very weak picture with an unimpressive future before it." Chester Morris was her nominal leading man. Of greater historical significance, Carole briefly shared footage with a studio newcomer and future co-star named Cary Grant.

Amid filming of *Sinners in the Sun*, the Depression struck Paramount a near-fatal blow. The company went into receivership, and was completely reorganized. B.P. Schulberg, replaced as production chief by Emanuel "Manny" Cohen, was reduced to producer status. Paramount's Astoria studio was closed, with its Hollywood roster of stars and featured players' future uncertain. William Powell had already left Paramount for Warner Brothers. Marlene Dietrich now ruled as queen of the lot, while Jeanette MacDonald was let go, leaving Miriam Hopkins, Claudette Colbert, Sylvia Sidney and, somewhat less securely, Nancy Carroll.

As for the Paramount men, Buddy Rogers was chopped while Maurice Chevalier was retained, despite his waning box-office appeal. Refusing to take the studio salary cuts accepted by fellow contractees, George Bancroft chose temporary retirement. Gary Cooper and Fredric March remained Paramount's most valued male stars, while secondary leads Richard Arlen and Jack Oakie stayed under contract. Of greater promise to the studio were such up-and-comers as Charles Laughton, Cary Grant and Randolph Scott. In the hope of raising public interest in the Paramount product, the company now took on gangster specialist George Raft, radio crooner Bing Crosby, silent screen comedian W.C. Fields and—challenging the Legion of Decency—the outrageously suggestive Mae West.

In 1932, radio provided a Depression-era challenge to moviegoing the same way that television later did. Emanuel Cohen's responsive ploy was to merge the two media by producing *The Big Broadcast* not only to showcase radio star Crosby, but also to feature the popular George Burns-Gracie Allen comedy team, the Boswell Sisters, the Mills Brothers and Kate Smith. On home broadcasts, audiences could only

The Biography

hear these entertainers; in movie theaters, one could also see them in action.

For *The Big Broadcast*, Cohen planned to interweave a thin storyline to feature Carole and Stuart Erwin among the specialty numbers and comedy bits. When she took an advance look at the screenplay and discovered how little she'd be required to do (not even a dance number), she refused the assignment. But Cohen was no Schulberg, and whereas Lombard's dealings with Paramount's previous production chief were more reasonable, her ambition to be cast instead in an Ernst Lubitsch picture was not negotiable. To make matters more discouraging, *The Big Broadcast* became the big success her career could have used.

Myron Selznick had negotiated a lucrative new Paramount contract for Lombard, plus a substantial raise. This was prior to the shake-up in management, which left Cohen in a quandary as to what to do about his problematic and costly leading lady. His gambit was a loan-out to whatever studio might show interest in her.

Lombard and her brother Stuart in 1932.

At low-rung Columbia, then only beginning to emerge from its Poverty Row beginnings, tough, foul-mouthed Harry Cohn ran his studio with crude and canny flair. And he offered to relieve Paramount of their dealings with Lombard by buying up her contract. That is, until he found out about her salary requirements and that her agent was the formidable Myron Selznick. However, Cohen willingly offered Columbia the *loan* of her services.

Carole undoubtedly faced the prospect of a Columbia picture with misgivings, and she was well aware of Cohn's blunt and vulgar reputation. For a star, being loaned out to that studio had the connotation of a humiliating jail sentence. If her home studio now considered her uncooperative, Powell gave his approval to her loan-out assignment, with Selznick advising her to "give Cohn more than the little bastard would bargain for."

The platinum-haired actress' beauty belied a strong mind and a brainy sense of humor that enabled her to cope with studio heads like Cohn. Their initial meeting was characteristically blunt: Cohn appraised Lombard and quipped, "Your hair's too white; you look like a whore." To which she quickly retorted, "I'm sure you know what a whore looks like, if anyone does." Cohn was immediately surprised, charmed and put in his place. From that moment on, the two would find a rapport destined to continue through five Columbia productions, one of which would be a Lombard milestone.

At Columbia, it would take her a month to film *Virtue* opposite up-and-coming Pat O'Brien, under the direction of Edward Buzzell. Robert Riskin's screenplay offered a punchy tale of a streetwalker's efforts to go straight, in the company of the cab driver she hoodwinked into marriage.

Lombard was accorded that studio's grandest dressing room and a relaxed atmosphere conducive to on-the-set visits from Bess Peters, William Powell and a number of her close friends. Madalynne "Fieldsie" Fields, who had forsaken acting to become Carole's personal assistant, advisor and best buddy from the outset of her Paramount contract, was a permanent presence on the *Virtue* set. At Paramount, Lombard was merely another leading lady; at Columbia, she was treated like a star. And what began as a close working relationship with screenwriter Riskin (his daily rewrites tightened the narrative) soon blossomed into mutual admiration and beyond.

Harry Cohn's introductory comment about her appearance may have had something to do with the subtle changes which now afforded her a more natural look, with less emphatic eye makeup and a slight darkening of her hair, from near-platinum to ash blonde. A softer hair style made her screen persona more like her real, off-screen self. It was a look she retained when she returned to Paramount, where she was assigned to *Hot Saturday*. That romantic comedy-drama was devised to test the leading-man possibilities of Cary Grant, who had been paying his studio dues in supporting roles. But once again, Lombard's career trajectory was altered by the temperamental whims of Miriam Hopkins, who objected to taking second-billing to Clark Gable, on loan from

The Biography

MGM, in *No Man of Her Own*. Since his billing was a non-negotiable Metro stipulation, Paramount had no choice but to replace the "indisposed" Hopkins with Lombard—who was then replaced by Nancy Carroll in *Hot Saturday*.

Lombard was very much aware of Gable's screen persona, from his tough-love teamings with MGM stars Joan Crawford, Jean Harlow and Norma Shearer. She also knew that he was married to the much-older socialite Ria Langham, although this did not appear to hamper his off-the-set relationships with his leading ladies. At Paramount, Nancy Carroll, who had acted onstage with Gable, alerted Lombard to his rascally reputation.

In the words of their director, Wesley Ruggles: "Carole was married to Bill Powell, which wouldn't have mattered to Clark, but it mattered to *her*. I think he was given to understand that, other than kissing her for the camera, she was off limits. But yes, they got along, and it was a delight, just working with them together."

At the studio party that marked the end of production for *No Man of Her Own*, amusing publicity was created around Lombard presenting Gable with a large ham with his image pasted over it. The gag was much-photographed and exploited in fan publications. But there's no evidence that the co-stars' on-set friendship continued in the wake of their only film together. With the movie's completion and Gable's return to MGM, Lombard appeared pleased to assure Paramount colleagues, "I'm one leading lady he didn't seduce!"

No Man of Her Own got a better press reception than her recent Paramount pictures. *The New York Times*' Mordaunt Hall was quite positive: "Miss Lombard and Mr. Gable are amusing and competent players. Between them they keep a rather usual sort of melodrama hustling along at a lively clip and sustain a pleasing illusion of handsome romantics and dashing humor."

Paramount was then casting *If I Had a Million*, an unusual project comprising a variety of eight short-story segments, each under the guidance of a different director, with a nine-day shooting schedule. Carole coveted the streetwalker sequence assigned to Wynne Gibson, but she was instead cast opposite Gary Cooper and Jack Oakie in a less substantial episode. She balked, and was replaced by Joyce Compton.

And so it was back to Harry Cohn at Columbia, at a time when *Virtue* was getting very positive audience feedback. This time, Paramount's "Orchid Lady" was rewarded with solo star billing in a well-made romantic comedy-drama fittingly called *No More Orchids* (after a suggestion Carole made to Cohn). She was well photographed by Joseph August, under the encouraging direction of Walter Lang, whom she would later credit for her success as a comedienne. (Lang later became the husband of her confidante "Fieldsie," and made Carole godmother to their son.) Years later, Lang remembered her as "a lovely person, a great person," adding, "We had so much fun, and the picture turned out so well, that the friendship grew from there till her death."

The year 1932 was a busy one for both Lombard and Powell: She had five pictures before the public, he had four, the most successful of which was Warners' *One Way Passage* with Kay Francis. For a time, Carole relished her work schedule at Paramount, where she continued to hope for her official acceptance as an *actress*. But twice that year she was unable to report for work because of ill health, and there were rumors about a possible nervous breakdown. The press was informed that she was under a doctor's care. Whatever the true situation, friends and family knew that all was not serene in the Powell household.

For the benefit of fan magazines, they remained one of movieland's devoted couples. But their divergent personalities and their age gap began to take a toll. At the beginning of 1933, the movie industry was seriously affected by the Depression, and at Warner Brothers, Powell was asked to accept a $2000 cut in his weekly salary, for Warners had sustained a loss of over $14 million the previous year. Despite everything, the actor appeared foolishly complacent about both his career and his homelife.

By now, the Lombard-Powell differences were becoming apparent, and that spring she suddenly left their Havenhurst Drive home and moved back in with her mother. Not only had their separate work schedules kept the couple frequently apart, but also Powell's career at Warners had not developed well, despite the popularity of *One Way Passage*. In fact, he was considered highly overcompensated for his worth to the studio. As for Carole, she remained a well-paid contract player at Paramount, which regularly fielded inquiries from other studios as to her availability. Winfield Sheehan even made a failed offer to acquire her pricey contract for Fox.

The Powells' official separation bewildered their public, especially since neither party would supply a concrete explanation for the split. Carole told the press that she still loved her husband, allowing merely that a separation was something that they had decided was needed. Privately, they hired an attorney and proceeded with an uncontested divorce. There would be no need for alimony or a property settlement. Employing the inaccurate but convenient charge of "mental cruelty,"

The Biography

Lombard staged a six-minute courtroom performance for the judge that quickly secured her freedom on August 16, 1933. At the post-trial press conference, she allowed that their divorce was amicable. A photographer's request for a smile brought the conference to a close when Carole responded: "I'm not at all happy about this, you know. So I am not going to give you a smile I don't mean. After all, a divorce is a divorce."

None of her four 1933 Paramount releases added anything important to the Lombard résumé. Somewhat reminiscent of MGM's big 1932 hit *Grand Hotel*, the smaller-scale *From Hell to Heaven* reflected the theme of varied stories in a single setting (here it was a racetrack) to offer a collection of colorful characters in a virtual parody of Metro's all-star blockbuster. At the head of the cast (Jack Oakie, Adrienne Ames, David Manners *et al.*), Lombard played a divorced socialite attempting to resume an old relationship with an opportunistic bookie (Sidney Blackmer). For Carole's fans, the movie's highlight could only have been her Travis Banton wardrobe. With much footage shot at the Santa Anita racetrack in chilly January, she shivered through her scenes attired in summery frocks, while crew members provided comforts like suitably warm clothing. When Carole had suffered enough, she yelled out; "All right, you warm, bloody bastards. What's good for one is good for all! I'm not shooting till I see every one of you down to your jockey shorts!" And she gleefully watched them comply.

Supernatural took her a definite step downward, under the clumsy direction of Victor Halperin, who had served Bela Lugosi much better with the uncanny 1932 thriller *White Zombie*. In the company of leading man Randolph Scott, she struggled vainly to make something of this spooky nonsense. Amid an especially challenging shoot, Lombard was forced to endure what seemed an eternity of remaining motionless while facial transformations were painstakingly achieved through makeup and stop-motion photography. The procedure drove her to exclaim, "God, this bastard's trying to paralyze me. Victor, God'll punish you for this!" Soon thereafter, when the deadly Long Beach earthquake of March 10, 1933, roared destructively through the studio, Lombard marched up to the suitably frightened Halperin, pointed an accusing finger and exploded, "Victor—that was only a warning!"

Carole's brief cameo appearance in the excellent anti-war drama *The Eagle and the Hawk* brought distaff name value to an otherwise all-male story of World War I fliers, most notably portrayed by Fredric March and Cary Grant. It's the former with whom she shares her eight-minute sequence, billed simply as "The Beautiful Lady."

The Biography

And then she returned to Columbia for her third loan-out, *Brief Moment*, based on the S.N. Behrman stage play. For a change, it's her leading man (Gene Raymond) playing the spoiled society individual, while Carole's the café torch singer who loves and tries to reform him. It's a standard domestic drama whose most notable attribute is the stunning cinematography of Ted Tetzlaff, whose artistry so impressed Lombard that she strove to have him photograph as many of her future pictures as could be arranged. The result: a total of nine movies at Columbia, Paramount, Universal and Warner Brothers.

Back at her home studio, she was not happy with plans to cast her in *The Way to Love*, opposite a waning Maurice Chevalier, and she refused the assignment. Paramount replaced her with Sylvia Sidney, who began filming, then quit the production for medical reasons and was herself replaced by Ann Dvorak.

Having also turned down Paramount's earlier effort to assign her to another minor-league feature, *The Girl Without a Room*, Lombard wasn't winning any popularity polls among her studio bosses—until their eccentric British character-star Charles Laughton put in a bid for her to be his leading lady in *White Woman*. Returning from England and his landmark portrayal in *The Private Life of Henry VIII* (1933), Laughton was eager to end his contractual obligations to Paramount with this trashy tropical melodrama. But he did not want to star opposite the studio's choice of Elissa Landi, with whom he had clashed amid the florid excesses of Cecil B. DeMille's *The Sign of the Cross* the previous year.

White Woman again cast Lombard as what John Douglas Eames (in *The Paramount Story*) described as "a vagrant blonde plying her trade as an 'entertainer,'" affording her a pair of Mack Gordon-Harry Revel songs, which she delivered in a bored style suggestive of Marlene Dietrich. Otherwise, this unlikely yarn about a cruel rubber plantation owner who marries an entertainer to prevent her deportation affords its portly star the opportunity for some coarse, over-the-top hamminess, in contrast to Lombard's effective underplaying. The sheer incongruity of their pairing renders this inferior movie watchable, with the added pleasure of Travis Banton's inappropriately stylish Lombard wardrobe. Acting with Laughton, she discovered, effectively challenged her. Her colleague proved more helpful to her performance than the picture's nominal director, Stuart Walker.

In the wake of their divorce, Lombard and Powell both continued to share a great mutual fondness, and they were often observed enjoying one another's company about Hollywood. Gossip sources

The Biography

A posed publicity portrait for *White Woman* with Charles Laughton.

had them on the verge of remarrying; no such reunion transpired. As a "bachelor girl," Carole enjoyed the attentions of numerous admirers, including screenwriter Robert Riskin and charismatic crooner Russ Columbo, who coached her singing for *White Woman*. In the case of Columbo, there was a serious love affair, and marriage seemed a likely culmination.

Not that Carole enjoyed a lot of free time for romance: Without a single day off, she had gone from filming *Brief Moment* to *White Woman* to her next Paramount assignment, replacing Miriam Hopkins opposite George Raft in *Bolero*.

An interesting footnote to the ongoing series of Carole Lombard-Miriam Hopkins casting juxtapositionings involved Columbia's attempt to borrow Hopkins from Paramount to star in Frank Capra's *It Happened One Night* opposite MGM leading man Robert Montgomery. But Miriam read the screenplay and dismissed it as "just another silly little comedy," passing the opportunity on to some other actress. When Montgomery balked at the idea of being farmed out to lowly Columbia, it became difficult to secure an important "name" actress. Harry Cohn urged Capra to employ Lombard, but the director expressed unfamiliarity with either her work or her image, and that was the end of that—until MGM's Louis B. Mayer countered Montgomery's decision by substituting Clark Gable, whom he exiled to Columbia for "punishment" reasons that remain unspecified. Carole liked Robert Riskin's script, but she overheard the rumor that Gable hoped to seduce her, now that she and Powell were divorced. However, her real reason for turning down *It Happened One Night* was that its production schedule would coincide with that of a Paramount film she coveted: *Bolero*.

Lombard relished the prospect of surprising studio bosses with her dancing ability in this period musical drama, and she found a most congenial teammate in her stone-faced leading man George Raft. In addition, she looks gorgeous in Travis Banton's uncharacteristic and elaborate 1910s-era costuming, as photographed by Leo Tover. For a welcome change to the course of her career, Carole was finally shown to advantage in a box-office winner.

Ray Milland, the film's secondary leading man, was just beginning his many years with Paramount. He recalled Lombard in his 1974 autobiography *Wide-Eyed in Babylon* as "a smashing girl, a true original, and a hell of an actress. ...She loved practical jokes and could tell a bawdy story with the best of them. In any company, her taste was impeccable."

Apparently Lombard didn't regret her decision to make *Bolero* instead of *It Happened One Night*, which co-starred Paramount's Claudette Colbert opposite Clark Gable and swept the 1934 Academy Awards. In hindsight, it's fascinating to contemplate the possible course of events had Lombard accepted the Capra movie offer in preference to *Bolero*. Might Lombard have won the Academy Award that went to Colbert?

Before *Bolero* had completed production, she was already involved in the filming of *We're Not Dressing*, loosely derived from James M. Barrie's play *The Admirable Crichton*. The dual assignments necessitated two weeks of hectic commutation between the two sets. The latter was yet another Lombard assignment once set for Miriam Hopkins—until the latter discovered the extent to which Paramount's screenwriters had altered the Barrie material, as a vehicle for their popular singer Bing Crosby. An even more discouraging prospect for highbrow Hopkins was the low-comedy supporting cast, featuring the likes of George Burns, Gracie Allen and Leon Errol. By now, Carole had become the unofficial go-to substitute whenever Paramount had trouble with the temperamental Miriam.

We're Not Dressing offered no problems for Lombard. She enjoyed working with Bing, found an immediate pal in Gracie, and reported that she'd never before had so much fun on a set. It's about shipwrecked, yachting socialites who become dependent on an enterprising deckhand (Crosby) for their survival. Among the screwball antics, there are also a collection of sound-alike Mack Gordon-Harry Revel songs, including "Once in a Blue Moon," in which Carole duets quite well with Bing.

In his autobiography *Call Me Lucky*, Crosby recalled his co-star with great fondness:

> Carole could lay tongue to more colorful epithets than any other woman I've ever known, and more than most men. She had a delicious sense of humor. The electricians, carpenters and prop men all adored her because she was so regular, so devoid of temperament.

A cheesecake portrait from 1934.

He also related a hilarious breakfast incident during the company's Catalina Island location hotel stay: Carole, in an effort to shake up the staid resort's elderly guests, shouted across the dining room one morning, "Oh, Bing, did I leave my negligee in your room last night?"

After the success of *Bolero*, the glamorous Lombard image was overshadowed by her image as a comedienne in *We're Not Dressing*, despite those slinky Travis Banton gowns.

We're Not Dressing completed production prior to the year's-end (1933) holidays. Amid persistent rumors that she and Powell might remarry, Carole hoped to take her mother on a much-needed holiday, during which they'd revisit Fort Wayne before traveling on to New York and a round of theater-going. But she got no cooperation from Paramount, where she'd recently rejected efforts to cast her in the trivial *Eight Girls in a Boat* (little-known Dorothy Wilson took the part) or loan her to Fox for *Worst Woman in Paris*, in exchange for whom Paramount would employ the services of Warner Baxter. Also, their uncooperative star was reminded that Paramount was paying her $2000 per week, not per picture, and they expected her to earn her keep. On the other hand, if she cared to take suspension of salary, she could enjoy as long a get-away as she chose. She did not.

There followed another detour to Columbia, where Harry Cohn continued to show his appreciation of her talents. The project was entitled *Sonata* (later released as *Sisters Under the Skin*), and Carole enjoyed rehearsing with co-stars Joseph Schildkraut and Frank Morgan. But before filming started, Paramount, faced with the sudden unavailability of Fay Wray, called Carole back for *Wharf Angel* (and dispatched Elissa Landi to Columbia to replace her). Lombard failed to appreciate this cavalier treatment, although she anticipated that *Wharf Angel* would be an intriguing change of pace. Yet another casting maneuver removed her from that picture, which went to Paramount newcomer Dorothy Dell. Fate had bigger plans for Carole Lombard at Columbia: *Twentieth Century*.

Her breakthrough movie was one producer-director Howard Hawks had negotiated to make for Columbia. He already had John Barrymore for the leading role of theatrical impresario Oscar Jaffe, but who'd be his leading lady? Who would portray Lily Garland, the former salesgirl Mildred Plotka, who becomes Jaffe's star and mistress? Onstage it had been Eugenie Leontovich, not only considered too old for the film, but also an unknown name in Hollywood. Hawks mused about stars of the stature of Tallulah Bankhead and Ina Claire, but neither one had ever taken hold in pictures. Among appropriate Hollywood names being mentioned, he expressed an interest in the ubiquitous Miriam Hopkins, which understandably prompted Harry Cohn to suggest Lombard.

Aware of her résumé, Hawks was receptive. And he thought perhaps her potential had not been fully explored. Cohn went to work on Paramount's Manny Cohen, with the suggestion that not only he, but also Hawks and Barrymore, wanted "what's-her-name, Lombard" for *Twentieth Century*. With the strong possibility that this movie could finally turn their expensive leading lady into a major box-office attraction, Paramount sprung her from *Wharf Angel* and sent her back to Columbia.

Carole was initially somewhat stunned. Without any lobbying on her part, a plum film role had just landed in her lap. And opposite the great Barrymore, with whom, but for her auto accident, she might once have appeared in *The Tempest*.

Ben Hecht, who had co-written this expansion of their farcical play with creative partner Charles MacArthur, admitted that the real casting challenge was in finding an actress who wouldn't be overshadowed by the extravagant, scene-stealing Barrymore. In her favor, Carole had gained an off-screen image as a party girl not given to inhibition, yet maintaining a high degree of glamour. In short, what the role most required was personality, and Lombard assuredly had that to offer. To become Barrymore's leading lady was more than she could have anticipated at this stage of her career.

Hawks wasn't then yet celebrated as a director of comedy, and was willing to leave the timing and pacing of such scenes to Barrymore. Lombard, who would later identify herself as "not a leader, but a follower," was only too happy to follow Barrymore, who immediately established a style and tempo with which she readily fell into step. Edward Bernds, the movie's sound engineer, later recalled: "I have never worked on a picture in which the scenes commanded such rapt attention from the crew. But Lombard and Barrymore were dynamite on the set. Anything could happen. We, the crew, were fascinated."

In the presence of seasoned pros Hawks and Barrymore, Carole completely metamorphosed into Lily Garland precisely as directed, enacting her part from the core of her being. Her co-star later proclaimed her "the greatest actress I have ever worked with." And, among the picture's laudatory notices, more than a few critics expressed surprise at the skill and vitality of her performance in this zany classic.

The Biography

Critic Andrew Sarris called *Twentieth Century* "the film which first established Carole Lombard as the finest comedienne of the Thirties."

Back at Paramount, she was dismayed to be handed the script of *Kiss and Make-Up*, a tired romantic comedy returning her to the familiar role of a Travis Banton clotheshorse. Its only redeeming prospect was co-star Cary Grant—hardly enough compensation for this perceived demotion. But, of course, at this juncture, her work in *Twentieth Century* had yet to be seen, so Paramount executives reasoned that the experience of teaming with John Barrymore had simply gone to her inflated head. Quite the contrary, of course. She described Barrymore to interviewer George Madden two years later: "It would take a book to describe all the things he did to help. But, perhaps the greatest was the subtle way he built my self-confidence and flattered me into believing I was good."

Lombard refused to do *Kiss and Make-Up*, offering to free the studio from its obligation to pay her high salary by severing their

As Lily Garland in *Twentieth Century*.

The Biography

relationship altogether. With Miriam Hopkins then concluding her Paramount contract, the studio was faced with a shortage of leading ladies, so they were not about to let go of Lombard. And then *Twentieth Century* was released to excellent notices. Less than a month later, the promising 19-year-old Dorothy Dell, who had replaced Lombard in *Wharf Angel* before scoring in the Shirley Temple hit *Little Miss Marker*, was killed in a traffic accident. Paramount had planned to groom Dell to take Hopkins' place on their actress roster, with her next assignment the Gary Cooper–Shirley Temple feature *Now and Forever*.

Myron Selznick advised Lombard to remain with Paramount and accept the studio's decision to give her *Now and Forever*, reasoning that Temple's presence alone would ensure a winner. And so it did. To her surprise, Carole loved little Shirley, who wasn't the calculating scene-stealer she had anticipated. But her aversion to stage mothers kept her from socializing with the ever-present Mrs. Temple. *Now and Forever* was nothing special in its tale of con man Cooper reformed by his diminutive daughter Shirley, with Lombard as the woman who adores them both. Never mind the unlikely plot; critics and audiences made it a hit.

Even though it didn't prove the box office hit Columbia had anticipated, *Twentieth Century*'s release finally caused the suits at Paramount to take note of Carole's talents. And since her biggest hit had been *Bolero*, why not reunite her with George Raft in a carbon-copy musical-drama called *Rumba*? With time required to prepare such a follow-up, the studio then allowed her a five-week vacation. Despite already having four pictures released in 1934, Carole accepted a bid from Harry Cohn to return to Columbia for *Lady by Choice*. After *Twentieth Century*, she figured she owed Harry Cohn a favor. It would be her fifth loan-out to his studio.

Frank Capra's 1933 comedy-drama *Lady for a Day* had been a big hit for Columbia with veteran character actress May Robson stealing the picture. Now she was back with a similar characterization in as near to a sequel as Cohn could come up with without the presence of either Capra or the prior film's screenwriter, Robert Riskin. Instead, Lombard had her *Brief Moment* director David Burton and a Jo Swerling script that was serviceable, if not classic. In it, she's a fan dancer who's essentially a stooge for an alcoholic old lady, played by 70-year-old Robson. As a Mother's Day publicity stunt, Lombard adopts the senior from a retirement home, with unexpected complications. Roger Pryor, a pal of Carole's off-screen boyfriend Russ Columbo, supplied the love interest.

Lombard always enjoyed the welcoming atmosphere of the sets at Columbia, and especially working with veteran performers like Robson and Walter Connolly, who played the movie's Judge Daly. She claimed that Robson knew more about comedy acting than anyone except Connolly: "He taught me how to cover a laugh. You have to sort of mark time after someone gets off a good line, because people in the theater will need time to laugh, but you don't want them to miss anything. So what do you do? You don't want to compete with your own script. Walter Connolly taught me to sort of freeze, except for the eyes and eyebrows, and start acting like hell with *them*."

After completing *Lady by Choice*, she reported back to Paramount for *Rumba*, only to find that casting problems had delayed George Raft on *Limehouse Blues*. This left Carole free to do an MGM picture on loanout. Since Metro was widely considered the cream of Hollywood studios, Carole had no hesitation in accepting whatever they had to offer. She hadn't even glimpsed their script for *The Gay Bride*, which would reunite her with *Sinners in the Sun*'s Chester Morris. Had she done so, she might have had second thoughts, for this was an uninspired blend of comedy and melodrama about a chorus girl and a gangster (Nat Pendleton), whose murder leaves her a widow who marries "office boy" Morris. MGM thought so little of *The Gay Bride* that they eschewed the customary trade paper ads altogether. Worse still, it played on the lower half of double bills. In *The New York Herald Tribune*, Richard Watts, Jr., wrote, "Miss Lombard achieves the feat of being almost as bad as her picture, and plays her part without humor or conviction."

Privately, she was harboring thoughts of abandoning her career altogether, for the prospect of love and marriage with Russ Columbo. Then, on September 4, 1934, tragedy struck. The fast-rising Italian-American crooner and Crosby sound-alike once enjoyed a reputation with the ladies, including a relationship with Carole's old friend Sally Blane. That changed in 1933 with Lombard: "His love for me was the kind that rarely comes to any woman."

As Columbo's own movie career was looking up with his initial starring vehicle *Wake Up and Dream*, he was suddenly killed in a freak accident. As the story goes, he was visiting a close friend, photographer Lansing Brown, when an antique pistol accidentally went off in Brown's hand. Shot through the eye by a ricocheting bullet, Columbo was rushed into surgery, but died hours later on the operating table. He was 26, the same age as Carole.

As Lombard later told Sonia Lee in a *Movie Classic* interview: "Russ and Lansing and I toyed with those two old dueling pistols a hundred times. We poked our fingers into the barrels and held them up to our eyes to squint up into them. Yet nothing ever happened. We never dreamed they were loaded." Although a servant described hearing a violent argument between the two men just prior to the gunshot, Columbo's tragic death was written off as accidental.

Lombard denied that they'd had marriage plans. She attended his funeral, and soon wished she hadn't, for she was unable to contain her grief. In Lee's *Movie Classic* magazine interview, Lombard said, "I believe that Russ' death was pre-destined. And I am glad that it came when he was so happy—so happy in our love and in his winning of stardom." Much later, as Mrs. Clark Gable, she'd admit to a *Life* interviewer, "Russ Columbo was the great love of my life ... and that very definitely is off the record."

In the wake of Columbo's death, Lombard sought to assuage her grief by exhibiting a façade of madcap fun. And she found distraction by staging a succession of theme parties that were the talk of Hollywood. The hospital party featured waiters dressed as doctors with dinner served in bedpans on operating tables, while guests were obliged to exchange their finery for hospital gowns. And the hillbilly party was created amid a barnyard motif with her living room floor covered in knee-deep hay. The most celebrated of them all involved Carole renting the entire Venice Amusement Pier at Oceanside Park for a star-studded evening. The hundreds of guests ranged from the likes of Cary Grant, Marlene Dietrich, Claudette Colbert and Randolph Scott to the behind-the-camera crew members with whom she was so popular. This was also her proclaimed swan song as a hostess. Now, Lombard determined to concentrate on her career at Paramount. Although she harbored serious doubts about ever falling in love again, she found some consolation in her ongoing friendship with her smitten co-star George Raft. And she was once again seen about town with Robert Riskin.

Rumba made money, but it couldn't hold a candle to its predecessor. While *Bolero* had flair and an exciting climactic dance number (set to Ravel's classic music), *Rumba* had neither. The studio advertising copy appeared to be approaching desperation: "The dancing lovers of *Bolero* in a dramatic romance as fiery as the Cuban dance of love itself." Well, not exactly!

The Biography

Lombard and Russ Columbo in 1934.

Continuing the Lombard-Raft pairing, she was assigned to his next picture *Stolen Harmony*, although she wasn't at all happy with either the role or its brevity. Then there was another executive shake-up at the studio, whose product had suffered a box office decline under Emanuel Cohen. Once again in charge of Paramount, Adolph Zukor appointed Ernst Lubitsch as his "superintendent of production." Lubitsch had long been a champion of Lombard's, with far less regard for Raft, and he reassessed her post–*Twentieth Century* work, after screening a rough cut of *Rumba*: "Those weren't Lombard pictures, they were just pictures and you merely were in them. So now, my dear Carole, we'll make some Lombard pictures."

Lubitsch's forte had always been comedy and, after the huge success of *It Happened One Night*, it seemed as though all the studios were putting an emphasis on humor. First, he freed Carole from *Stolen Harmony* (the role was reassigned to starlet Grace Bradley), and also delivered her from *Wedding Present* and *My American Wife* (Joan Bennett

The Biography

(From left) Lombard, Cary Grant, Marlene Dietrich and Richard Barthelmess at the Venice Pier Party in 1935.

and Ann Sothern took on those parts). Lombard rejected the script of *Sailor Beware*, slated for her and Bing Crosby, opining that it was unworthy of the studio's prime singing star. Instead, Lubitsch gave her a much-needed vacation while he set about tailoring a "vehicle" for her.

In 1934, after residing with her mother for a time, Lombard moved into a place of her own in the middle of Hollywood, setting up a "bachelor girl" residence with her pal "Fieldsie." And, with time off from Paramount during the first half of 1935, she had the leisure and the inspiration to make of her new house a true home, where she became celebrated for her parties. Concern for the beverage choices of her guests moved Carole to note their preferences beforehand. Thus, each new arrival could soon expect to find the appropriate drink in his (or her) hand. The hostess herself drank Scotch on the rocks or, when in the company of studio crew members, a beer. To these carpenters, electricians and other behind-the-cameras personnel, she was like one of the boys: boisterous, joking and, of course, not to be outmatched when it came to colorful language. Unofficially, Lombard was Hollywood's "profane angel." However, when in the company of Bess Peters and *her* friends, Carole's language was above reproach.

Lombard once admitted that she was somewhat of a chameleon:

> I like to be liked, but everyone might not like me as I am, so I bend. It's a kind of acting and psychology and lying all mixed up, trying to be what people want and expect. But I don't apologize. I like people to reveal themselves to me, and not devote all their time and attention to trying to assimilate me. You see, most people can't be flexible. I can, so I am. I take on the attitudes and tastes of other people. And they like that.

Carole's plans to enjoy a European vacation with her mother in the spring of 1935 were derailed by the death of her father in Ann Arbor, Michigan. At 59, Fred Sr. had been recovering from brain surgery, performed in a hopeless attempt to relieve him of the mental torments remaining from his long-ago accident. Memories of Russ Columbo's recent funeral motivated Carole to skip her father's Fort Wayne services. As she explained: "My father is entitled to some dignity and respect in death, and if I were there it would turn into the worst kind of theatrical event." Instead, Lombard sojourned in Florida.

Back at Paramount, she reported for *The Bride Comes Home*, which was being tailored for her under the direction of Wesley Ruggles (*No Man of Her Own, Bolero*). At the same time, Columbia put in another bid for her services, this time for a comedy being touted as a winner. Carole read the screenplay of *She Married Her Boss* and agreed, anticipating the pleasure of working with co-star Melvyn Douglas and a reunion with director Gregory La Cava (*Big News*). Ernst Lubitsch was understandably averse to relinquishing Lombard to benefit Harry Cohn, whom he personally loathed. Meantime, Paramount's Claudette Colbert, in the wake of her recent Academy Award for *It Happened One Night*, opted to return to Columbia for *She Married Her Boss*. This made Colbert's next scheduled Paramount vehicle, *Hands Across the Table*, available for Lombard. Lubitsch assured Lombard that, as written by the team of Norman Krasna, Vincent Lawrence and Herbert Fields, it was the best comedy script in Hollywood. Also, he promised that he would supervise all aspects of its production. Wesley Ruggles, who was currently engaged on the Sylvia Sidney starrer *Accent on Youth*, was slated to direct. But, Lubitsch informed her, if she'd agree to another director, the production could begin almost at once. Carole immediately asked for her old friend Mitchell Leisen, a Paramount director of such

The Biography

dramatic fare as *Cradle Song*, *Death Takes a Holiday* and *Four Hours to Kill*. In view of the latter's surprising success, Lubitsch agreed.

Hands Across the Table was prepared with the kind of care Carole had not previously experienced at her home studio. She and Leisen met in advance to discuss the production. Of course, there was no question that Ted Tetzlaff would photograph it and that Travis Banton would design the costumes. But, for the first time, she was invited to select her leading man from the studio's contract list. Cary Grant was her first choice, but Katharine Hepburn had already requested him for *Sylvia Scarlett*, so he was off to RKO. Although Gene Raymond and Lloyd Nolan were tentatively announced, Lombard wasn't satisfied, and suggested Ray Milland. Leisen thought Milland could handle it, but (difficult to believe in hindsight) the actor protested, "Please don't ask me to do it, because I know I can't play comedy." Then they discussed borrowing Franchot Tone from MGM, before finally settling on Paramount contractee Fred MacMurray. Tall, dark and handsome Fred had only been in Hollywood a short time, but he'd already scored one comedy hit opposite Claudette Colbert in *The Gilded Lily*, and again registered with movie fans as Hepburn's leading man in *Alice Adams*, on loan to RKO.

In all of Lombard's years at Paramount, no leading man was better suited to her in every way than MacMurray. Their blonde-brunette contrast worked in perfect complement, while his quiet brand of masculinity offered balancing support for her without competing for audience attention. Eventually, he would win industry-wide acceptance as an expert farceur, but when he began work on *Hands Across the Table*, MacMurray challenged the faith put in him by Lombard and Leisen. As the director recalled to his biographer David Chierichetti, "Fred had a natural flair for comedy, but he was terribly shy in those days and he was afraid to try anything. We really had to draw it out of him, and Carole was a great help there. She felt that all the others had to be good or it wouldn't matter how good *she* was. She got right in there and pitched."

At the time they made *Hands Across the Table*, neither Lombard nor MacMurray was wed, so Paramount's press department tried to capitalize on the possibility of an off-screen romance by supplying the movie magazines with candid shots of the pair, who enjoyed a close on-the-set friendship, but nothing more.

Paramount's Thanksgiving picture, *Hands Across the Table* became one of their box office hits of 1935. Following their initial pairing, MacMurray was cast in a picture once slated for Lombard, *The Bride Comes*

The Biography

Home, but this time opposite Claudette Colbert. For the two Paramount ladies, it was apparent that their film roles had become interchangeable.

There were now plans to re-team Lombard and MacMurray in *The Princess Comes Across*, but Fred was having a problem with the studio. While his name appeared in star billing after Carole's, his salary remained what he had started at under a modest Paramount stock contract. Lombard advised him to go on strike and not report to work, encouraging him to ignore the threatening notes dispatched to him daily by the studio. She assured MacMurray that he was worth a lot more money, and told him she'd refuse to make *The Princess Comes Across* with anyone else. And she was right; the studio finally renegotiated his contract, stipulating four Paramount movies per year, with loan-outs to other studios when they had nothing for him on the home lot. And along with a substantial salary increase came renewed respect. In Fred's retrospective view, "I owe all of that to Carole."

At a time when Paramount had no films lined up for her, she persuaded Lubitsch to loan her to Universal for *Love Before Breakfast*, because her friend Walter Lang (*No More Orchids*) was set to direct it and was seeking a glamorous star experienced at light comedy. Lubitsch was reluctant to lease her services to a studio he considered second-rate, so Lombard took a characteristically earthy tack with him: "We'll make a deal. I do the picture at Universal, and if it turns out a stinker, you can have your way with me in the fancy hotel of your choice." She then grabbed his trademark cigar, concluding, "On the other hand, if *Love Before Breakfast* is a hit, I'll take over your job and shove this black thing up your ass!"

Carole enjoyed making *Love Before Breakfast*, which teamed her romantically with both Preston Foster and her then-persistent off-screen beau Cesar Romero. While pleasantly entertaining, it's nothing special. However, as it completed production, *Hands Across the Table* was released to great popular and critical acclaim, which meant that Universal now had a potentially bigger audience-pleaser than they had anticipated with *Love Before Breakfast*. Consequently, a new advertising campaign was developed to herald what promised to be that modest studio's big movie event for the spring of 1936. And so it was, although Lombard did not hold Lubitsch to their "deal."

On January 23, 1936, Lombard presided over filmland's annual Mayfair Club Ball, the social highlight of the year, held at the Victor Hugo on Rodeo Drive. She specified all-white gowns for the ladies on their formal invitations, so she was infuriated when Norma Shearer, on the arm of her producer-husband Irving Thalberg, showed up in scarlet.

The Biography

In his witty Hollywood memoir *Bring on the Empty Horses*, actor David Niven recalls Lombard's very audible reaction: "Who the fuck does Norma think she is? The house madam?"

Carole's official date for that occasion was Cesar Romero, but her duties as hostess kept them more or less separated. Among the many celebrity guests were Clark Gable (slightly drunk) and his wife Ria, 17 years his senior. But the Gables were famously estranged, and each had arrived with a separate escort.

At some point in the evening, guests noticed that Lombard was missing, as was Gable. They had last been seen together. Later, when they returned, each did so separately, although admitting that they'd *left* together. Lombard's explanation was that he had drawn her outside to prevent her confronting Shearer over that inappropriate attire, which she eventually did, anyway—to Gable's dismay. It wasn't how one treated the revered Miss Shearer. His disapproval of Carole's behavior led to his immediate departure from the ball, followed by a two-day bender. When he finally returned to his rooms at the Beverly Wilshire Hotel, he discovered her olive branch: a pair of white doves in a cage. Thus began one of Hollywood's great love stories.

Lombard's reputation as a madcap Hollywood prankster was solidified shortly thereafter at a noontime party hosted by socialite John Hay Whitney. Since it was an event for which guests were encouraged to devise entertaining gags, Lombard came up with a landmark prank. She arrived in an ambulance and was rushed to the center of the party on a stretcher, where the guests witnessed what looked like a deceased Lombard, her body covered by the sheet. When she sat up with a shout of "Surprise!" her friends were more aghast than amused.

Back at Paramount, the success of *Hands Across the Table* enabled agent Myron Selznick to forge a lucrative new three-picture contract for Lombard. While she'd previously been earning $3000 a week, her new box office value prompted Selznick to stipulate $150,000 per *film*, making her movieland's top-earning star. Under this agreement, she now had approval of both her director and supporting cast, and could choose her own cameraman, hairdresser, makeup artist and other technicians. She could also film one outside movie per year.

Carole's unusual concern for others is illustrated by her activism on behalf of Pat Drew, a Paramount electrician so seriously crippled during the production of *Annapolis Farewell* (1935) that the studio attempted to let him go. Instead, she demanded his employment on all of her pictures, and brushed off his efforts to thank her.

The Biography

Margaret Tallichet, a young actress Lombard once tried to help with her career, later shared her theory about the star's off-color language: "I used to puzzle about it, because I found it so unusual. I was young and not terribly perceptive, but even then I understood that it had to have begun as a sort of defense mechanism. I felt then and I feel now, that that was the defense she built for herself so as not to be as vulnerable as she probably was."

She began work on *The Princess Comes Across*. Originally, Lombard was to have played once again opposite George Raft. But after she engineered script changes to emphasize comedy elements over mystery, Raft pulled out, citing his objection to her insistence on having her favorite Ted Tetzlaff as cinematographer. Raft's complaint was that Tetzlaff favored Lombard with his camerawork; he also objected (off the record) to her script changes and the downsizing of *his* role. Carole suggested Fred MacMurray as Raft's replacement, continuing a copasetic association eventually destined to encompass four pictures.

This oddball mix of comedy, romance and mystery offers Lombard a field day portraying a New York showgirl whose ambition to become a movie star inspires her to an elaborate ploy, posing as a Swedish "princess" on a transatlantic liner. She gets involves first with bandleader MacMurray, then with blackmailer Porter Hall, who uncovers her Brooklyn origins before being mysteriously murdered. Under William K. Howard's direction, this entertaining but uneven film proved a hit, with the Paramount publicity machine heralding the Lombard-MacMurray team as "America's Box-Office Royalty."

At Universal, the screwball social comedy *My Man Godfrey* was already in production with William Powell, borrowed from MGM. Having failed to make it big at Warner Brothers, Powell had moved on to Metro, where 1934's *The Thin Man* had scored a big hit for him and Myrna Loy, making them the screen's most popular love team. Now, under the direction of the inventive Gregory La Cava, Powell was in a position to name his preferred leading lady. His choice was Carole Lombard. One glance at the screenplay, and she realized that her ex-husband had handed her a major prize and a role the likes of which she hadn't had since *Twentieth Century*'s Lily Garland. Inspired and encouraged by that earlier career breakthrough, she immersed herself in the script so cleverly devised by Morrie Ryskind and Eric Hatch (and the uncredited La Cava). La Cava encouraged his cast to experiment with improvisation in their dialogue.

Accoutered with a reported 24 outfits designed by her beloved Travis Banton, Lombard is wackily delightful as a brain-challenged rich girl

The Biography

who takes on what she thinks is the rehabilitation of "forgotten man" Powell, pulling him away from a hobo village to install him as the new family butler in a household rife with jealousy and madness. An unlikely romance blooms. Viewing *My Man Godfrey* today, it's evident that Powell and Lombard still took great pleasure in acting together, and it's a joy to observe their mutual give-and-take. *Variety*'s critic wrote:

> Miss Lombard's role is the more difficult of the two, since it calls for pressure acting all the way, and it was no simple trick to refrain from overworking the insanity plea in a many-sided assignment. It's Powell's job to be normal and breezily comic in the madcap household, and that doesn't require stretching for him.

Lombard later admitted to an interviewer, "Irene in *Godfrey* was the most difficult part I ever played. Because Irene was a complicated and, believe it or not, essentially a tragic person. Back of every good belly-laugh there is a familiarity with things not funny at all."

My Man Godfrey was released to enthusiastic response in the fall of 1936. Clark Gable was especially impressed, informing friends that Lombard's performance therein was responsible for his realization that he had fallen in love. This landmark "screwball" comedy brought Carole her first (and only) Best Actress nomination for an Academy Award. In turn, Powell was also nominated that year, although each lost: she to Luise Rainer (*The Great Ziegfeld*) and he to Paul Muni (*The Story of Louis Pasteur*). It is believed that the film has entered the public domain, as the copyright was apparently not renewed. However, the source material, the 1935 book *1101 Park Avenue*, had its copyright renewed in 1963.

As her career attained greater Hollywood status, Lombard's relationship with the still-married Gable grew deeper. When asked whether he was serious about Lombard, he retorted, "No, I just like the way she wiggles her derriere in a tight satin dress." When Lombard was questioned about Gable, her disarmingly frank comment was unprintable in the newspapers of 1936. Although Clark and Ria Gable had been living separate lives, Ria was not about to grant him an easy divorce. His womanizing ways, well-known around Movie-Town, had caused her no end of embarrassment in the past, and her financial demands for a legal split made it impossible for him to acquiesce. Meanwhile, Carole and Clark spent their leisure time together, and were frequently seen dining about town. In search of greater privacy, she moved from her Hollywood Boulevard home to St. Cloud Road in upper-class Bel Air, where she could meet him in reasonable seclusion. In addition, she now enjoyed more space for her collection of pets in a house that was also more accommodating for parties. Around this time, she had her name legally changed from Jane Peters Powell to Carole Lombard.

In 1937, Paramount's *Swing High, Swing Low* reteamed her with Fred MacMurray in a remake of *The Dance of Life*, filmed by the studio eight years earlier with Nancy Carroll. The source of both pictures was the stage play *Burlesque*, which had been a career booster for a young (pre–Hollywood) Barbara Stanwyck. Under Mitchell Leisen's guidance, this much-altered adaptation centers on the on-and-off relationship of a musician (MacMurray) and a hapless hairdresser-entertainer (Lombard) who marry and divorce, enter into other relationships (Dorothy Lamour, Harvey Stephens) and have a rather iffy reunion at the film's close. This remained a favorite role of Lombard's. *Swing High, Swing Low* obviously appealed to her public as well, for it proved one of Paramount's big moneymakers that year.

Among the movie's mixed critical reception, the fan magazine *Photoplay* seemed best to reflect popular opinion:

> That vivid climb toward stardom started by Carole Lombard in *Twentieth Century* three years ago here reaches glory for, while this photoplay is the smoothest possible blend of laughter and tears, of torch numbers, fine production, direction and camera work, it is Lombard's art that makes this a great emotional experience.

Leisen recalled working with Carole: "She was visually at her best on the first take. After that she got bored with it, and would lose spontaneity. Since Fred often needed the first couple of takes to get into the swing of it, I'd give her a new bit of business or something each time, and they'd both be great on the third or fourth take."

Dorothy Lamour, who'd only recently debuted in *The Jungle Princess*, recalled the star's treatment of a newcomer: "The moment I stepped onto that set, Carole Lombard took one look at me and said, 'This poor girl's eyebrows are too thin. Get Wally Westmore.' She refused to shoot anything until Westmore came down to the set and fixed my eyebrows. I have never known anybody to be as kind and generous as Carole."

As her three-picture Paramount contract neared its conclusion, Myron Selznick hammered out an even better deal with his producer-brother David O. Selznick. Her contract with Selznick-International, based on Carole's strong desire to play Scarlett O'Hara in David's long-planned *Gone with the Wind*, was for three years and worth more than a half million dollars. David was generating much

The Biography

Posing for a portrait photographer in 1937.

publicity with his search for a Scarlett, with such starry names as Bette Davis and Katharine Hepburn, and such authentic Southern belles as Tallulah Bankhead and Miriam Hopkins, all reportedly in contention for the part. But nobody had actually been signed, so Carole felt she might still be considered.

Her initial Selznick feature would be her first in Technicolor and its screenplay was tailored for Lombard by the noted Ben Hecht. The result, derived from a *Saturday Evening Post* magazine story, was *Nothing Sacred*, a screwball satire. She played Hazel Flagg, a Vermont girl turned national celebrity when she's misdiagnosed as dying; Hazel went right onto Carole's short list of favorite parts. It was also more physically exhausting than any of her other pictures, including strenuous scenes of wrestling combat with co-star Fredric March. Especially difficult for Carole were her love scenes with March, a notorious womanizer whose

A typical glamour portrait from 1937.

attentions she discouraged in a humiliating incident years earlier, when both were contracted to Paramount. It's a gauge of their talents to see how well the two perform together here, especially in the sequence where he knocks her out with a punch, only to have her retaliate in kind.

Lombard biographer Larry Swindell summed up *Nothing Sacred*: "Mistaken as a great film almost immediately, it was never that. But it was a great screenplay, and one of Hollywood's rare examples of satire achieved within a farce structure."

Lombard was an undeniable box office asset to Paramount, and she looked forward to that one last picture that would fulfill her studio contract. William LeBaron had by now taken over the studio's artistic-supervisor reins from Ernst Lubitsch, and she was stunned by the general low quality (or the complete unsuitability) of the screenplays sent her way, among them *John Meade's Woman*, *Exclusive* and *The Last Train from Madrid*. Fortunately, she had her approval of scripts, and what did interest her was an ambitious Technicolor project called *Men with Wings*. But that production was delayed. Meanwhile, Wesley Ruggles offered up a script that Claude Binyon had expressly tailored for her comedic talents, and Lombard was encouraged. So much so that she completed *Nothing Sacred* on a Friday afternoon and began *True Confession* the following Monday morning.

True Confession was Lombard's last teaming with her most agreeable co-star, Fred MacMurray. It's unfortunate that their final film together isn't more substantial, for Ruggles had guided two of her better pictures at the studio, *No Man of Her Own* and *Bolero*, and was thus the only one officially to direct Carole three times. Also, through her own maneuvering, she was able to repay her debt to John Barrymore for *Twentieth Century*. Once billed as "America's Greatest Actor," Barrymore was now accorded feature billing in Paramount B-movies, such as the Bulldog Drummond series. Lombard used her clout to secure him a supporting role; made sure that screenwriter Claude Binyon built up the part sufficiently to honor the Barrymore name, and also insisted that he get above-the-title billing along with its two leading players. In *True Confession*, Barrymore's is a jarringly eccentric part and he is not altogether successful, although he has his scene-stealing moments.

As for Lombard, while *My Man Godfrey* presented her as lovably scatterbrained, in *True Confession* she's downright stupid, as well as a compulsive liar. For undiscriminating audiences, the movie offered amusing entertainment, vying with *Nothing Sacred* for moviegoers' attendance amid 1937's year-end holiday season.

Paramount's multi–Oscar-winning costume designer Edith Head, who had paid her dues for years as Travis Banton's assistant, had nothing but praise for Lombard:

> The girls in the workroom worshipped her. The fitters begged to work with her. That's a true barometer. Her fittings were gay, hilarious, you could hear them for six blocks off. She had great clothes sense and a true clotheshorse figure, but she didn't take clothes or herself seriously. Nothing was sacred, nothing was a crisis.

For a time, Paramount continued to send Lombard scripts for consideration, although the most attractive project, *Bluebeard's Eighth Wife*, opposite Gary Cooper, went to Claudette Colbert. The studio's promising screenwriter Preston Sturges tailored his *Remember the Night* for the Lombard-MacMurray team, but somehow it was never offered to her. In 1940, that script was expertly served by Barbara Stanwyck, opposite MacMurray.

The Biography

A fashion portrait from 1937.

At the budget-straining salary of $175,000 a picture, Myron Selznick was now offering Lombard's services to any and all of the studios. By now, however, she was more preoccupied with Clark Gable than her career. Selznick almost secured her a one-picture contract at Metro, but she refused to take it, lest she have to work when Gable was free. It was a possibility she would not countenance.

At a time when her agent appeared to have lost interest, Carole impulsively made her own deal with Warner Brothers, the one movie company where she hadn't worked. Since Warners seemed to lack for a major female comedy star, she now infuriated Selznick by lowering her price to $150,000 and simply offering them her services. Under the agreement, her co-star would be the briefly popular Continental import Fernand Gravet, and a script was be devised for them. The critics had approved his first Warners picture *The King and the Chorus Girl*, if not the public. Studio boss Jack Warner, who knew next to nothing about creating comedy, appeared vague about the required screenplay, beyond

The Biography

glamorous fashions and broad humor for Lombard and smoldering romance for Gravet. Many hands and brains worked on the script that Mervyn LeRoy attempted to direct, but to little avail. The result was *Fools for Scandal*, a comedy without laughs, generating such negative reviews (*Variety*: "pretty dull stuff") and word-of-mouth that its audiences grew ever more sparse.

Released in the spring of 1938, *Fools for Scandal* was the only Lombard picture that year. Dismay had set in before shooting was completed. Carole knew that she was in a loser and tried in vain to make something out of the movie, before finally throwing in the proverbial towel. Depressed over what had happened to her brilliant career, she stopped giving interviews and, with no worthwhile projects in sight, determined to devote herself to Gable. She'd be away from the cameras for the next ten months.

Ever since that Mayfair Ball episode at the start of 1936, Carole and Clark had been a serious romantic item, so much so that they were by now identified as filmdom's most visible unmarried couple. He, of course, remained legally attached to Ria, who not only felt humiliated by his cavalier public behavior, but also knew that a divorce would be worth major compensation from America's biggest star. Confirming his tight-fisted reputation, Gable balked at her demands for half a million, expecting her price to come down. Instead, it went up.

Seriously in love with him despite their differences (i.e., she loved moviemaking; he considered it merely his job), Lombard made it her goal to adapt to Gable's favorite pastimes, especially hunting and fishing, at which she became proficient.

It seemed that all of Hollywood, as well as the country's novel-reading public, envisioned Clark Gable as *Gone with the Wind*'s Rhett Butler—everyone except Gable. After his box office disaster of the historical drama *Parnell* (1937), he had developed an aversion to costume pictures of any kind, considering himself strictly a contemporary actor. Nor did Lombard want to ponder her dimming chances of being cast as Scarlett.

Meanwhile, David Selznick had tailored the romantic comedy *The Young in Heart* for Carole. She was partial to that screenplay about a family of charming con artists, but more concerned about her personal life, deciding to pass on the project, which then went to Janet Gaynor. Among Carole's preoccupations was the unexpected departure of her personal assistant "Fieldsie," whose marriage to director Walter Lang precipitated her retirement into domesticity. Without a full-time secretary and business manager, Lombard suddenly realized how much she'd depended on her friend in so many ways—self-discipline for one. In place of "Fieldsie," there emerged Jean Garceau, a former employee of the Myron Selznick Talent Agency, whose terms centered on a businesslike work schedule. Eventually she proved equally useful to both Gable and Lombard.

Carole was very much aware of Clark's charisma, both on the set and off, and she made it her business to keep an eye on him, sometimes to his annoyance. Amid the production of his 1938 picture *Too Hot to Handle*, she was a constant presence, discouraging any young MGM starlets who might have harbored romantic ideas about her man. At times, Lombard's attentiveness led to quarrels. Some of her ideas about conventional unions were surprisingly advanced for the late '30s. In her view, the best argument for marriage was a couple's intent to raise a family. She and Gable both wanted children, and they carried on serious conversations about retiring from their profession altogether in favor of private family life.

In the 1987 ABC-TV documentary *Gone with the Wind: The Making of a Classic*, Marcella Rabwin, a veteran executive assistant to producer Selznick, revealed a surprising twist in the casting of Rhett Butler. It seems that Louis B. Mayer quietly offered the estranged Mrs. Gable half a million dollars to divorce him, on the condition that she persuade her husband to accept that role. And so she did. But not quickly enough.

On August 25, 1938, Gable officially signed with David Selznick to play Rhett Butler. Following the producer's prolonged negotiations with Mayer, it was announced that MGM would release *Gone with the Wind*, receiving 50 percent of the profits. In exchange, Selznick would get Gable plus Metro's investment of $1,250,000. With the knowledge that, once the Selznick epic got into production, their top leading man would be unavailable for a substantial period of time, Mayer kept Gable busy in a succession of Metro pictures.

After fan mail took an overwhelmingly dim view of Norma Shearer's playing Scarlett O'Hara, MGM sought to appease her by letting her have Gable as her leading man in *Idiot's Delight*. Lombard, who had never forgiven Shearer for the red dress incident at her white Mayfair Ball, was not amused, especially with the possibility that the Widow Thalberg (Irving died in 1936) might be after Clark for herself. This, despite Shearer being regularly seen about Hollywood with Carole's old friend George Raft. Gable didn't *appear* interested in Shearer, quipping

The Biography

to an on-the-set photographer, "I wish this broad would get the hell out of here."

But he did seem intrigued with several lesser females in the cast, especially Virginia Grey. There were rumors about Gable and Grey, but on-the-set visitor Lombard sensed vibrations with yet another of the movie's scantily clad bit players, and she staged an uncharacteristic scene, shouting to the director: "Get that whore out of here. Either she goes or Gable goes!" Carole held no official power at Metro, but when she returned to the set the following day, her wish had been fulfilled.

In a *Motion Picture* magazine interview, Lombard had some interesting comments to tell Gladys Hall about star temperament:

> I'm not temperamental about myself. But I do get temperamental when I hear some little would-be Napoleon of a director, some little killer-diller of a petty czar cursing out extras, grips, electricians. I've walked off sets when

Lombard uses a motorized bike to get around the Paramount backlot in 1938.

things like that happen. And I will again, if and when they happen again. I've said to the pettifogging nappies, "Why don't you bawl *me* out if that's the way you feel about it?" You don't dare to bawl the stars out, do you? They could bark right back at you, couldn't they? So you have to light on the little fellows, the ones who can't talk back, don't you? It's an obsession with me, the bullying of men who can't defend themselves by men who, not necessarily stronger, are in stronger positions. I've tweaked more than one nose for that sort of thing.

David Selznick finally came up with a script that both met with her approval and coincided with Gable's work schedule, since she now agreed to film only at a time when he, too, was similarly engaged. Lombard's project, casting her opposite James Stewart, was the romantic comedy-drama *Made for Each Other*, about struggling newlyweds. Under John Cromwell's sensitive direction, the result was a well-received tearjerker that *Newsweek* termed "the best performance of her career." Lombard was gratified that her wish to escape from zany comedy had gone so well. On the other hand, she may have expressed a private quip or two about Selznick publicist Russell Birdwell's advertising campaign for the picture, which immodestly proclaimed: "CAROLE CRIES! It's a David O. Selznick stroke of showmanship to make Lombard go dramatic!"

With *Made for Each Other* completed, she entertained renewed optimism that she and Gable would shortly be free to wed and set about finding a future home that would accommodate their needs. This turned out to be a 20-acre San Fernando Valley ranch that belonged to director Raoul Walsh. Gable shared her enthusiasm for the spread, but balked at the asking price of $50,000. The prospect of meeting Ria Gable's huge financial demands would hardly allow for such domestic expenditure. Lombard offered to cover the ranch costs herself, leaving them with only one problem: the divorce itself.

Favorable reaction to her work in *Made for Each Other* promoted some Oscar nomination speculation, as well as renewed rumbles about the Scarlett O'Hara casting. At year's end, *Hollywood Reporter*'s predictions actually favored Lombard. At the same time, she and Gable were unnerved by a surprisingly frank article in the January 1939 *Photoplay*, Kirtley Baskette's "Hollywood's Unmarried Husbands and Wives." An immediate sell-out in the movie community, this notorious piece detailed the "domestic arrangements" of such familiar twosomes as Barbara Stanwyck and Robert Taylor, Charlie Chaplin and Paulette Goddard—and Gable and Lombard. Angered at first, Clark

The Biography

and Carole had eventual cause for gratitude: apparently, the article finally served to hasten a humiliated Ria Gable's move for a divorce. On March 8, that became official. Three weeks later, during a short *Gone with the Wind* shooting hiatus, Gable and Lombard eloped to Kingman, Arizona, putting an end to all the speculation on March 29, 1939.

Filming on the Selznick production had famously begun with the burning of Atlanta, performed by studio stand-ins for the picture's stars. Gable was unhappy at the outset: Neither David Selznick nor director George Cukor were among his favorite Hollywood people, and he entertained forebodings. Legend has it that it was Myron Selznick's appearance on the set during that initial fire scene that settled the chief casting problem when he introduced his brother David to Vivien Leigh with the words, "David, I want you to meet Scarlett O'Hara."

March 29, 1939, the day of her marriage to Clark Gable in Kingman, Arizona.

The Biography

When Leigh's casting was made public, Myron, who represented her, had his hands full, dealing with the heartbroken Lombard. In an effort to pacify her, he negotiated a promising two-year contract for Carole with RKO that guaranteed two films annually. In addition, she would enjoy a percentage of the profits (long before such arrangements became standard practice for stars), along with her $150,000-per-picture salary. Inaugurating the deal would be a romantic melodrama, *Memory of Love*, coincidentally dealing with the situation of a woman's love for an unhappily married man whose estranged wife refuses him a divorce. Art imitating life?

Memory of Love was filmed while Gable was dealing with David Selznick, George Cukor and *Gone with the Wind*, which was constantly being rewritten. In addition to which, his costumes didn't fit, he refused to master the requisite Southern accent, and Selznick had just sent him a 92-page memo detailing how he should play Rhett Butler. To make matters worse, the fussy Cukor appeared to be favoring Leigh over Gable.

After two and a half weeks of shooting, the picture was five days behind schedule. Selznick closed down the production. Cukor was

From left to right, producer David O. Selznick, Vivien Leigh, director Victor Fleming, Lombard, and Clark Gable in 1939.

The Biography

fired and replaced by Gable's pal Victor Fleming, while Ben Hecht was brought in to rewrite Sidney Howard's screenplay. *Gone with the Wind* underwent numerous additional rewrites, including those of the producer himself.

At RKO, *Memory of Love* had originally been intended for Katharine Hepburn before she temporarily left Hollywood under the damning label "Box-Office Poison." Retitled *In Name Only* before its release, the picture reunited Lombard with a pair of colleagues from her Paramount years, Cary Grant and Kay Francis, under the direction of John Cromwell. While she enjoyed the two-month (April–June) shooting schedule on her picture, Gable endured the long January–July production of Selznick's magnum opus, in addition to its retakes in August. With *Gone with the Wind*'s completion, Gable had only harsh words for David Selznick, centering on his treatment of Victor Fleming, who suffered a physical collapse prior to the close of production. When Gable refused to join the starry contingent on Selznick's plane to the Atlanta premiere, Lombard pulled strings to arrange a separate accommodation for Clark, herself and publicists Howard Strickling and Otto Winkler. Selznick later credited her for saving the occasion.

When Gable also avoided Selznick's party following the Hollywood premiere, Lombard apologized for him. And although Selznick said he understood, she was the recipient of a private memo from the producer:

> Neither of us is used to such strained and peculiar situations as that on the night of the local opening of *Gone with the Wind*, when I like to believe we should have been in each other's arms. I certainly recognize the awkward position you are in, and cannot expect to come out on the right side when your loyalties are divided. And perhaps some day in the future, attitudes may change, as they do in the business, and it will again be possible for you to do a picture for me with the wholehearted pleasure that we once both knew in our endeavors.

Gable may have had nothing to lose by treating the producer with contempt, but Lombard did, for there remained another Selznick picture on her contract. And yet no such movie was ever made.

More than anything, Lombard wanted to win an Oscar. Gable already had his for *It Happened One Night*, and she harbored the hope of balancing their mantelpiece with a statuette of her own. Now she was counting on her forthcoming RKO hospital drama, *Vigil in the Night*, to put her in the running for the first time since *My Man Godfrey*. With the distinguished George Stevens directing, *Vigil in the Night* was anticipated to be an impressive acting showcase, if not a moneymaker, and the studio's prestige movie for 1940. As nursing sisters, she and Anne Shirley delivered admirable performances, yet audiences appeared not to care. Lombard's name had been considered strong enough to attract the public, but now it seemed that they only wanted her in comedies.

Unable to find an RKO comedy script that she liked, she decided on a more serious project. So, while Clark filmed *Boom Town* with Spencer Tracy, Claudette Colbert and Hedy Lamarr, Carole took on another strong dramatic role in *They Knew What They Wanted*. It was anything but a happy shoot, chiefly due to the temperamental Charles Laughton's never-ending battles with director Garson Kanin. Having dealt with the British actor's eccentricities seven years earlier during the filming of *White Woman* (when *he* commanded top billing), Lombard had little patience with the filming delays caused by his behavior, and frequently called his bluff. Laughton's ego made it hard to understand why her name should now precede his, until she informed him that RKO billed according to salary, adding, "Come to think of it, maybe my letters should be *twice* as big as yours."

While coping with Laughton's nonsense, Kanin had only admiration for Lombard's professionalism—and the fact that she had no use for temper tantrums. And she was even known to show up on the set on her days off. As Kanin recalled in his book *Hollywood*, "[S]he wanted to be around, to stay with the feel of things. She did not want to lose the momentum of work. On these days, she would hang around the set, watching; come along and look at the rushes; talk to various members of the cast. She was valuable."

Gable accompanied his wife when *They Knew What They Wanted* filmed on location in California's Napa Valley. Back in Hollywood, there were rumors linking him and beautiful Hedy Lamarr (with whom he teamed again in *Comrade X*). Lombard made it a point to check out his MGM dressing room as often as she could for signs of hanky-panky. Meanwhile, her own desire to become pregnant had borne no results.

During the summer of 1940, RKO submitted a script called *Mr. & Mrs. Smith* that she liked, especially with the idea of returning to light comedy. In interviews, she admitted that her apparent decline in popularity concerned her:

> I'm definitely going back into comedy, and I mean permanently. Some people will say I've been scared off by drama, and that's not true. I know what I can do, and perhaps I'll do an occasional heavy story, but primarily I've got to go the screwball route. It's obvious that the public prefers I do comedy, and I think I owe them something. After all, they've made me rich. But

the truth is, I regard comedy as more difficult than drama. In a straight part you react as you would react in real life. In comedy you have to do the unexpected.

Carole first met Alfred Hitchcock when David Selznick imported the English director to helm *Rebecca*, and she was well aware of his flair for melodrama. But she observed a sense of humor in his films, and inquired whether he'd consider doing a screwball comedy. While not intrigued with the idea, Hitchcock allowed as how *her* involvement might help him decide. And when she asked him to direct her in *Mr. & Mrs. Smith*, he consented.

After unsuccessfully seeking to engage Cary Grant to play her vis-à-vis, their second choice for light comedy expertise was Robert Montgomery, with whom Lombard had realized extraordinary comic rapport. For the "other man" role, Carole remembered her *Brief Moment* co-star, affording Gene Raymond's career a needed shot of adrenaline. For the occasion, Raymond sought a change of image by dying his trademark blond hair black.

Obviously, this lark about a couple who discover that their marriage isn't legal, isn't characteristic of Hitchcock. He'd later allow that he only made it to please Lombard, whom he greatly admired. As he explained to François Truffaut, "I more or less followed Norman Krasna's screenplay. Since I really didn't understand the type of people who were portrayed in the film, all I did was to photograph the scenes as written."

Hitchcock was unduly modest: *Mr. & Mrs. Smith* contains a number of his sly comic touches. It was released at the end of January 1941, to great box-office success, thanks to increasingly enthusiastic word-of-mouth. Five months later, when *Mr. & Mrs. Smith* was adapted for *Lux Radio Theatre*, Carole was heard opposite Bob Hope, at his comic-timing best. Unfortunately, she and Hope never filmed together.

Lombard had long been unhappy about her professional representation by Myron Selznick, whom she thought had become increasingly negligent of her career. She finally moved to sever their affiliation, although doing so cost her $17,500. Soon thereafter, Gable's friend Nat Wolff became her agent, negotiating her subsequent contracts as a freelance talent. Wolff also advised her that her price was too high. Lombard wouldn't film again for nearly a year.

Late in 1940, she and Clark visited Baltimore's Johns Hopkins Medical Center, he for a painful old shoulder injury (but certainly a potency check) and she for gynecological tests, which reported everything normal. But still she failed to become pregnant, and there were rumors of domestic unrest at the Gable home. Carole's jealous streak flared when Clark paired with sexy young Lana Turner in *Honky Tonk*. In her autobiography, *Lana: The Lady, the Legend and the Truth*, Turner denied that she ever had a relationship with Gable and wrote, "[O]urs was a closeness without intimacy."

There were rumors of a separation, partly fueled by their suddenly putting their ranch on the market, then taking it off again. Lombard explained that the place had become too well-known, but then they realized its sentimental importance and reversed their decision. When Gable wasn't filming at MGM, he and Lombard took extended vacations, generally in outdoor locations like Lake Meade and Baja California that he favored. She continued to share an interest in his favorite pastimes, while he remained absent from her sophisticated circle of friends and their more intellectual pursuits.

She thought that perhaps a co-starring vehicle for the Gables might be the answer to ending her long period of inactivity, and she championed a Metro screenplay called *Miss Achilles Heel*, but to no avail. (As *Design for Scandal*, it became a 1941 madcap showcase for Rosalind Russell and Walter Pidgeon.) Continuing to read scripts, Carole entertained an offer from her old friend Harry Cohn at Columbia. Although he couldn't afford her going rate, he was willing to offer profit-sharing, if she approved the screenplay for a comedy called *He Kissed the Bride*. She told him she was looking for something stronger as her comeback and after that she would consider doing *He Kissed the Bride*.

Speaking of comebacks, Ernst Lubitsch thought he had just such a prospect for Miriam Hopkins in *To Be or Not to Be*, for which he was seeking radio comedian Jack Benny. Actually, this was more of a vehicle for its male star, so Hopkins demanded to have the leading lady's lesser role built up for her. The filmmaker was understandably reluctant to order such a rewrite merely to suit his favorite star. Lubitsch was preparing this as an independent production, since none of the Hollywood studios would sanction a farce lampooning the Nazis, and he was having problems raising the money for such a venture.

Lombard heard about this dilemma through Nat Wolff, who couldn't visualize *To Be or Not to Be* for her. But Carole persisted. She'd always longed to do a Lubitsch movie, and trusted his judgment. If he had enough faith in a project to produce it independently, that was enough encouragement for her. Lubitsch was surprised and flattered by her interest, explaining that hers would essentially be a

The Biography

supporting part. Carole read the script and immediately sensed its comic possibilities.

With Lombard's participation, Lubitsch soon found his financing. Jack Benny signed on, but had one misgiving: Carole would receive top billing, to which she responded: "Isn't it only fair, Jack, since you already have all the lines?"

Filmed in less than two months in the autumn of 1941, *To Be or Not to Be* proved a memorable production for all concerned, including many from the old gang at Paramount. Lombard termed it the happiest experience of her career. Not only was she glad to be working again, but the comradeship shared by the hand-picked cast and crew was rare. Lubitsch said she hoped to make many more pictures with his beautiful leading lady, and he expressed the hope of starring her in a comedy about Catherine the Great.

Agreeing to do Columbia's *He Kissed the Bride* (and chopping her asking price to $112,500), Lombard looked forward to having Melvyn Douglas as her co-star. The picture was scheduled to begin production in early 1942. The movie's schedule would coincide with Gable's assignment to make MGM's *Somewhere I'll Find You*, again opposite the enticing Lana Turner. That news enraged Lombard.

And then the world changed on December 7, 1941, with the Japanese attack on Pearl Harbor. President Roosevelt's subsequent Day of Infamy speech so moved Gable and Lombard that they drafted a telegram to the commander in chief, volunteering their services in any way that might be helpful. A White House response assured them that their contribution to the entertainment industry was of continued importance to the country.

With Gable named chairman of the Screen Actors Division of the Hollywood Victory Committee, he was requested by presidential advisor Harry Hopkins to visit his home state of Ohio, selling U.S. Defense Bonds. Gable immediately responded in the negative, informing Hopkins: "I'll help you any way I can, other than personal appearances. But I hate crowds and don't know how to act when I'm in one. Besides, I'm no salesman." Responding to pressure from Lombard, he urged *her* to sell Defense Bonds. Lombard tried to get her husband to accompany her, but MGM refused to delay the start of *Somewhere I'll Find You*. And so she went without him, in the company of her mother and Metro publicist Otto Winkler, boarding an eastbound train for a war bond rally in Indiana. Arriving in a cold and windy Indianapolis on January 15, 1942, Carole Lombard toured the city and spoke in front of the Indiana

A publicity portrait for *To Be or Not to Be*.

State House. At a bond sale, she offered her autograph for every purchase made. The expected goal of $500,000 was far exceeded. Drawing a crowd estimated at 12,000, she infused her fellow Hoosiers with such patriotic enthusiasm that at day's end, some $2,000,000 had been raised. The star capped her appearance by leading a rousing delivery of the National Anthem and a "V for Victory" salute.

The happily exhausted Hollywood trio was scheduled to return home by train, as directed by government advisors interested in the actress' safety. Both Winkler and Bess Peters, who suffered from a fear of flying, strongly urged Carole to stick to prearranged plans. But Lombard, who had never been separated from Gable for more than two days at a time, was anxious to get back. There had been a failed attempt to reach him at home, as well as the studio, and

The Biography

she had uneasy feelings about his well-known rapport with alluring *Somewhere I'll Find You* co-star Lana Turner. Discovering that TWA had three cancellations on a 4:00 a.m. flight to Burbank, she insisted that they avoid the three-day railway journey and return by air. Mother and daughter engaged in a serious argument, and Mrs. Peters, citing negative numerology, was heard to exclaim: "Carole, we must not take that plane!" In her mind were too many coincidental repetitions of the bad-luck number three: their DC-3 plane would be Flight 3 from New York; they were a party of three people, and Carole's age was then 33 and three months. A coin was flipped, Lombard successfully called tails, and the matter was settled.

Lombard and Howard D. Mills of the U.S. Treasury Dept. on January 12, 1942, the day she left Los Angeles for the fateful bond-selling tour.

Their plane, a 21-passenger Douglas "Skyclub," had begun its multi-stop flight in New York, and was slated to reach Los Angeles shortly before six p.m. Flight delays put them two hours behind schedule as they successively stopped in St. Louis, Kansas City, Wichita, Albuquerque and Las Vegas, where they refueled. At 7:07 p.m., the plane left Las Vegas—and 15 minutes later crashed into Double-Up Peak, a near-vertical cliff in the Sierra Nevada Mountains southwest of the city. Its 19 passengers and crew of three were all killed on impact.

An investigation by the Civil Aeronautics Board stated: "[T]he probable cause of the accident to aircraft NC 1946 on January 16, 1942, was the failure of the captain, after departure from Las Vegas, to follow the proper course by making use of the navigational facilities available to him." Among the contributing factors cited were an erroneous compass course, a wartime blackout of most of the area's beacons, and the pilot's failure to confine his flight movements to the actual on-course signals.

The Biography

In Las Vegas, reports of the crash quickly reached the police, and ambulances were dispatched to the area. Darkness and the rugged countryside seriously challenged first-responders. In fact, there was no hope whatever of reaching the crash site before daybreak on the 17th.

At the Gable ranch, Carole's brothers had joined Clark for a surprise homecoming when MGM's Eddie Mannix called with the fragmentary information that Lombard's plane was reported down in Nevada. Hopeful that she was still alive, Gable chartered an immediate flight to Las Vegas, accompanied by Mannix and pal Buster Collier (they were joined there by Spencer Tracy). Their worst fears were confirmed. Of the plane's many military passengers, five had been thrown clear of the wreckage. All others had been so badly burned that only dental records could confirm their identification. The only salvable vestiges of Lombard were a lock of blonde hair and a charred diamond-and-ruby clip.

Two days later, a devastated Gable accompanied three sets of fragmented remains home. Services were held at Forest Lawn's Church of the Recessional on January 22. There were no hymns or prayers, only the Twenty-Third Psalm and the reading of a poem Lombard loved. Most of Hollywood was too shocked and saddened to comment; an uncharacteristically serious Errol Flynn told a *New York Times* reporter: "Carole Lombard's death means that something of gaiety and of beauty has been taken from the world at a time such things are needed most."

President Roosevelt dispatched a telegram to Gable:

> Mrs. Roosevelt and I are deeply distressed. Carole was our friend, our guest in happier days. She brought great joy to all who knew her and to millions who knew her only as a great artist. She gave unselfishly of her time and talent to serve her government in peace and in war. She loved her country. She is and always will be a star, one we shall never forget nor cease to be grateful to.

Released by United Artists a month after her death, *To Be or Not to Be* garnered Lombard some of the most glowing notices of her career, and there are those who consider this her finest moment on the screen. Very much of an ensemble work, it's essentially Jack Benny's picture, although one cannot help appreciate the grace and skill with which she plays "straight man" to him amid this edgy mix of absurd comedy and sobering drama. Some three decades after its release, film historian Leonard Maltin saluted *To Be or Not to Be* as "a brilliant topical comedy whose wisdom and humor transcend the passage of years to make it as effective in the seventies as it was in 1942."

Lombard had willed her entire estate to Gable. Her brothers never spoke to him again. Gable's life, in the wake of Carole's sudden demise,

The Biography

has been much written-about: how he'd dealt with rumors of marital discord and infidelity and of his subsequent war service in the Army Air Corps. And there were two more Gable wives, both blonde, as he appeared to be seeking the elusive impossibility of another Carole Lombard.

Silent star Patsy Ruth Miller, who first knew Lombard when she was still Jane Peters, recalled in her 1988 memoir *My Hollywood: When Both of Us Were Young*, an evening shared with Carole shortly before her final visit to Indiana:

> She was in bed, having just come home from the hospital where she had what she referred to as very, very minor surgery. She laughed and said, "Oh, it was nothing. Just one of those little readjustments we girls sometimes have to have ... you know, so we can have a baby."

Lombard never told Miller that she was pregnant, yet the question remains unanswered.

In a thoughtful, in-depth *Liberty* magazine article, published shortly after the star's death, Adela Rogers St. Johns quoted Lombard on the subject of spiritual beliefs: "I don't get solemn about it, and some people might not understand. That's why I never talk about it. I think it's all here—in the mountains and the desert. I don't think God is a softie, either. In the end it's better if people are forced back into—well—into being right, before they're too far gone. I think your temple is your everyday living."

In the time leading up to her death, Lombard was considered for two pictures that went to Loretta Young, *Bedtime Story* and *Lady from Cheyenne*. Perhaps more definite prospects were *Ball of Fire* and the previously mentioned comedy *He Kissed the Bride*. Barbara Stanwyck earned an Oscar nomination for the former, while *They All Kissed the Bride* (as it was re-titled) went before the cameras with Carole's old Charleston-dancing rival Joan Crawford as the star. Crawford donated her salary to war charities, in Lombard's memory.

The April 1942 *Photoplay* posthumously featured an interview conducted by William French, in which Lombard, evincing the wish that she would die "in full bloom," recalled the untimely 1937 passing of her 26-year-old friend Jean Harlow. To his question of how *she'd* like to be remembered, Carole replied: "Jean had it, a humanness that makes your passing leave a void no one can ever quite fill. If I had that, the other fellow could have the Oscars."

And Hollywood's "Profane Angel" had it.

THE FILMS
(in Order of Release)

A Perfect Crime
Associated Producers–Fox, 1921

Credits: Director-Screenwriter: Allan Dwan, based on the *Saturday Evening Post* story by Carl Clausen. Cinematographer: Lyman Broening. Five reels. Released March 27, 1921.

In *A Perfect Crime* with Monte Blue.

THE FILMS: *Gold Heels / Dick Turpin*

Cast: Monte Blue (*Wally Griggs*); Jacqueline Logan (*Mary Oliver*); Stanton Heck ("*Big Bill*" *Thaine*); Hardee Kirkland (*President Halliday*); Jane Peters [Carole Lombard] (*Wally's Sister*).

In this minor melodrama, an unbilled Jane Peters made her movie debut at 12, portraying the tomboy kid-sister of star Monte Blue. Blue played an ordinary bank messenger who leads a more adventurous life in his spare time. Young Jane's three scenes, all with Blue, were shot in two days at the Fox Studio on Western Avenue, not far from the Peterses' apartment. *A Perfect Crime* received several respectable notices but rather limited distribution as an independent production acquired by an indifferent Fox. Several years passed before Jane Peters' second screen appearance.

Gold Heels
Fox, 1924

Credits: Director: W.S. Van Dyke. Screenwriters: John Stone and Frederic Chapin, based on *Checkers: A Hard Luck Story* by Henry Martin Blossom. Cinematographer: Arthur Todd. Six reels. Released November 30, 1924.

Cast: Robert Agnew (*Boots*); Peggy Shaw (*Pert Barlow*); Lucien Littlefield (*Push Miller*); William Norton Bailey (*Kendall, Jr.*); Carl Stockdale (*Barlow*); Fred Butler (*Kendall Sr.*); Harry Tracey (*Tobe*); Jane Peters [Carole Lombard] (*Girl*).

This minor melodrama derives its title from the name of a broken-down racehorse, bought by a hopeless optimist (Robert Agnew) who trains the animal for competition—and wins both the big race and the girl (Peggy Shaw), despite the machinations of a criminal element. Lombard played a bit part.

Dick Turpin
Fox, 1925

Credits: Director: John G. Blystone. Screenwriters: Charles Kenyon and Charles Darnton. Cinematographer: Dan Clark. 72 minutes. Released February 1925.

Cast: Tom Mix (*Dick Turpin*); Kathleen Myers (*Alice Brookfield*); Philo McCullough (*Lord Churlton*); James Marcus (*Squire Crabstone*); Lucille Hutton (*Sally*); Alan Hale (*Tom King*); Fred Kohler (*Taylor*); Bull

The Films: *Gold and the Girl / Marriage in Transit*

Montana (*Bully Boy*); Fay Holderness (*Barmaid*); Carol [Carole] Lombard (*Girl*); Jack Herrick (*Bristol Bully*).

As "Carol Lombard" (five years before the "e" was added), the 16-year-old made her official debut as a Fox contract starlet in this uncharacteristic Tom Mix vehicle in which he played the fabled eighteenth-century English highwayman. Lombard's one scene with Mix and leading lady Kathleen Myers landed on the cutting room floor, but she can still be spotted elsewhere in the film, among a group of players.

Gold and the Girl
Fox, 1925

Credits: Director: Edmund Mortimer. Screenwriter: John Stone. Cinematographer: Allen Davey. 53 minutes. Released April 1925.

Cast: Buck Jones (*Dan Prestiss*); Elinor Fair (*Ann Donald*); Bruce Gordon (*Bart Cotton*); Lucien Littlefield (*Weasel*); Claude Peyton (*Rankin*); Alphonz Ethier (*Sam Donald*); Carol [Carole] Lombard (*Girl*).

In the first of her three films with Buck Jones, an unbilled Lombard makes a brief walk-on appearance in this Western melodrama about the theft of gold shipments.

Marriage in Transit
Fox, 1925

Credits: Director: Roy William Neill. Screenwriter: Dorothy Yost, based on a story by Grace Livingston Hill. Cinematographer: G.O. Post. 53 minutes. Released March 29, 1925.

Cast: Edmund Lowe (*Holden/Cyril Gordon*); Carol [Carole] Lombard (*Celia Hathaway*); Adolph Milar (*Haynes*); Frank Beal (*Burnham*); Harvey Clarke (*Aide*);

Lombard and Edmund Lowe in *Marriage in Transit*.

Fred Walton (*Valet*); Byron Douglas, Fred Butler, Wade Boteler, Fred Becker and Edward Chandler (*Conspirators*).

In her first leading role, Lombard played opposite the older and already-established Edmund Lowe in a romantic mystery melodrama in which he's a secret agent out to retrieve an important government code by impersonating the conspirators' ringleader. Quite unaware, Lombard weds the undercover man, eventually adjusting to his true identity. Made up to look older, the 16-year-old is acceptably partnered with the 30-something Lowe. *Motion Picture News* found her displaying "good poise and considerable charm."

Hearts and Spurs
Fox, 1925

Credits: Director: W.S. Van Dyke. Screenwriter: John Stone, based on a story by Jackson Gregory; Cinematographer: Allen Davey. 52 minutes. Released June 7, 1925.

In *Hearts and Spurs* with Buck Jones.

Cast: Charles "Buck" Jones (*Hal Emory*); Carol [Carole] Lombard (*Sybil Estabrook*); William Davidson (*Victor Dufresne*); Freeman Wood (*Oscar Estabrook*); Jean LaMotte (*Celeste*); J. Gordon Russell (*Sid Thomas*); Walt Robbins (*Jerry Clark*); Charles Eldridge (*The Sheriff*).

Carol's second leading role at Fox romantically cast her opposite Buck Jones in this minor Western tale of ranchers, gamblers and stagecoach robbery. Director W.S. "Woody" Van Dyke won critical praise for his use of picturesque location backgrounds and for making an unlikely story convincing. A decade later, Van Dyke became one of MGM's most respected directors.

Durand of the Badlands

Fox, 1925

Credits: Director-Screenwriter: Lynn Reynolds, based on a story by Maibell Heikes Justice; Cinematographer: Allen Davey; 62 minutes. Released November 1, 1925.

Cast: Charles "Buck" Jones (*Dick Durand*); Marion Nixon (*Molly Gore*); Malcolm Waite (*Clem Allison*); Fred De Silva (*Pete Garson*); Luke Cosgrove (*Kingdom Come Knapp*); George Lessey (*John Boyd*); Buck Black (*Jimmie*); Ann Johnson (*Clara Belle Seesel*); James Corrigan (*Joe Gore*); Carol [Carole] Lombard (*Ellen Boyd*).

Fox could not have held contractee Lombard in very high esteem, for they relegated her to tenth place in the cast of this, her follow-up Buck Jones Western. She plays the well-to-do young miss who loses him to leading lady Marion Nixon, but only after Jones rescues Carol from the bad guys, who imprisoned her in a mine.

The Road to Glory

Fox, 1926

Credits: Director: Howard Hawks. Screenwriter: L.G. Rigby, based on a story by Howard Hawks. Cinematographer: Joseph August. 93 minutes, Released February 7, 1926.

Cast: May McAvoy (*Judith Allen*); Leslie Fenton (*David Hale*); Ford Sterling (*James Allen*); Rockliffe Fellows (*Del Cole*); Milla Davenport (*Aunt Selma*); John MacSweeney (*Butler*); Carol [Carole] Lombard (*Girl*).

Cast in a minor role in this drama, Lombard had scarcely begun filming when a serious automobile accident necessitated her replacement with another actress. However, she remains visible in two scenes as an unidentified character. *The Road to Glory* was Howard Hawks' directorial debut.

The Johnstown Flood
Fox, 1926

Credits: Director: Irving Cummings. Screenwriters: Edfrid Bingham and Robert Lord. Cinematographer: George Schneiderman. Assistant Director: Charles Woolstenhulme. 70 minutes. Released February 28, 1926.

Cast: George O'Brien (*Tom O'Day*); Florence Gilbert (*Gloria Hamilton*); Janet Gaynor (*Ann Burger*); Anders Randolf (*John Hamilton*); Paul Nicholson (*Peyton Ward*); Paul Panzer (*Joe Burger*); George Harris (*Sidney Mandel*); Max Davidson (*David Mandel*); Walter Perry (*Pat O'Day*); Sid Jordan (*Mullins*); Carol [Carole] Lombard (*Bridesmaid*); Clark Gable (*Bar Patron*); Gary Cooper (*Flood Survivor*); Kay Deslys (*Dance Hall Queen*); Florence Lawrence (*Townswoman*); George Reed (*Dinty*); Dick Rush (*Conspirator*); Fred Warren (*Piano Player*).

Impressive special effects distinguish this disaster drama that marked Janet Gaynor's feature film bow. Lombard's brief appearance as one of Florence Gilbert's four bridesmaids may be attributable to her auto accident. She is glimpsed in several key scenes eavesdropping on George O'Brien's proposal to Gilbert; then as Gilbert dresses for her wedding, and finally amid the bridal ceremony. Reportedly, Carol tested unsuccessfully for the leading ingénue role, played by Gaynor. Coincidentally, future Lombard mate Clark Gable can be glimpsed in a barroom sequence, six years prior to their only co-starring appearance in *No Man of Her Own*. Gary Cooper, also destined to be one of Lombard's leading men a few years hence, also has a bit part.

The Fighting Eagle
Pathé, 1927

Credits: Director: Donald Crisp. Screenwriters: Douglas Z. Doty and John Krafft, from the story *The Exploits of Brigadier Gerard* by Sir Arthur Conan Doyle. Cinematographer: Arthur Miller. Art Director: Mitchell Leisen. Editor: Barbara Hunter. Costumes: Adrian. 85 minutes. Released August 29, 1927.

THE FILMS: *Smith's Pony / A Gold Digger of Weepah*

Cast: Rod La Rocque (*Etienne Girard*); Phyllis Haver (*Countess de Launay*); Sam de Grasse (*Tallyrand*); Max Barwyn (*Napoleon Bonaparte*); Julia Faye (*Josephine*); Carol [Carole] Lombard (*Girl*).

According to both director Donald Crisp and star Rod La Rocque, Lombard played a bit part in this Napoleonic costume drama, produced by the Cecil B. DeMille unit at Pathé. In 1970, the Conan Doyle story served as source material for *The Adventures of Gerard* with Peter McEnery and Claudia Cardinale.

Smith's Pony

Sennett-Pathé, 1927

Credits: Director: Alf Goulding. Producer: Mack Sennett. Two reels. Released September 18, 1927.

Cast: Raymond McKee, Ruth Hiatt, Mary Ann Jackson, Carol [Carole] Lombard, Billy Gilbert

Lombard sought to resurrect her career following the hiatus mandated by her months of recovery from the October 1925 auto accident and facial surgery. Her savior: comedy-shorts producer Mack Sennett, who was less interested in Lombard's scarred cheek than her fetching figure, and offered her a year of employment. In *Smith's Pony*, the first of her 18 Sennett shorts, she was cast as a pretty young thing wrongly suspected of conducting a shipboard love affair with a married man.

A Gold Digger of Weepah

Sennett-Pathé, 1927

Credits: Director: Harry Edwards. Producer: Mack Sennett. Screenwriters: Harry McCoy, Jefferson Moffitt and Vernon Smith. Cinematographers: George Unholz, Vernon L. Walker and William Williams. Editor: William Hornbeck. Two reels. Released October 2, 1927.

Cast: Billy Bevan, Sunshine Hart, Matty Kemp, Alma Bennett, Johnny Burke, Andy Clyde, William McCall, Barney Hellum, Nancy Cornelius, Mary Mayberry, Ernie Alexander, Anita Barnes, Alice Belcher, Hubert Diltz, Billy Gilbert, George Gray, Young Griffo, Minnette Gross, Jules Hanft, Jimmy Hertz, Patrick Kelly, Martin Kinney, Carol [Carole] Lombard, Alice Lyndon, Paul Ross, Valery Schramm, William Searby, Kathryn Stanley, Ted Stroback, Ronald Tilley, Tiny Ward, Peggy Wynne.

THE FILMS: *The Girl from Everywhere*

Lombard (second from left) with Billy Bevan and unidentified players in *A Gold Digger of Weepah*.

Lombard's second Sennett featurette afforded her the opportunity to work with silent comedy veteran Billy Bevan.

The Girl from Everywhere
Sennett-Pathé, 1927

Credits: Director: Edward Cline. Producer: Mack Sennett. Screenwriters: Harry McCoy, Vernon Smith, Betty Browne and Al Giebler. Two reels. Released December 11, 1927.

Cast: Daphne Pollard, Dot Farley, Mack Swain, Carol [Carole] Lombard, Irving Bacon, Madalynne Fields, Anita Barnes, Marie Pergain, Kathryn Stanley, Nancy Cornelius, Leota Winters, Madaline Hurlock, Andy Clyde, William McCall, Barney Hellum, Sterling Holloway.

This comedy short not only introduced Lombard to Sennett superstars Pollard and Swain, but also inaugurated a lifelong friendship with comedienne Madalynne "Fieldsie" Fields.

THE FILMS: *Run, Girl, Run / The Beach Club / Smith's Army Life*

Run, Girl, Run

Sennett-Pathé, 1928

Credits: Director: Alf Goulding. Producer: Mack Sennett. Screenwriters: Harry McCoy and Paul Perez. Editor: William Hornbeck. Two reels. Released January 15, 1928.

Cast: Daphne Pollard, Carol [Carole] Lombard, Irving Bacon, Jim Hallett, Lionel Belmore, Anita Barnes, Leota Winters, Kathryn Stanley, Lucille Miller, Barbara Tennant, Andy Clyde, Ben Wise, Margie Angus, Mary Angus, Betty Arlen and Myron Babcock.

After three Sennett shorts in which she was part of the acting ensemble, Lombard emerged here as a featured player. She's the star sprinter of Sunnydale Girls' School who, after breaking training, regains her colleagues' respect by winning an important footrace for coach Daphne Pollard in competition with a rival academy. Some sequences were filmed in the early two-strip Technicolor process.

The Beach Club

Sennett-Pathé, 1928

Credits: Director: Harry Edwards. Producer: Mack Sennett. Screenwriters: Jefferson Moffitt, Al Giebler and Harry McCoy. Two reels. Released January 22, 1928.

Cast: Billy Bevan, Madeline Hurlock, Carol [Carole] Lombard, Vernon Dent, Johnny Burke, Mary Mayberry, Nancy Cornelius, Barney Hellum, Andy Clyde, Matty Kemp, Irving Bacon, Marie Pergain, William McCall, Marcella Arnold, Patsy Barlowe, Anita Barnes, Nita Cavalier, Diana Dare, William Davis, Hubert Diltz, Rosita Foucher, Rupert Franklin, Billy Gilbert, Young Griffo, Ruby Groh, Minette Gross, Charley Hahm, Jack Herrick, Jimmy Hertz, Dena Hill, Myra Kinch, Gordon Lewis, Alice Lyndon, Evelyn McNames, Lucille McNames, Ernest Melanson, Patsy Meredith, Pat Moyer, Betty Nelson, Iris Nicholson, Captain Pepper, Beth Peters, Ralph Rigard.

Smith's Army Life

Sennett-Pathé / 1928

Credits: Director: Alf Goulding. Producer: Mack Sennett. Screenwriters: Jefferson Moffit and Vernon Smith. Editor: William Hornbeck. Two reels. Released February 5, 1928.

THE FILMS: *The Best Man / The Swim Princess*

Cast: Raymond McKee, Ruth Hiatt, Mary Ann Jackson, Vernon Dent, Glen Cavender, William McCall, Irving Bacon, Andy Clyde, Barney Hellum, John Quillan, Mary Mayberry, Balto, Anita Barnes, Eleanor Black, Jimmy Hertz, Willie Keeler, Matty Kemp, Gordon Lewis, Carol [Carole] Lombard, Sam Lufkin, Art Rowlands, William Searby, George Spear, Harry Spear, Kathryn Stanley, Ted Stroback, Ronald Tilley, Tiny Ward.

This was an entry in Sennett's ongoing "Smith Family" two-reel comedy series.

The Best Man
Sennett-Pathé, 1928

Credits: Director: Harry Edwards. Producer: Mack Sennett. Screenwriters: Dudley Early and Harry Edwards. Supervisor: John A. Waldron. Two reels. Released February 19, 1928.

Cast: Billy Bevan, Alma Bennett, Vernon Dent, Carol [Carole] Lombard, Andy Clyde, William Searby, Nancy Cornelius, Irving Bacon, William McCall, Marie Pergain, Mary Mayberry, Barney Hellum, Sunshine Hart, Betty Amann, Peggy Gaddis, Gertrude Garrett, Young Griffo, Minette Gross, Jules Hanft, Pat Harmon, Bill Harris, Ralph Hennessey, Jimmy Hertz, Agnes Holden, Fred Holmes, Sally Hurst, Lyman Jones, Len Lander, Gloria Lee, Gordon Lewis, Joy Lind, Ruth Lind, Alice Lyndon, Pat Moyer, Paul Ross, Art Rowlands, Sam Sendler, Walter Shaw, Wanda Sibbald, Kathryn Stanley, Orvis Thomas.

Carol Lombard can be glimpsed in one scene as a wedding guest.

The Swim Princess
Sennett-Pathé / 1928

Credits: Director: Alf Goulding. Producer: Mack Sennett. Supervisor: John A. Waldron. Screenwriters: James Tynan and Frank Capra. Editor: William Hornbeck. Two reels. Released February 26, 1928.

Cast: Daphne Pollard, Andy Clyde, Carol [Carole] Lombard, Cissie Fitzgerald, Jim Hallett, Barney Hellum.

As in *Run, Girl, Run*, Lombard is again the main focus of the picture, this time as the star swimmer of her school. Some key scenes were shot in color. Note the early appearance of Frank Capra's name, here as co-author of the screenplay.

THE FILMS: *The Bicycle Flirt / Half a Bride*

Lombard (at right) with unidentified players in *The Swim Princess*.

The Bicycle Flirt
Sennett-Pathé, 1928

Credits: Director: Harry Edwards. Producer: Mack Sennett. Screenwriters: Vernon Smith and Harry McCoy. Two reels. Released March 18, 1928.

Cast: Billy Bevan, Vernon Dent, Carol [Carole] Lombard, Dot Farley.

Mustachioed Billy Bevan has the title role as a suitor who unsuccessfully courts Lombard on a bike supported by an automobile.

Half a Bride
Paramount, 1928

Credits: Director: Gregory La Cava. Screenwriters: Doris Anderson, Percy Heath and Julian Johnson. Cinematographer: Victor Milner. Editor: Verna Willis. 70 minutes. Released June 16, 1928.

Cast: Esther Ralston (*Patience Winslow*); Gary Cooper (*Captain Edmunds*); William Worthington (*Mr. Winslow*); Freeman Wood (*Jed*

The Films: *The Divine Sinner*

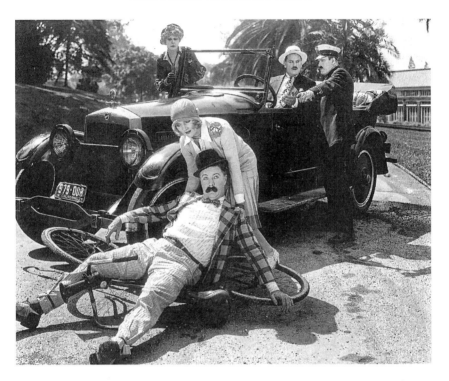

In *The Bicycle Flirt*, Lombard assists Billy Bevan, with Dot Farley and Vernon Dent in the background. The policeman is an unidentified bit player.

Session); Mary Doran (*Betty Brewster*); Guy Oliver (*Chief Engineer*); Ray Gallagher (*Second Engineer*).

Two years before becoming a Paramount contract player (and star), Lombard had a brief scene with Gary Cooper in this Paramount picture; it was not included in the release version of this entertaining adventure drama. Director Gregory La Cava would play a more important role in her future with *Big News* and, especially, *My Man Godfrey*.

The Divine Sinner
Trem Carr-Rayart, 1928

Credits: Director: Scott Pembroke. Producer: Trem Carr. Screenwriter: Robert Anthony Dillon. Cinematographer: Hap Depew. Editor: J.S. Harrington. 60 minutes. Released July 15, 1928.

Cast: Vera Reynolds (*Lillia Ludwig*); Nigel De Brulier (*Minister of Police*); Bernard Siegel (*Johann Ludwig*); Ernest Hilliard (*Prince Josef*

THE FILMS: *The Girl from Nowhere*

Miguel); John Peters (*Luque Bernstorff*); Carol [Carole] Lombard (*Millie Claudert*); Harry Northrup (*Ambassador D'Ray*); James Ford (*Heinrich*); Alphonse Martel (*Paul Coudert*).

Amidst shooting her many Sennett comedy shorts, Lombard had an unimportant supporting role in this long-forgotten Poverty Row quickie that garnered but a few Los Angeles bookings. Vera Reynolds, a former DeMille star on the decline, had the title role of an Austrian girl who falls in with the Paris underworld before finding romance with prince Ernest Hilliard.

The Girl from Nowhere
Sennett-Pathé, 1928

Credits: Director: Harry Edwards. Producer: Mack Sennett. Screenwriters: Ewart Anderson and Jefferson Moffitt. Two reels. Released August 5, 1928.

Cast: Daphne Pollard, Dot Farley, Mack Swain, Sterling Holloway, Madalynne Fields, Carol [Carole] Lombard.

Lombard (at left) with Madalynne Fields and Daphne Pollard in *The Girl from Nowhere*.

Carol played an aspiring movie actress in this Hollywood farce about a wardrobe mistress (Pollard) and a temperamental director (Swain).

His Unlucky Night
Sennett-Pathé, 1928

Credits: Director: Harry Edwards. Producer: Mack Sennett. Supervisor: John A. Waldron. Screenwriters: Vernon Smith and Nick Barrows. Editor: William Hornbeck. Two reels. Released August 12, 1928.

Cast: Billy Bevan, Vernon Dent, Carol [Carole] Lombard, Dot Farley, Bud Jamison, Andy Clyde, Carmelita Geraghty, William McCall, Sunshine Hart, Art Rowlands, Alice Belcher, Sammy Blum, Bill Boardway, Harry Carlie, Vaughn Clark, Possums the Cat, Barbara Clayton, Mariana Cummings, William Dale, William Davis, Hazel Delmar, Jean Douglas, Florence Dudley, Bill Dunn, Jack Eshbaugh, Madalynne Fields, Harry Fleming, Otto Fries, Jane Fuller, Betty Geary, Austin George, George Gofert, George Gray, Fronzie Gunn, Frances Hamilton, Charles Hammond, J.E. Harrison, Nancy Hellman, Barney Hellum, Sally Hurst, Olaf Hytten, Eugene Jones, Ray Jones.

Lombard was featured as telephone operator Peggy, who helps traveling salesman Billy Bevan in his matchmaking efforts with pal Vernon Dent.

Smith's Restaurant
Sennett-Pathé, 1928

Credits: Director: Phil Whitman. Producer: Mack Sennett. Screenwriters: St. Elmo Boyce and Frank Terry. Editor: William Hornbeck. Supervisor: John A. Waldron. Assistant Director: Harry Connett. Two reels. Released August 19, 1928.

Cast: Raymond McKee, Ruth Hiatt, Mary Ann Jackson, Daphne Pollard, William Searby, Vernon Dent, Madalynne Fields, Andy Clyde, William McCall, Barney Hellum, Mary Mayberry, Patrick Kelly, Balto, Irving Bacon, Charles Hamme, Joe Kessel, Len Lauder, Gloria Lee, Carol [Carole] Lombard, Helen Miller, Pat Moyer, Margaret Rimkus, Paul Ross, Valery Schramm, Wanda Sibbald, Alice Ward, Kathrin Clare Ward, Albert Whitlock, Ernie Alexander.

This was the 21st entry in Sennett's "Smith Family" series.

Power

Pathé, 1928

Credits: Director: Howard Higgin. Producer: Ralph Block. Screenwriters: Tay Garnett and John Krafft. Cinematographer: Peverell Marley. Editor: Doane Harrison. Art Director: Mitchell Leisen. Assistant Director: Robert Fellows. 65 minutes. Released September 23, 1928.

Cast: William Boyd (*Husky*); Alan Hale (*Handsome*); Jacqueline Logan (*Lorraine La Rue*); Jerry Drew (*The Menace*); Joan Bennett *(A Dame)*; Carol [Carole] Lombard (*Another Dame*); Pauline Curley (*Still Another Dame*).

Lombard's inauspicious feature-film bow for Pathé was a small, nameless role as "Another Dame" in this male-oriented tale of rival skirt-chasing ironworkers (William Boyd and Alan Hale) on a dam-building assignment. Carol's fellow "dames" included Pauline Curley and a film-debuting Joan Bennett, 18 years old and still a natural blonde.

The Campus Vamp

Sennett-Pathé, 1928

Lombard (lower right) and unidentified players in *The Campus Vamp*.

THE FILMS: *Motorboat Mamas / Me, Gangster*

Credits: Director: Harry Edwards. Producer: Mack Sennett. Screenwriters: Ewart Adamson and Carl Harbaugh. Cinematographer: Fred Dawson. Editor: William Hornbeck. Two reels. Released September 23, 1928

Cast: Daphne Pollard, Matty Kemp, Sally Eilers, Carol [Carole] Lombard, Johnny Burke, Leota Winters, Kathryn Stanley, Lucille Miller, Anita Barnes, Alice Ward, Mary Wiggins and Jack Cooper.

Lombard was a bathing beauty comic foil in this beach comedy.

Motorboat Mamas
Sennett-Pathé, 1928

Credits: Directors: Harry Edwards and Phil Whitman. Screenwriters: Betty Browne and Bennett Cohen. Two reels. Released September 30, 1928.

Cast: Billy Bevan, Alma Bennett, Vernon Dent, Carmelita Geraghty, Barbara Tennant, Sunshine Hart, Louise Carver, William McCall, George Gray, Barney Hellum, Irving Bacon, Jimmy Hertz, Billy Gilbert, Minette Grosse, Cecilia Cameron, Jack Carlyle, James Conaty, Frank Crayne, Douglas Dale, William Davis, Hazel Delmar, Gene Douglas, Bob Erickson, Jack Eshbaugh, Cecille Evans, Dot Farley, Jimmy Fortier, Clem Fuller, Peggy Gaddis, Gertrude Garrett, Greta Granstedt, Doris Hamilton, Jules Hanft, Bill Howell, Ray Jones, H. Joseph, Malcolm Letts, Gordon Lewis, Joy Lind, Carol [Carole] Lombard, Helen Louise, Frank Mason, Lucille McNames, Harold McNulty, Kitty Menge, Elinor Merry, Marie Messinger.

Lombard was briefly seen as an automobile passenger.

Me, Gangster
Fox, 1928

Credits: Director: Raoul Walsh. Screenwriters: Charles Francis Coe, William Kernell and Raoul Walsh, based on the *Saturday Evening Post* story by Charles Francis Coe. Cinematographer: Arthur Edeson. Editor: Louis Loeffler. Assistant Director: Archibald Buchanan. 70 minutes. Released October 14, 1928.

Cast: June Collyer (*Mary Regan*); Don Terry (*Jimmy Williams*); Anders Randolf (*Russ Williams*); Stella Adams (*Lizzie Williams*); Al Hill (*Danny*); Burr McIntosh (*Bill Lane*); Walter James (*Police Captain Dodds*); Gustav von Seyffertitz (*Factory Owner*); Herbert Ashton (*Sucker*); Harry Castle (*Philly Kidd*); Joe Brown (*Joe Brown*); Arthur

Stone (*Dan the Dude*); Nigel De Brulier (*Danish Looie*); Carol [Carole] Lombard (*Blonde Rosie*); Bob Perry (*Tuxedo George*).

Me, Gangster was a prestigious Fox melodrama with a top director in Raoul Walsh. Again, Lombard's role was small. As the trampish "Blonde Rosie," she sported exaggerated makeup and had one good scene. None of the critics appeared to notice.

Show Folks

Pathé, 1928

Credits: Director: Paul L. Stein. Producer: Ralph Block. Screenwriters: Jack Jungmeyer, George Dromgold and John Krafft, based on a story by Phillip Dunning. Cinematographers: Peverell Marley and David Abel. Art Director: Mitchell Leisen. Editor: Doane Harrison. Song: "No One but Me" by Al Koppel, Billy Stone and Charles Weinberg. Assistant Director: Robert Fellows. 70 minutes. Released October 21, 1928.

With Eddie Quillan in *Show Folks*.

THE FILMS: *Hubby's Weekend Trip / The Campus Carmen*

Cast: Eddie Quillan (*Eddie*); Lina Basquette (*Rita*); Carol [Carole] Lombard (*Cleo*); Robert Armstrong (*Owens*); Crauford Kent (*McNary*); Bessie Barriscale (*Kitty*); Joan Bennett (*Nightclub Patron*).

For middle-ranking Pathé, *Show Folks* was quite an important picture, and especially for Lombard. Cast as the movie's third lead, she was the comedy's unscrupulous "other woman," who nearly steals vaudeville-hoofer star Eddie Quillan away from dancing partner Lina Basquette.

With the rapid approach of sound, *Show Folks*, like many other silents of its era, featured a talking sequence (approximately ten minutes) to help attract an audience. There was some understandable confusion among moviegoers, generated by the similar title of MGM's same-year, more prestigious feature *Show People*. For the film's secondary female, there was finally some notice by the press: *Picture Play* observed, "Carol Lombard, a very pretty blonde, is worth watching."

Hubby's Weekend Trip
Sennett-Pathé, 1928

Credits: Director: Harry Edwards. Producer: Mack Sennett. Screenwriters: Ewart Adamson, Betty Browne, Jefferson Moffitt, Vernon Smith and Maurice Stephens. Two reels. Released November 1, 1928.

Cast: Billy Bevan, Dot Farley, Vernon Dent, Carmelita Geraghty, Alice Ward, Anita Barnes, Lucille Miller, Kathryn Stanley, Leota Winters, Betty Amann, Lionel Backus, Irving Bacon, Eugene Beday, Walter Byron, Hal Craig, William Davis, Hubert Diltz, James Dime, Yvonne Dumont, Charles Dunbar, Elmer Fain, Ardon Faught, Harry Fleming, Otto Fries, Austin George, Billy Gilbert, Greta Granstedt, George Gray, Lois Hardwick, Pat Harmon, Frank Heath, Jimmy Hertz, Matthew Jones, Natalie Joyce, Carol [Carole] Lombard, William McCall, Patsy Meredith, Pat Moyer, Jack Paul, Evelyn Revier, Ronald R. Rondell, Paul Ross, Art Rowlands, Thelma Salter, Valery Schramm, Norman Senior, Hyca Slocum, Myer Steinfeld, Ted Stroback, Harry Wagner.

The Campus Carmen
Sennett-Pathé, 1928

Credits: Director: Alf Goulding. Producer: Mack Sennett. Screenwriters: Jefferson Moffitt and Earle Rodney. Two reels. Released November 25, 1928.

Cast: Carol [Carole] Lombard, Sally Eilers, Daphne Pollard, Madalynne Fields, Matty Kemp, Johnny Burke, Carmelita Geraghty, Vernon Dent.

Once again, Sennett employed Technicolor segments to highlight a short silent farce, this time focusing on an amateurish college production of Bizet's opera *Carmen*.

Ned McCobb's Daughter

Pathé, 1929

Credits: Director: William J. Cowen. Screenwriters: Beulah Marie Dix and Edwin Justus Mayer, based on the play by Sidney Howard. Cinematographer: David Abel. Editor: Anne Bauchens. Art Director: Edward Jewell. Assistant Director: Roy Burns. 71 minutes. Released January 12, 1929.

Cast: Irene Rich (*Carrie McCobb*); Theodore Roberts (*Ned McCobb*); Robert Armstrong (*Babe Callahan*); George Barraud (*George Callahan*); Edward Hearn (*Butterworth*); Carol [Carole] Lombard (*Jennie*); Louis Natheaux (*Kelly*).

Variety had nothing but praise for this adaptation of Sidney Howard's stage hit about bootlegging, murder and romantic complications in Down East Maine. Lombard had the supporting part of an impertinent waitress employed in a spa run by the film's star, Irene Rich. *Film Spectator* took note: "Carol Lombard repeats the good impression she made on me in *Show Folks*."

Good though it may have been, *Ned McCobb's Daughter*, like many another picture released late during 1928 and early 1929, suffered from being a silent movie at a time when talkies were fast taking over the motion picture industry. Pathé considered remaking the film as a talking picture, using Howard's original stage script, but the costs were discouraging; it was decided to simply add synchronized sounds such as crying seagulls and crashing waves, but no voices. *The New York Times* cited the film for containing "some excellent dramatic passages," but audiences were not impressed.

Matchmaking Mamas

Sennett-Pathé, 1929

Credits: Director: Harry Edwards. Producer: Mack Sennett. Supervisor: John A. Waldron. Screenwriters: Jefferson Moffitt and Carl

Harbaugh. Editor: William Hornbeck. Two reels. Released March 31, 1929.

Cast: Johnny Burke, Matty Kemp, Sally Eilers, Carol [Carole] Lombard, Daphne Pollard, Irving Bacon, Andy Clyde, Ronald Tilley.

This comedy short centered on a couple's marriage plans for their children, Sally Eilers and Lombard.

High Voltage
Pathé, 1929

Credits: Director: Howard Higgin. Screenwriters: Elliott Clawson, James Gleason and Kenyon Nicholson. Cinematographer: John Mescall. Editor: Doane Harrison. Song: "Colleen O'Kildare" by George Green and George Waggner. Assistant Director: Leigh Smith. Art Director: Edward Jewell. 57 minutes. Released April 3, 1929. DVD availability: public domain (various sources).

Cast: William Boyd (*Bill Dougherty*); Carol [Carole] Lombard

Lombard (right) in *High Voltage* with Diane Ellis and William Boyd.

(*Billie Davis*); Owen Moore (*Detective Dan Egan*); Phillips Smalley (*J. Milton Hendricksen*); Billy Bevan (*Gus Engstrom*); Diane Ellis (*Diane*).

Lombard's first all-talkie was this minor melodrama about a small group of bus passengers, stranded by a High Sierras snowstorm, finding refuge in an abandoned church occupied by escaped convict William Boyd. She's a felon being escorted to prison by detective Owen Moore. Boyd and Owen both take a romantic interest in Lombard, and although she and Boyd attempt to run away together, they ultimately decide to stay and pay their social debts. Boyd's profession had been that of a telephone lineman, but apart from that barely mentioned fact, *High Voltage* is a meaningless title.

The movie's laughably foolish screenplay, which somehow took three writers to devise, featured dialogue too inept for even a better director than Howard Higgin to make credible.

Don't Get Jealous

Sennett-Pathé, 1929

Credits: Director: Phil Whitman. Producer: Mack Sennett. Screenwriters: Harry Edwards, Carl Harbaugh, Lee Hugunin, Jefferson Moffitt, James J. Tynan and Phil Whitman. Two reels. Released May 19, 1929.

Cast: Billy Bevan, Vernon Dent, Carmelita Geraghty, Edna Mae Cooper, Andy Clyde, Spencer Bell, James Hanft, Matthew Jones, Carol [Carole] Lombard, William McCall, Art Rowlands, Ted Stroback, Tiny Ward.

Carol's final comedy short for Sennett relegated her to yet another small supporting role. It was also her last silent.

Big News

Pathé, 1929

Credits: Director: Gregory La Cava. Screenwriters: Walter DeLeon and Jack Jungmyer, based on the play *For Two Cents* by George S. Brooks. Cinematographer: Arthur Miller. Editor: Doane Harrison. Sound: D.A. Cutler and Clarence M. Wickes. 75 minutes. Released September 7, 1929. DVD availability: public domain (various sources).

Cast: Robert Armstrong (*Steve Banks*); Carol [Carole] Lombard (*Marg Banks*); Sam Hardy (*Reno*); Tom Kennedy (*Patrolman Ryan*);

The Films: *Big News*

Lombard in *Big News* with Robert Armstrong.

Louis Payne (*Hensel*); Wade Boteler (*O'Neil*); Charles Sellon (*Addison*); Warner Richmond (*District Attorney*); Robert Dudley (*Telegraph Editor*); Gertrude Sutton (*Helen*); James Donlan (*Deke*); Cupid Ainesworth (*Society Editor*); Fred Bahrle (*Elevator Man*); Colin Chase (*Birn*).

Among the first of many newspaper-focused melodramas released during the early days of talking pictures, *Big News* was originally planned as a silent film prior to the sound revolution. It's a standard program picture for which its director, Gregory La Cava, held little respect, confiding to his leading lady: "If we rattle the dialogue real fast, people won't be able to reflect on how rotten it is. I guess the main thing is to be busy all the time, just keep moving. Stand still and the picture might die."

Lombard played the steadfast wife neglected by her tough, hard-drinking reporter-spouse Robert Armstrong. Complications ensue when he investigates a dope ring, masterminded by gangster Sam Hardy, one of Armstrong's paper's valued advertisers. *New York Times* critic Mordaunt Hall called Lombard "a step above the ingénue film heroine and manages her part with sufficient restraint."

The Racketeer
Pathé, 1929

Credits: Director: Howard Higgin. Associate Producer: Ralph Block. Screenwriters: Paul Gangelin and A.A. Kline. Cinematographer: David Abel. Art Director: Edward Jewell. Set Decorator: T.E. Dickson. Editor: Doane Harrison. Costumes: Gwen Wakeling. Assistant Director: George Webster. Sound: A.A. Cutler and Clarence M. Wickes. Music: Josiah Zuro. 66 minutes. Released November 9, 1929. DVD availability: public domain (various sources).

Cast: Robert Armstrong (*Mahlon Keene*); Carol [Carole] Lombard (*Rhoda*); Roland Drew (*Tony*); Jeanette Loff (*Millie*); John Loder (*Jack*); Paul Hurst (*Mehaffey*); Winter Hall (*Mr. Simpson*); Winifred Harris (*Mrs. Simpson*); Kit Guard (*Gus*); Al Hill (*Squid*); Bobby Dunn (*The Rat*); Hedda Hopper (*Mrs. Lee*); Budd Fine (*Bernie Weber*).

Lombard's last Pathé film again teams her with Robert Armstrong (in the title role), who's sufficiently attracted to the young blonde to arrange a concert featuring her violinist-boyfriend (Roland Drew). Out of gratitude, she accepts crime boss Armstrong's marriage offer. But before they can be wed, he's killed in a gun battle, leaving Carol to return to her musician.

Variety termed the movie a "hackneyed, stereotyped production," while *Film Daily* sang the praises of its leading lady: "Carol Lombard proves a real surprise, and does her best work to date. In fact, this is the first opportunity she has had to prove that she has the stuff to go over. With looks and a good trouping sense, she also has the personality."

Dynamite
MGM, 1929

Credits: Director-Producer: Cecil B. DeMille. Screenwriters: Jeanie Macpherson, John Howard Lawson and Gladys Unger. Assistant Director: Mitchell Leisen. Cinematographer: Peverell Marley. Editor: Anne Bauchens. Art Directors: Cedric Gibbons and Mitchell Leisen. Costumes: Adrian. Music: Herbert Stothart. Song: "How Am I to Know?" by Dorothy Parker and Jack King. Sound: J.K. Brock and Douglas Shearer. 118 minutes. Released December 13, 1929.

Cast: Conrad Nagel (*Roger Towne*); Kay Johnson (*Cynthia Crothers*); Charles Bickford (*Hagon Derk*); Julia Faye (*Marcia Towne*); Joel

McCrea (*Marco*); Muriel McCormac (*Katie Derk*); Robert Edeson, William Holden and Henry Stockbridge (*Three Wise Fools*); Leslie Fenton and Barton Hepburn (*Young "Vultures"*); Tyler Brooke (*The Life of the Party*); Ernest Hilliard, June Nash, Nancy Dover, Neely Edwards, Jerry Zier and Rita LaRoy (*Good Mixers*); Clarence Burton and James Farley (*Officers*); Robert T. Haines (*The Judge*); Douglas Frazer Scott (*Bobby*); Jane Keckley (*Bobby's Mother*); Fred Walton (*The Doctor*); Ynez Seabury, Blanche Craig and Mary Gordon (*Neighbors*); Scott Kolk (*Radio Announcer*); Russ Columbo (*Mexican Prisoner*).

Dynamite represents the only occasion upon which Lombard was fired from a picture: Cecil B. DeMille, directing his first talkie, didn't think she took her part seriously as she fluffed her lines and, characteristically, joked about it. He would later declare that he "discharged her for a lack of talent," while allowing, "I'm not the world's greatest talent scout."

As to which role Lombard was to play, there seems to be some controversy: Her biographer Larry Swindell has her cast as the ingénue eventually enacted by Muriel McCormac, while Mitchell Leisen told interviewer David Chierichetti, "Lombard was originally announced for the role Kay Johnson played." Whatever the facts, it seems that Lombard filmed for several days before her dismissal, and that she can be briefly spotted in the release print.

Dynamite was released in December of 1929, following the release of *Big News* and *The Racketeer*, both made after Carol wad dismissed from the DeMille film.

The Arizona Kid
Fox, 1930

Credits: Director: Alfred Santell. Screenwriters: Ralph Block and Joseph Wright. Cinematographer: Glen MacWilliams. Editor: Paul Weatherwax. Art Director: Joseph Wright. Costumes: Sophie Wachner. Assistant Director: Marty Santell. Sound: George Leverett. 83 minutes. Released May 27, 1930.

Cast: Warner Baxter (*The Arizona Kid*); Mona Maris (*Lorita*); Carol [Carole] Lombard (*Virginia Hoyt*); Soledad Jiminez (*Pulga*); Theodore von Eltz (*Nick Hoyt*); Arthur Stone (*Snakebite Pete*); Walter P. Lewis (*Sheriff Andrews*); Hank Mann (*Bartender Bill*); Jack Herrick (*The Hoboken Hooker*); Wilfred Lucas (*Manager*); De Sacia

The Films: *The Arizona Kid*

Lombard, left, with Mona Maris and Warner Baxter in *The Arizona Kid*.

Mooers (*Molly*); James Gibson (*Stage Driver*); Larry McGrath (*Homer Snook*).

Temporarily free of studio commitments, Lombard returned to Fox for this sequel to their 1929 hit *In Old Arizona*. (Its star Warner Baxter had won a Best Actor Academy Award for his performance.) For Lombard, it was a throwback to the sagebrush flicks of her mid–1920s days at Fox, but on a greatly elevated level. With his Cisco Kid of the earlier film now known as the *Arizona* Kid, Baxter essentially recreated his original lawless characterization, with Carol in the chief supporting role of a villainess! With her husband (Theodore von Eltz), posing as a brother and sister from the East, she charms her way into the Kid's emotional confidence with the hope of discovering the location of his secret gold mine for their own selfish benefit. But, before the end titles, she has lost both her "brother" and the Kid, who rides off with dance hall girlfriend Mona Maris.

The New York Times admired Lombard's beauty, but expressed doubts as to "whether she is suited to the role of Virginia." *Photoplay* thought she did well with a disagreeable part.

Safety in Numbers
Paramount, 1930

Credits: Director: Victor Schertzinger. Screenwriters: Marion Dix, George Marion, Jr., and Percy Heath. Cinematographer: Henry Gerrard. Editor: Robert Bassler. Songs: "My Future Just Passed," "The Pickup," "Business Girl," "Pepola," "I'd Like to be a Bee in Your Boudoir," "You Appeal to Me" and "Do You Play, Madame?" by George Marion, Jr., and Richard A. Whiting. Choreographer: David Bennett. Sound: Eugene Merritt. 78 minutes. Released June 7, 1930.

Cast: Charles "Buddy" Rogers (*William Butler Reynolds*); Kathryn Crawford (*Jacqueline*); Josephine Dunn (*Maxine*); Carol [Carole] Lombard (*Pauline*); Geneva Mitchell (*Cleo Carewe*); Roscoe Karns (*Bertram Shapiro*); Francis McDonald (*Phil Kempton*); Virginia Bruce (*Alma McGregor*); Richard Tucker (*C. Carstairs Reynolds*); Raoul Paoli (*Jules*); Lawrence Grant (*Commodore Brinker*); Louise Beavers (*Messaline*).

Safety in Numbers, a one-film assignment at Paramount, anticipated Lombard's longest association with any Hollywood studio: 22 movies in eight years. In this vehicle for their reigning juvenile Charles "Buddy" Rogers, she's billed fourth after the star and leading ladies Kathryn Crawford and Josephine Dunn (both now long-forgotten). The foolish plot casts Rogers as a 20-year-old aspiring songwriter who will realize a fortune on his next birthday. He's naïve about women; to correct this shortcoming, his uncle sets him up in a New York City apartment, in the company of three Broadway showgirls, to "educate" him. Plot complications involve his efforts to write a musical revue with parts for the trio, despite production problems and the interference of a conniving chorine (Virginia Bruce). In the finale, Rogers ends up with Crawford.

Lombard gets to parade a glamorously revealing wardrobe, as well as render the amorous number "You Appeal to Me" featuring the suggestive lyric "You have the key to my ignition." Most importantly, it landed her a seven-year contract at Paramount.

Fast and Loose
Paramount, 1930

Credits: Directors: Fred Newmeyer and (uncredited) Bertram Harrison. Screenwriters: Doris Anderson, Jack Kirkland and Preston Sturges, based on the play *The Best People* by Avery Hopwood.

THE FILMS: *Fast and Loose*

With Frank Morgan in *Fast and Loose*.

Adaptation: David Gray. Cinematographer: William Steiner. Sound: C.A. Tuthill. 75 minutes. Released November 8, 1930.

Cast: Miriam Hopkins (*Marion Lenox*); Carole Lombard (*Alice O'Neil*); Frank Morgan (*Bronson Lenox*); Charles Starrett (*Henry Morgan*); Henry Wadsworth (*Bertie Lenox*); Winifred Harris (*Carrie Lenox*); Herbert Yost (*George Grafton*); David Hutcheson (*Lord Rockingham*); Ilka Chase (*Millie Montgomery*); Herschel Mayall (*Judge Summers*).

The Best People enjoyed a Broadway success in 1924; Paramount brought it to the silent screen the following year with Margaret Morris, Warner Baxter and Esther Ralston in the roles played in this 1930 remake by Miriam Hopkins, Charles Starrett and Lombard. With the addition of sound in 1930, it was retitled *Fast and Loose* and, to accommodate film-debuting stage luminary Hopkins, it was shot, like many of the studio's late-silent and early-talkie productions, mainly at their East Coast studio in Astoria, Queens, New York. This often made it possible to film on Long Island during the day with New York actors appearing on Broadway stages at night.

A Broadway fixture throughout much of the 1920s, Hopkins

stars in this slight comedy as a willful, capricious debutante slated to wed stuffy Englishman David Hutcheson to please her snobbish high-society parents. But there's no love attached to this marriage of convenience, and her subsequent rebellion gains the full support of her black-sheep partying brother (Henry Wadsworth), who plans to marry his quite-respectable chorus-girlfriend (Lombard) even though his parents will be outraged. Hopkins falls for a hunky mechanic (Charles Starrett) while Wadsworth strategizes to make his class-conscious family accept Lombard, who has encouraged her suitor to mend his dissolute ways. Eventually, social reform is accomplished, and this fluffy comedy of manners concludes on a note of unbelievable happiness for all concerned.

With her carefully enunciated stage speech, which occasionally lapsed into a Georgia twang, Hopkins offered a different sort of movie star, with her unglamorous but attractive appearance. Obviously, she would need to rely on ability rather than looks. Fortunately, she had the talent. On the other hand, second lead Lombard, already a screen veteran at 22, displayed both the talent and the beauty. The role of chorine Alice O'Neil doesn't allow her much footage to make an impression, but everything does work.

Fast and Loose did little to capture the interest of 1930 audiences. *The New York Times* praised the movie's "brilliant" camerawork and called the film "a highly amusing feature with competent acting."

Incidentally, this was the movie that permanently altered the Lombard spelling of "Carol" to "Carole." Apparently, someone in Paramount's publicity department—amid the picture's last-minute title change from *The Best People* to *Fast and Loose*—mistakenly added the "e" to her first name on an advertising poster. Initially upset by the gaffe, she gave the matter careful consideration before deciding that she approved. And thus "Carole" became the official spelling.

It Pays to Advertise
Paramount, 1931

Credits: Director: Frank Tuttle. Screenwriters: Arthur Kober and Ethel Doherty, based on the play by Roi Cooper Mergrue and Walter Hackett. Cinematographer: Archie J. Stout. 66 minutes. Released February 28, 1931.

Cast: Norman Foster (*Rodney Martin*); Carole Lombard (*Mary Grayson*); Skeets Gallagher (*Ambrose Peale*); Eugene Pallette (*Cyrus*

Martin); Lucien Littlefield (*Andrew*); Helen Johnson (*Comtesse de Beaurien*); Louise Brooks (*Thelma Temple*); Morgan Wallace (*Donald McChesney*); Marcia Manners (*Miss Burke*); Tom Kennedy (*Perkins*); Junior Coghlan (*Office Boy*); John Howell (*Johnson*); John Sinclair (*Window Cleaner*).

As Carole's first leading role at Paramount, the studio cast slow-rising Norman Foster, in the vain hope of developing a new screen team along the lines of Fox's Janet Gaynor and Charles Farrell. In this light comedy satirizing the world of advertising, she's the adoring secretary to his young ad executive as he schemes to rival his father (Eugene Pallette) in the soap business. It's all about a product called "Thirteen— unlucky for dirt."

Hard times had forced Paramount to cut down on expenses, which accounts for the picture's skimpy three-week shooting schedule. As a footnote to *It Pays to Advertise*, it's worth noting the "cameo" presence of the now-legendary Louise Brooks, billed seventh as a glamorous movie queen, a role that reflected her brief former glory as an iconic Paramount star of the late '20s.

Theatre magazine's critic wrote: "Although slightly outmoded and rather obvious for this sophisticated generation, *It Pays to Advertise* is still good fun. The old stage play has been jazzed up considerably and the picture is capably acted. Miss Lombard is an excellent and appealing secretary."

The movie's working title was *Have You Got It?* Paramount filmed an earlier adaptation of the play in 1919 with Bryant Washburn and Lois Wilson.

Man of the World

Paramount, 1931

Credits: Director: Richard Wallace. Screenwriter: Herman J. Mankiewicz. Cinematographer: Victor Milner. 71 minutes. Released March 27, 1931. DVD availability: Universal Studios Home Entertainment: "Carole Lombard: The Glamour Collection."

Cast: William Powell (*Michael Trevor*, aka *Jimmy Powers*); Carole Lombard (*Mary Kendall*); Wynne Gibson (*Irene Harper*); Guy Kibbee (*Harold Taylor*); Lawrence Gray (*Frank Thompson*); Tom Ricketts (*Mr. Bradkin*); André Cheron (*Victor*); George Chandler (*Fred*); Tom Costello (*Spade*); Maude Truax (*Mrs. Jowitt*).

At a time when Paramount was determined to complete the

THE FILMS: *Man of the World*

With William Powell in *Man of the World*.

transition of their valued star William Powell from sinister character actor to romantic lead, they engaged screenwriter Herman J. Mankiewicz to tailor a vehicle that would reflect the man's off-screen charm and suave sophistication. This was *Man of the World*.

Man of the World was considered a prestige production among the studio's many 1931 programmers. At a time when Paramount was working to refine its blonde starlet's glamour image, Lombard relished the opportunity to appear with Powell, on whom she already had a romantic crush. From their first "approval" meeting in director Richard Wallace's office, that crush quickly accelerated into mutual admiration—and beyond. Later, when some thought that she had given an indolent performance, Carole was inclined to agree, admittedly preoccupied with the love of her leading man.

The setting is Paris, where Powell, a former newspaperman from the States, now operates a clandestine blackmail business in league with Wynne Gibson and George Chandler. Amidst pulling a clever deception on philandering American tourist Guy Kibbee, he meets and immediately falls for the man's socialite niece (Lombard). A romance develops, despite her engagement to away-on-business Lawrence Gray. Powell suffers a bout of conscience, presents himself to Lombard as a blackmailing cad, and leaves with Kibbee's payoff check for $10,000. Carole returns to her fiancé while Powell, pressured into leaving Paris or face the consequences, sails for South Africa with longtime girlfriend Gibson, who watches him destroy Kibbee's check.

Attired in an eye-catching wardrobe, Lombard delivers what's required of her, although she's overshadowed by the more forceful Gibson in a role of equal size. The movie really belongs to Powell, whose strong and confident acting makes even the most unlikely plot twists believable.

Ladies' Man
Paramount, 1931

Credits: Director: Lothar Mendes. Screenwriter: Herman J. Mankiewicz, based on the novel by Rupert Hughes. Cinematographer: Victor Milner. Costumes: Travis Banton. Sound: H.M. Lindgren. 70 minutes. Released April 26, 1931.

Cast: William Powell (*James Darricott*); Kay Francis (*Norma Page*); Carole Lombard (*Rachel Fendley*); Gilbert Emery (*Horace Fendley*); Olive Tell (*Mrs. Helene Fendley*); Martin Burton (*Anthony Fendley*); John Holland (*Peyton Weldon*); Frank Atkinson (*The Valet*); Maude Turner Gordon (*Therese Blanton*).

William Powell considered himself an *actor* and not any kind of "great lover" movie star, and so was understandably disturbed by this film's title, an obvious tie-in to his previous Paramount picture. Again, Lombard is featured as his romantic interest, although it's second-billed Kay Francis he really loves.

Ladies' Man offers Powell as a debonair cad who employs his charms to receive gifts and jewelry from female admirers sufficient to assure him a considerable income when he converts everything into cash. Among his benefactresses is Olive Tell, whose daughter (Lombard) falls in love with him despite what she knows about her mother's past association with the man. Lombard's father (Gilbert Emery), discovering the extent of Powell's involvement with his wife *and* daughter, confronts the gigolo and precipitates his death in a fatal fall.

It's a strange and offbeat tale, to say the least, and the fact that Lothar Mendes directs his cast to play it for comedy doesn't help

THE FILMS: *Up Pops the Devil*

audiences accept the film's unexpectedly tragic ending. On the plus side, Lombard comes off well in her emotional scenes with Powell, convincingly registering inebriation, vengefulness and thoughts of suicide.

In its understated review of *Ladies' Man, Motion Picture* termed the blend of subtle comedy and ultimate tragedy "a trifle disconcerting," while summing it all up as "film fare for the sophisticate, rather than for grandma."

Up Pops the Devil
Paramount, 1931

Credits: Director: A. Edward Sutherland. Screenwriters: Arthur Kober, Eve Unsell and Preston Sturges, based on the play by Albert Hackett and Frances Goodrich. Cinematographer: Karl Struss. Costumes: Travis Banton. Sound: Harold Lewis. 85 minutes. Released May 30, 1931.

Cast: Skeets Gallagher (*Biney Hatfield*); Stuart Erwin (*Stranger*); Carole Lombard (*Anne Merrick*); Lilyan Tashman (*Polly Griscom*);

(From left) Lombard with Stuart Erwin, Lilyan Tashman and Skeets Gallagher in *Up Pops the Devil*.

Norman Foster (*Steve Merrick*); Edward J. Nugent (*George Kent*); Theodore von Eltz (*Gilbert Morrell*); Joyce Compton (*Luella May Carroll*); Eulalie Jensen (*Mrs. Kent*); Harry Beresford (*Mr. Platt*); Effie Ellsler (*Mrs. Platt*); Sleep'N'Eat [Willie Best] (*Laundryman*); Guy Oliver (*Waldo*); Pat Moriarity (*Kelly*); Matty Roubert (*Subscription Boy*).

Lombard was teamed with Norman Foster for the second time during her busy year of 1931 but, although they worked well together in *Up Pops the Devil*, they were not destined to be the studio's new "love team." In fact, Foster soon forsook acting, leaving his type of Paramount roles to studio newcomers like Cary Grant, Kent Taylor and Randolph Scott. Foster went on to a more stable future as a director.

Based on the successful stage play, *Up Pops the Devil* was a pleasant marital comedy of role reversal with Foster as a stay-at-home husband, struggling to complete his Great American Novel, and Lombard as the breadwinner, who dances in a stage show. Mutual misunderstandings involve her with a publisher (Theodore von Eltz) who gives her money, while the husband associates with a flirtatious visitor (Joyce Compton). This results in a serious argument that leads to a separation. However, following the successful publication of his book, the couple reunites.

Mordaunt Hall of the *New York Times* had only praise for Carole: "The shining light of this film is Miss Lombard, whose sincerity in her portrayal is only surpassed by her exquisite beauty."

In 1938, Paramount remade *Up Pops the Devil* as a musical showcase for Bob Hope and Shirley Ross under the title *Thanks for the Memory*. Because of entangled literary rights, neither version is available for home viewing.

I Take This Woman

Paramount, 1931

Credits: Directors: Marion Gering and Slavko Vorkapich. Screenwriter: Vincent Lawrence, based on the story "Lost Ecstasy" by Mary Roberts Rinehart. Cinematographer: Victor Milner. Costumes: Travis Banton. 74 minutes. Released June 27, 1931.

Cast: Gary Cooper (*Tom McNair*); Carole Lombard (*Kay Dowling*); Helen Ware (*Aunt Bessie*); Lester Vail (*Herbert Forrest*); Charles Trowbridge (*Mr. Dowling*); Clara Blandick (*Sue Barnes*); Gerald Fielding (*Bill Wentworth*); Albert Hart (*Jack Mallory*); Guy Oliver (*Sid*); Syd Saylor (*Shorty*); Mildred Van Dorn (*Clara Hammell*); Leslie Palmer (*Phillips*);

The Films: *I Take This Woman*

Lombard and Gary Cooper in *I Take This Woman*.

Ara Haswell (*Nora*); Frank Darien (*Station Agent*); David Landau (*Circus Boss*).

This 1931 Gary Cooper dramedy bears no relationship to MGM's 1940 picture of the same title, other than that both were major flops. Its basic plot formula was better served in the 1938 Cooper film *The Cowboy and the Lady*.

For Lombard, *I Take this Woman* was yet another unexciting Paramount assignment, this time casting her as a well-heeled New York debutante dispatched west to the family ranch to avoid a minor scandal. Once there, she clashes with mild-mannered cowboy Cooper, who balks at being ordered about by the Easterner. Confronted with this challenge, she changes her tactics, plays up to him and, perhaps just for the thrill of it all, marries this ruggedly simple individual.

Lombard submits to the new experience of ranch life, but it's a losing battle. They separate, and she returns to the glamorous world she knows best. Cooper turns to rodeo stunt-riding but after he's thrown from his horse and seriously injured, she returns to take care of him, presumably for the long term.

While less than charmed by some aspects of the lady's on-screen character, *Variety* opined: "[S]he climbs on top of the part and becomes a distinct personality. She has a face that photographs from all angles and in her playing never falters. Miss Lombard ought to advance rapidly from this point."

The House That Shadows Built
Paramount, 1931

To celebrate the studio's 20th anniversary, Paramount produced this 55-minute documentary featuring filmclips from its most successful productions, profiles of its then-current stars, and scenes from upcoming pictures. Included were excerpts from Lombard's forthcoming 1932 picture *No One Man*.

No One Man
Paramount, 1932

Credits: Director: Lloyd Corrigan. Screenwriters: Sidney Buchman, Percy Heath and Agnes Brand Leahy, based on the novel by Rupert Hughes. Cinematographer: Charles Lang. Costumes: Travis Banton. Sound: Earl Hayman. 73 minutes. Released January 30, 1932.

Cast: Carole Lombard (*Penelope Newbold*); Ricardo Cortez (*Bill Hanaway*); Paul Lukas (*Dr. Karl Bemis*); Juliette Compton (*Sue Folsom*); George Barbier (*Alfred Newbold*); Virginia Hammond (*Mrs. Newbold*);

With Paul Lukas in *No One Man*.

THE FILMS: *Sinners in the Sun*

Arthur Pierson (*Stanley McIlvaine*); Frances Moffett (*Delia*); Irving Bacon (*License Clerk*).

The movie's title derives from Lombard's screen character—yet another spoiled heiress—who philosophizes, "No one man could have all the virtues."

Conferring Carole top billing, *No One Man* offers little more than sudsy drama about a well-to-do divorcee who seems unable to settle on the right husband. Torn between the attentions of Viennese physician Paul Lukas and American playboy Ricardo Cortez, she weds the latter, only to find him surreptitiously involved with Juliette Compton. After the script conveniently dispatches Cortez with a fatal heart attack, Lombard and Lukas are reunited. Will this be the man for her? Could anyone really care?

Not unexpectedly, the glamorous star, outfitted beautifully by Paramount's master couturier Travis Banton, looks gorgeous in the film's production stills. But, as photographed for the first time by Charles Lang, Lombard isn't seen to her best advantage in the film. As *Variety*'s critic noted: "The lens has been none too kind to her here. The reproduction on the screen for her is such as to cause audible unfavorable comment from women in the audience." The reasons appear attributable to illness, for the star had suffered an attack of food poisoning during her recent Hawaiian honeymoon, exacerbated by a mild case of malaria.

Accommodating Paramount's busy filming schedule, she had probably succumbed to studio pressure and returned to work too soon. Although well-lit still photography could fool Lombard's public, the motion picture cameras could not.

Sinners in the Sun
Paramount, 1932

Credits: Directors: Alexander Hall and William C. DeMille. Screenwriters: Vincent Lawrence, Waldemar Young and Samuel Hoffenstein, based on the *College Humor* story "The Beachcomber" by Mildred Cram. Cinematographer: Ray June. Costumes: Travis Banton. 70 minutes. Released May 13, 1932.

Cast: Carole Lombard (*Doris Blake*); Chester Morris (*Jimmie Martin*); Adrienne Ames (*Claire Kinkaid*); Alison Skipworth (*Mrs. Blake*); Cary Grant (*Ridgeway*); Walter Byron (*Eric Nelson*); Rita La Roy (*Lil*); Reginald Barlow (*Mr. Blake*); Zita Moulton (*Mrs. Florence Nelson*); Luke Cosgrove (*Grandfather Blake*); Ida Lewis (*Grandmother Blake*);

THE FILMS: *Sinners in the Sun*

Lombard and Chester Morris in *Sinners in the Sun*.

Russ Clark (*Fred Blake*); Frances Moffett (*Mrs. Blake*); Pierre De Ramey (*Louis*); Veda Buckland *(Emma)*.

Travis Banton's stylish wardrobe provided the main attraction for this uninspired soap opera about a fashion model and an auto mechanic, young lovers portrayed by Lombard and Chester Morris. Their marriage plans are thwarted by her insistence on waiting until he has enough capital to finance his own garage. As a result, they quarrel and break their engagement. Each goes on to form upwardly mobile romantic alliances, she with unhappily married Walter Byron, he with wealthy Adrienne Ames, whom he marries but eventually leaves to become a car salesman. Lombard splits from Byron to become a fashion-cutter. And the anticipated lovers' reunion eventually transpires as expected.

Variety termed it a tale "told on the screen too frequently, and usually better than in *Sinners in the Sun*," concluding that Lombard and Morris were "called upon to make believable a script which sinks from its own weight." Mordaunt Hall of *The New York Times* thought Lombard "competent" but Morris "miscast." Perhaps he would have

THE FILMS: *Virtue*

preferred Paramount's original plan to team Carole with Phillips Holmes, when it was still known as *The Beachcomber*, before Lombard's post-honeymoon illness caused its postponement.

Lombard shares two scenes with studio newcomer Cary Grant, billed fifth in the movie's supporting cast. Seven years later, they co-starred for *In Name Only*.

Virtue

Columbia, 1932

Credits: Director: Edward Buzzell. Screenwriter: Robert Riskin, based on the story by Ethel Hill. Cinematographer: Joseph Walker. Editor: Maurice Wright. Assistant Director: Sam Nelson. Sound: Edward Bernds. 67 minutes. Released October 25, 1932.

Cast: Carole Lombard (*Mae*); Pat O'Brien (*Jimmy Doyle*); Ward Bond (*Frank*); Shirley Grey (*Gert Hanlon*); Mayo Methot (*Lil Blair*); Jack La Rue (*Toots*); Willard Robertson (*Mackenzie*); Lew Kelly and Edward

Lombard in *Virtue* with Pat O'Brien.

The Films: *Virtue*

LeSaint (*Magistrates*); Fred Santley (*Hank*); Jessie Arnold (*Landlady*); Edwin Stanley (*District Attorney*).

At a period of relative production inactivity, when insolvent Paramount was concerned with survival, Columbia's Harry Cohn offered to buy up Lombard's contract, only to renege when he discovered that she was in the big-money class. But Paramount's Emanuel Cohen expressed his willingness to lease her services to Columbia, and so she experienced her first loan-out. Having met brash, profane Cohn's initial insolence with equal four-letter sass, Lombard immediately gained his respect, with the result that she was given the royal treatment, including that modest studio's grandest dressing room. Carole had initially experienced embarrassment at the idea of being loaned to another studio but, during the four weeks of *Virtue*'s production, she much enjoyed herself.

After some of her recent pictures for Paramount, she could only have appreciated the skills of Robert Riskin, whose well-written script packs a lot of plot into its 67 minutes. Lombard and co-star Pat O'Brien are well-matched here, delivering solid, interesting characterizations under the steady hand of director Edward Buzzell, a former musical-comedy actor before graduating to directing early sound comedy shorts. *Virtue*'s lighter moments underscore his background in comedy.

The movie's plot—about a "bad" girl's efforts to go straight—shows its pre–Code origins, since she never has to pay "the ultimate price" for her transgressions. We're never told what set this beautiful gal on a streetwalking career but, as the movie begins, she's one of several New York City hookers given a suspended sentence, provided they leave town. Carole's handed a one-way ticket to New Haven, Connecticut, a destination she fails to reach, for she willingly disembarks at Manhattan's 125th Street and hails a taxi. It's driven by O'Brien, a friendly fellow whom she cheats out of his fare and runs off. Suffering a bout of conscience, she later tracks him down and pays what she owes. And so a begrudging friendship blossoms into romance when she finds respectable employment as a lunch counter waitress. After a brief courtship, they marry, only to have Lombard arrested for violating the court order. Her past is then revealed to O'Brien, who's shocked but stands by her, providing a marriage license that appeases the law.

Further plot complications involve the young couple in shady alliances that lead to larceny, accidental murder and mutual misunderstandings. The film's more upbeat conclusion finds O'Brien the proud owner of his own filling station, with Lombard his gas-pump girl.

THE FILMS: *No More Orchids*

Thanks to Buzzell's direction and intelligent screenwriting, Lombard, O'Brien & Co. deliver a neat little melodrama—tough, hard and clean, with none of the sentimentality that often clung to early-'30s Hollywood.

No More Orchids
Columbia, 1932

Credits: Director: Walter Lang. Screenwriter: Gertrude Purcell, based on the novel by Grace Perkins. Adaptation: Keene Thompson. Cinematographer: Joseph August. Editor: Jack Dennis. Costumes: Robert Kalloch. Sound: Edward Bernds. Assistant Director: Sam Nelson. 68 minutes. Released November 25, 1932. DVD availability: Sony Pictures Home Entertainment, Turner Classic Movies Vault Collection: "Carole Lombard in the Thirties."

Cast: Carole Lombard (*Anne "Smudge" Holt*); Walter Connolly (*Bill Holt*); Louise Closser Hale (*Grandma Holt*); Lyle Talbot (*Tony Gage*); Allen Vincent (*Dick*); Ruthelma Stevens (*Rita*); C. Aubrey Smith (*Jerome Cedric*); William V. Mong (*Burkhart*); Charles Hills Mailes (*Merriwell*); Jameson Thomas (*Prince Carlos*); Harold Minjir (*Modiste*); Sidney Bracey (*Holmes*); Edward LeSaint (*Ship Captain*); Arthur Houseman (*Serge*); William Worthington (*Cannon*); Broderick O'Farrell (*Benton—Butler*); Belle Stoddard Johnstone (*Housekeeper*).

Lombard's second loan-out to Columbia came in the wake of her refusal to appear with Gary Cooper and Jack Oakie in the "Three Marines" segment of Paramount's episodic all-star comedy-drama *If I Had a Million*. That brief waitress role went to Joyce Compton, and Carole was sent back to Harry Cohn's domain. There she took on an untitled comedy-drama that Cohn thought of calling *Roses for Annie* because, despite a tough exterior, the man was fond of flowers. Fed up with her home studio's attempts to promote her as their "Orchid Lady," Carole's response to his title idea was: "Roses, snapdragons, lilies ... call it any flower except orchids. I'm ready for some other angle. No more orchids for me." And a film title was born, accompanied by an explanatory line of dialogue in the picture.

No More Orchids offers the familiar story of a rich girl (Lombard) in love with a poor boy (Lyle Talbot). When her banker father (Walter Connolly) suddenly faces financial ruin, she seeks the aid of her disapproving uncle (C. Aubrey Smith), whose terms hinge on her abandoning

Talbot to marry a wealthy prince (Jameson Thomas). She consents, but a downbeat twist of plot involves Connolly's suicide. The original lovers are reunited.

Variety called this "[a] smart, polished production replete with good acting, smooth direction and clever lines," but had reservations about the self-destructive denouement. And it noted "something a little forced and over-strained in Carole Lombard's delivery," while admiring her clothes and appearance. Perhaps the tension of her disintegrating marriage to William Powell, complicated by a clandestine relationship with Columbia screenwriter Robert Riskin, may have been at least partially responsible.

No Man of Her Own
Paramount, 1932

Credits: Director: Wesley Ruggles. Producer: Albert Lewis. Screenwriters: Maurine Watkins and Milton H. Gropper, based on a story by Edmund Goulding and Benjamin Glazer. Cinematographer: Leo Tover. Costumes: Travis Banton. Editor: Otho Lovering. Sound: Earl Hayman. 85 minutes. Released December 30, 1932. DVD availability: Universal Studios Home Entertainment: "Cinema Classics."

Cast: Clark Gable (*Jerry "Babe" Stewart*); Carole Lombard (*Connie Randall*); Dorothy Mackaill (*Kay Everly*); Grant Mitchell (*Vane*); George Barbier (*Mr. Randall*); Elizabeth Patterson (*Mrs. Randall*); J. Farrell MacDonald (*Dickie Collins*); Tommy Conlon (*Willie Randall*); Walter Walker (*Mr. Morton*); Paul Ellis (*Vargas*); Lillian Harmer (*Mattie*); Frank McGlynn, Sr. (*Minister*).

Carole's one and only film partnership with future

No Man of Her Own with Lombard and Clark Gable.

The Films: *No Man of Her Own*

husband Clark Gable, then a fast-rising attraction at MGM, came about by way of a canny talent swap: Paramount let Metro have crooner Bing Crosby for the Marion Davies vehicle *Going Hollywood*, while acquiring Gable to replace George Raft in *No Man of Her Own*.

The original plan was for Gable to appear opposite Miriam Hopkins, which was fine with Miriam—until she learned that MGM demanded top billing for their star, relegating her to a secondary position. This she found unacceptable, claiming that "illness" prevented her from working. And so Lombard was taken off her scheduled teaming with contract players Cary Grant and Randolph Scott in *Hot Saturday*. As confusing as it may be, this kind of production-juggling was standard procedure.

No Man of Her Own was filmed prior to *No More Orchids*, when Lombard's marriage to William Powell still remained solid. She and Gable worked well together, but she did not find him charming enough to jeopardize her private life. As she later told director Garson Kanin: "We did all kinds of hot love scenes and everything. And I never got any tremble out of him at all. You know, he was just the leading man. So what? A hunk of meat."

Wesley Ruggles, the force behind 1931's Academy Award–winning *Cimarron*, directed this uneven blend of comedy and romantic melodrama, with Gable as a Manhattan cardsharp working in league with glamorous shill Dorothy Mackaill. Their operation is being monitored by suspicious detective J. Farrell MacDonald, which prompts Gable to take temporary refuge in a small, sleepy town where he meets and impresses bored librarian Lombard. A quick courtship leads to marriage and a move to the big city, where Gable resumes his old livelihood, while telling his bride he works on Wall Street. Mackaill's jealous reappearance threatens to ruin their marriage, until Gable gives himself up and serves a three-month jail sentence. Upon his release, a happier future appears likely for the married couple.

Years later, director Ruggles recalled *No Man of Her Own* to Lombard biographer Larry Swindell:

> I thought Carole was the revelation. Somebody complained that she didn't seem to be acting, which was one hell of a complaint. Because it didn't *look* like acting, it was so damn natural. Look at the picture today. It's dated, but her work hasn't. She's very fresh. She's playing straight, but using comedy technique, too. Those idiots who'd taken over the studio—they couldn't even see that. Well, the critics didn't see it either. She was wonderful but it just passed by.

THE FILMS: *From Hell to Heaven*

In 1950, Paramount recycled the movie's title for a Barbara Stanwyck vehicle that bore no relation to the 1932 *No Man of Her Own*.

From Hell to Heaven
Paramount, 1933

Credits: Director: Erle C. Kenton. Screenwriters: Percy Heath and Sidney Buchman, based on the play *Good Company* by Lawrence Hazard. Cinematographer: Henry Sharp. Costumes: Travis Banton. 67 minutes. Released February 24, 1933.

Cast: Carole Lombard (*Colly Tanner*); Jack Oakie (*Charlie Bayne*); Adrienne Ames (*Joan Burt*); David Manners (*Wesley Burt*); Sidney Blackmer (*Cuff Billings*); Verna Hillie (*Sonny Lockwood*); James C. Eagles (*Tommy Tucker*); Shirley Grey (*Winnie Lloyd*); Bradley Page (*Jack Ruby*); Walter Walker (*Pop Lockwood*); Berton Churchill (*Toledo Jones*); Donald Kerr (*Steve Wells*); Nydia Westman (*Sue Wells*); Cecil Cunningham (*Mrs.*

With Sidney Blackmer in *From Hell to Heaven*.

THE FILMS: *Supernatural*

Chadman); Thomas Jackson (*Lynch*); Allen Wood (*Pepper Murphy*); Rita La Roy *(Elsie)*; Clarence Muse (*Sam*); Dell Henderson (*McCarthy*).

In the wake of MGM's great success with its all-star, episodic *Grand Hotel*, mixing comedy and tragedy within a single setting, other studios sought to cash in on that success formula. Metro returned with *Dinner at Eight*, while Warner Brothers offered *Union Depot* and Paramount followed *If I Had a Million* with *From Hell to Heaven*, albeit with nowhere near the luminaries that helped *Grand Hotel* score a box-office bulls-eye.

Mirroring *Grand Hotel*'s top international hostelry in Berlin, Paramount's venue was something called the Luray Springs Hotel, where assorted folks gather to bet on the nearby races. Intermixing the elements of romance, comedy and melodrama, the Percy Heath-Sidney Buchman screenplay blends various stories, with its central focus on top-billed Lombard. With an eye to Travis Banton's striking fashion designs, she's presented as a wealthy divorcee and horse owner who's at the racetrack to rekindle a relationship with Sidney Blackmer, a man who once left her to wed an upper-class Bostonian.

In *The New York Times*, Mordaunt Hall wrote, "It is not as ambitious a picture as *Grand Hotel*, but it is interesting. Carole Lombard serves this film well." But the movie added no luster to her career, as observed by *Variety*: "Miss Lombard gets nowhere in particular here, being the girl who, in need of coin, bets her virtue with the bookmakers against a horse she picks off the cuff."

A Good Thing and *Eleven Lives* were the movie's working titles during production.

Supernatural

Paramount, 1933

Credits: Director-Producer: Victor Halperin. Associate Producer: Edward Halperin. Screenwriters: Harvey Thew and Brian Marlow, based on a story and adaptation by Garnett Weston. Cinematographer: Arthur Martinelli. Costumes: Travis Banton. Dialogue Director: Sidney Salkow. 64 minutes. Released May 12, 1933. DVD availability: Universal Home Entertainment: "Vault Series."

Cast: Carole Lombard (*Roma Courtney*); Randolph Scott (*Grant Wilson*); Vivienne Osborne (*Ruth Rogen*); Alan Dinehart (*Paul Bavian*); H.B. Warner (*Dr. Carl Houston*); Beryl Mercer (*Madame Gourjan*);

The Films: *Supernatural*

In *Supernatural* with Alan Dinehart (being choked by Lombard) and Randolph Scott.

William Farnum (*Robert Hammond*); Willard Robertson (*Warden*); George Burr MacAnnan (*Max*); Lyman Williams (*John Courtney*).

    The Halperin brothers, Victor and Edward, had recently scored a success with their 1932 minor masterpiece of the macabre *White Zombie*, when they were engaged by Paramount to bring similar atmospherics to their production of *Supernatural*. Assigned to its leading role, Lombard found herself, under the direction of Victor, dealing with a bumbling novice who constantly misguided his cameraman to focus on the slightly scarred side of her beautiful face, among other blunders. It was not a happy set. Nor was the resulting "spook show" successful enough to merit all the *Sturm und Drang* that had accompanied its production. At one point, Carole was heard to question, "Who do you have to screw to get off this picture?"

    Yet again, the star was cast as an heiress, this time menaced by phony spiritualist Alan Dinehart, who's after her family fortune. In a séance designed to summon the spirit of her dead brother, Dinehart skillfully manipulates visual effects to suggest that the boy was murdered by her guardian, William Farnum. Wildly melodramatic plot twists then involve a psychologist (H.B. Warner) and a condemned murderess (Vivienne Osborne), who has her own personal score to settle with Dinehart. After her execution, Osborne's vengeful spirit enters Lombard's body and she drives Lombard to kill Dinehart. The killing is prevented by the intervention of Carole's fiancé, Randolph Scott. Ultimately, Dinehart is killed in a shipboard accident, and Osborne's spirit leaves Lombard's body, freeing her to find solace with Scott. There's a lot of hokum packed into this spooky programmer's 64 minutes!

In *The New York Times*, Mordaunt Hall somehow found the proceedings interesting, "not withstanding the incredibility of many of its main incidents." But *Motion Picture Herald* was less accepting: "The too-obvious effort to appear mystical, mysterious and weird causes it at times to descend of its own weight to something approaching absurdity."

Of all her post-silent films, *Supernatural* remains the one for which Lombard held the least affection.

The Eagle and the Hawk
Paramount, 1933

Credits: Directors: Stuart Walker and (uncredited) Mitchell Leisen; Producer: Bayard Veiller. Screenwriters: Bogart Rogers and Seton I. Miller, based on the story "Death in the Morning" by John Monk Saunders. Cinematographer: Harry Fischbeck. Special Effects Photography: Farciot Edouart. Costumes: Travis Banton. 68 minutes. Released May 19, 1933. DVD availability: Turner Classic Movies, Universal Studios Home Entertainment.

Cast: Fredric March (*Jerry Young*); Cary Grant (*Henry Crocker*); Jack Oakie (*Mike Richards*); Carole Lombard (*The Beautiful Lady*); Sir Guy Standing (*Major Dunham*); Forrester Harvey (*Hogan*); Kenneth Howell (*John Stevens*); Leland Hodgson (*Kingsford*); Virginia Hammond (*Lady Erskine*); Crauford Kent (*General*); Douglas Scott (*Tommy*); Robert Manning (*Voss*); Adrienne D'Ambricourt (*Fifi*); Jacques Jou-Jerville (*French General's Aide*); Russell Scott (*Flight Sergeant*); Paul Cremonesi (*French General*); Yorke Sherwood (*Taxi Driver*).

Lombard's unexpected cameo in this male-oriented drama of

THE FILMS: *The Eagle and the Hawk*

In *The Eagle and the Hawk* with Fredric March.

World War I fliers came about because of the intervention of her friend Mitchell Leisen: "Carole was already an established leading lady, and it was unheard of for somebody of her stature to accept such a small part, but I asked her to do it and she agreed."

In David Chierichetti's book *Mitchell Leisen: Hollywood Director*, it is revealed that it was actually Leisen who directed this picture, with Stuart Walker never more than his assistant. But Walker had a contractual clause that guaranteed him full directorial credit, regardless of the circumstances. And so he became the nominal director—until *The Eagle and the Hawk* was reissued in 1939, at which time Paramount's revised advertising art stated, "Directed by Stuart Walker and Mitchell Leisen." The re-release print was cut by four minutes to comply with the changes in Production Code restrictions.

In a realistic story reminiscent of Warners' 1930 drama *The Dawn Patrol* (both are from stories by John Monk Saunders), Fredric March plays a stressed-out member of the British Flying Corps who romantically encounters Lombard's character (identified simply as "The Beautiful Lady") during a ten-day leave in London. Her cameo, eight minutes in the original release version, appears to be there simply to give the picture a box office boost. *The Eagle and the Hawk* was several cuts above her previous two films.

Variety's critic considered the story "adroitly told in both dialog and action," but added: "Carole Lombard contributes little in spite of sincere playing."

The film's working title was *Fly On*.

Brief Moment
Columbia, 1933

Credits: Director: David Burton. Screenwriters: Brian Marlow and Edith Fitzgerald, based on the play by S.N. Behrman. Cinematographer: Ted Tetzlaff. Editors: Gene Milford and Gene Havlick. Assistant Director: Wilbur McGaugh. Art Director: Steve Goosson. 70 minutes. Released September 8, 1933. DVD availability: Sony Pictures Home Entertainment, Turner Classic Movies: "Carole Lombard in the Thirties."

Cast: Carole Lombard (*Abby Fane*); Gene Raymond (*Rodney Deane*); Monroe Owsley (*Harold Sigrift*); Donald Cook (*Franklin Deane*); Arthur Hohl (*Steve Walsh*); Reginald Mason (*Mr. Deane*); Jameson Thomas (*Prince Otto*); Theresa Maxwell Conover (*Mrs. Deane*); Florence Britton (*Kay Deane*); Irene Ware (*Joan*); Herbert Evans (*Alfred*); Edward LeSaint (*Manager*).

At a juncture when her home studio could offer nothing better than the very minor *Girl Without a Room* opposite fast-waning Charles Farrell, Lombard paid Harry Cohn's Columbia a visit to offer her services. This was a most unusual move, for Cohn was used to begging the more important studios for the loan of their stars. But he liked Carole. They talked the same language, she was beautiful and talented, and she had already done well by Columbia on two prior occasions.

Showing her a list of studio properties with a characteristic "anything here that'll wet your pants?" Cohn caught her attention with the title *Brief Moment*, an S.N. Behrman Broadway hit for which Cohn had once unsuccessfully sought to get Gertrude Lawrence. With the property agreed upon, Columbia now had to formally request her services from Paramount. Lombard advised him how best to proceed: "Ask for Miriam [Hopkins]. You won't be able to get her anyway, so ask. It won't seem fishy if I'm second choice."

Two weeks later, when she checked in to begin filming, Cohn told her: "They thought I was a lunatic asking for Hopkins, and after they stopped laughing, they said could they send me Lombard instead? I asked who else was available. They said Frances Drake and I said who the fuck is Frances Drake and never mind, I'll take Lombard." Just an idea of how negotiations were handled in Hollywood in the 1930s, and perhaps still are.

Playwright Behrman regretted that he wasn't available to do the screen adaptation himself, but there remained enough of his clever dialogue for Carole to appreciate, especially in comparison to her recent scripts at Paramount.

Brief Moment presents Lombard as a nightclub torch singer who falls for irresponsible playboy Gene Raymond, whom she weds and attempts to reform, encouraging him to find employment. She asks his supportive father (Reginald Mason) to cut off Raymond's income, and the older man compromises by giving his son a job in the family business. When Lombard discovers that Raymond frequently deserts his desk for the racetrack, she leaves him and goes back to work at the club. Her departure motivates Raymond to change his name and find honest employment elsewhere. Eventually, they reconcile.

Motion Picture Herald thought *Brief Moment* "not more than average entertainment, somewhat lacking in action and punch." *The New York Times*' Mordaunt Hall: "Miss Lombard and Mr. Raymond treat it as though it were entirely new. An audience cannot help being lured into a favorable reaction."

Perhaps *Brief Moment*'s most noteworthy aspect was Ted Tetzlaff's photography, for he was particularly sensitive to lighting his leading ladies to emphasize their best features. In Lombard's case, not only was he cognizant of her slight facial scar, but also of the fact that her classic visage, if not carefully lit, could take on an unflattering hardness, as had sometimes occurred in her earlier pictures. When she saw the finished product, Lombard was so appreciative of her "look" in *Brief Moment* that she fought to have Tetzlaff shoot many of her later films at various other studios.

White Woman

Paramount, 1933

Credits: Director: Stuart Walker. Screenwriters: Samuel Hoffenstein and Gladys Lehman, based on the play *Hangman's Whip* by

THE FILMS: *White Woman*

A poster for *White Woman*.

Norman Reilly Raine and Frank Butler. Cinematographer: Harry Fischbeck. Editor: Jane Loring. Sound: Joseph Foohey. Songs: "Yes, My Dear" and "He's a Cute Brute, a Gentleman and a Scholar" by Harry Revel and Mack Gordon. Art Directors: Hans Dreier and Harry Oliver. Costumes: Travis Banton. 68 minutes. Released November 10, 1933. DVD availability: Universal Studios Home Entertainment: "Vault Series."

Cast: Charles Laughton (*Horace Prin*); Carole Lombard (*Judith Denning*); Charles Bickford (*Ballister*); Kent Taylor (*David Von Elst*); Percy Kilbride (*Jakey*); Charles B. Middleton (*Fenton*); James Bell (*Hambley*); Claude King (*Chisholm*); Ethel Griffies (*Mrs. Chisholm*); Jimmie Dime (*Vaegi*); Marc Lawrence (*Connors*); Noble Johnson (*Native Chief No. 1*); Gregg Whitespear (*Native Chief No. 2*).

White Woman was arguably little more than trashy melodrama in a jungle setting, and prestigious British émigré Charles Laughton only agreed to star in it to fulfill his Paramount contract and complete his obligation to a studio where he'd grown disenchanted with his assignments. Nor would he accept Elissa Landi as his leading lady; they'd not gotten along on the set of Cecil B. DeMille's *The Sign of the Cross* the previous year, and so he requested that she be replaced with Lombard, whom he'd met on the studio lot.

While *White Woman* was in production, *The Private Life of Henry VIII* was released. The critics shouted huzzahs for Laughton, who would end up winning a Best Actor Academy Award for that performance. Such unbridled praise from the critics apparently encouraged him to play way-over-the-top in this production. Lombard, on the other hand, found herself considerably challenged and stimulated by his florid acting style, which offered an effective contrast to her characteristic naturalism.

The setting is Malaya, where she's an entertainer on the verge of deportation, a fact which motivates her to marry rubber plantation overseer Laughton. Cruel by nature and jealous of her friendship with employee Kent Taylor, he tries unsuccessfully to have the young man killed by headhunters. Amidst a native uprising, fugitive convict Charles Bickford helps Lombard and Taylor escape, leaving himself and Laughton to face certain death.

White Woman wasn't the sort of melodrama to charm the critics. *The New York Times* quipped that, despite Laughton's presence, the film "is as original as a happy ending and as close to life as a love story in a confession magazine."

Never mind the movie's outlandish story and foolish plotting: Lombard's unlikely parade of exotic white (and occasionally black) Travis Banton creations provided the main attraction here. That, and her world-weary delivery of two songs written for her by Mack Gordon and Harry Revel, "Yes, My Dear" and "He's a Cute Brute, a Gentleman and a Scholar."

A remake, 1939's *Island of Lost Men,* featured Anna May Wong in the Lombard role, with J. Carrol Naish no match for Laughton.

Bolero

Paramount, 1934

Credits: Directors: Wesley Ruggles and (uncredited) Mitchell Leisen. Associate Producer: Benjamin Glazer. Screenwriter: Horace Jackson, based on a story by Carey Wilson, Kubec Glasman and Ruth Ridenour. Cinematographer: Leo Tover. Editor: Hugh Bennett. Art Directors: Hans Dreier and Ernst Fegte. Costumes: Travis Banton. Music: Ralph Rainger, incorporating Maurice Ravel's "Bolero."

THE FILMS: *Bolero*

Choreographer: LeRoy Prinz. Sound: Earl Hayman. 83 minutes. Released February 23, 1934.

Cast: George Raft (*Raoul De Baere*); Carole Lombard (*Helen Hathaway*); Sally Rand (*Annette*); Frances Drake (*Leona*); William Frawley (*Michael De Baere*); Gertrude Michael (*Lady Claire D'Argon*); Raymond [Ray] Milland (*Lord Robert Coray*); Gloria Shea (*Lucy*); Del Henderson (*Theater Manager*); Frank G. Dunn (*Hotel Manager*); Martha Baumattie (*Belgian Landlady*).

Granite-faced and monotoned George Raft, whom Paramount curiously continued to promote as a second Rudolph Valentino, was slated to do this picture opposite the ubiquitous Miriam Hopkins. But hard-to-please Miss Hopkins didn't care for the script. Although she was eager to complete her studio contract and return to her first love, the stage, she was only too happy to claim "illness" and relinquish the assignment to Lombard. Carole *did* want to do the picture, because she had known Maurice Mouvet, the ballroom dancer on whom the film was thinly based, plus she wanted an opportunity to display her dancing ability. As it turned out, she and Raft enjoyed a great rapport, both on and off screen. As he recalled to biographer Lewis Yablonsky, "I

Lombard and George Raft in *Bolero*.

The Films: *Bolero*

truly loved Carole Lombard. She was the greatest girl that ever lived, and we were the best of pals."

It's almost a half-hour into *Bolero* before Lombard appears. Before that, we have the pre–World War I story of "Belgian" brothers (the very Noo Yawk–accented Raft and William Frawley) who work to promote the dancing ambitions of Raft, with Frawley as his manager. At first Raft teams with Frances Drake in a nightclub act, but it's disrupted by her tempestuous infatuation with him. He, it seems, wants only a business relationship and he dumps her. Eventually he meets Lombard, an ex–Follies girl, with whom he soon realizes the heights of success as "Raoul and Helen."

At the opening of his swank Paris club, where Raft and his lovely partner are about to introduce their "Bolero" number, his patrons appear more concerned with the country's entry into the World War. Lombard proudly witnesses his speech to the audience, announcing his intention of enlisting the following day. When he later confesses that this was merely a cynical ploy to attract business, she leaves him in disgust to marry a persistent admirer (Ray Milland, then known as Raymond), who also happens to be an English lord.

Raft does go to war, and returns from service with a weakened heart. He ignores the advice of doctors to rest and resumes his dancing career, this time in partnership with Sally Rand, whose drinking jeopardizes their opening night. Frawley discovers Lombard in attendance and persuades her to step in and perform a one-night-only comeback, partnering Raft in their "Bolero" routine from five years earlier. This they do, to great acclaim. But when Raft is changing his costume for an encore number, his heart gives out and he suddenly collapses and dies.

At the end of shooting, Paramount executives weren't satisfied with the climactic Raft-Lombard "Bolero" and enlisted contractee Mitchell Leisen to step in and re-take the sequence. It took him two days with the stars. In cleverly lit long shots, professional dancers executed some of the more athletic adagio steps that might have been beyond the skills of experienced nightclub dancer Raft.

Years later, Raft named *Bolero* as his special favorite among his many movies. And yet, reappraisal of the picture reveals a rather one-note performance from its male star, displaying his limitations outside of the gangster genre for which he is best known. Lombard offers a warm and sympathetic portrayal and, of course, looks stunning throughout, as lit and photographed by Leo Tover, in a succession of Travis Banton's inspired period creations. In the wake of *White Woman*,

From Hell to Heaven and especially *Supernatural*, *Bolero* was a major improvement.

We're Not Dressing
Paramount, 1934

Credits: Director: Norman Taurog. Screenwriters: Horace Jackson, Francis Marion and George Marion, Jr., based on Benjamin Glazer's adaptation of James M. Barrie's play *The Admirable Crichton*. Cinematographer: Charles Lang. Editor: Stuart Heisler. Art Directors: Hans Dreier and Ernst Fegte. Costumes: Travis Banton. Songs: "Love Thy Neighbor," "Good Night, Lovely Lady," "May I?" "She Reminds Me of You," "Once in a Blue Moon" and "It's a New Spanish Custom" by Harry Revel and Mack Gordon. 77 minutes. Released April 27, 1934. DVD availability: Universal Studios Home Entertainment: "Carole Lombard: The Glamour Collection."

Cast: Bing Crosby (*Stephen Jones*); Carole Lombard (*Doris Worthington*); George Burns (*George Martin*); Gracie Allen (*Gracie Martin*); Ethel Merman (*Edith*); Leon Errol (*Hubert*); Jay Henry (*Prince Alexander Stofani*); Raymond [Ray] Milland (*Prince Michael Stofani*); John Irwin (*Old Sailor*); Charles Morris (*Captain*); Ben Hendricks (*First Ship's Officer*); Ted Oliver (*Second Ship's Officer*).

James M. Barrie's play about shipwrecked aristocrats may have been the source of this Bing Crosby musical-comedy, but there's little or nothing of *The Admirable Crichton* that remains—although Bing and Carole Lombard winkingly compare their situation to the Barrie original amidst the proceedings. It's a predictable tale of class differences and romance, with its slight story seasoned with the typical nonsense-humor of George Burns and Gracie Allen, coupled with the song-and-dance humor of Ethel Merman and Leon Errol. Surrounded by all this, Lombard may have felt out of her element, but she displays good sportsmanship and does her best to appear interested in her bland and inexpressive—but constantly crooning—co-star.

Once again, Lombard took over a role intended for Miriam Hopkins—until Miriam discovered how much low-comedy had replaced J.M. Barrie's prose. *We're Not Dressing* was shot mostly on California's Catalina Island, which kept Lombard busily commuting between there and the Paramount studio, where *Bolero* was simultaneously in production.

Riding on Crosby's ongoing radio popularity, *We're Not Dressing* garnered very decent notices. *The New York Times*' Mordaunt Hall noted: "It is nicely photographed and cleverly directed, the sort of thing that, while it may have too many moaning melodies, is invariably diverting. Miss Lombard is attractive and competent."

In the hands of Cecil B. DeMille, this Barrie yarn had provided an important career milestone for Gloria Swanson in the 1919 silent film *Male and Female*. And in 1957, British filmmakers produced yet another—more Barrie-faithful—*Admirable Crichton*.

Twentieth Century
Columbia, 1934

Credits: Director-Producer: Howard Hawks. Screenwriters: Ben Hecht and Charles MacArthur, based on their stage play. Cinematographer: Joseph August. Editor: Gene Havlick. Assistant Director: C.C. Coleman. Sound: Edward Bernds. 91 minutes. Released May 11, 1934. DVD availability: Sony Pictures Home Entertainment.

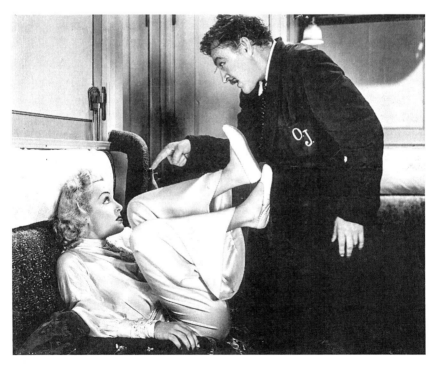

Lombard and John Barrymore in *Twentieth Century*.

The Films: *Twentieth Century*

Cast: John Barrymore (*Oscar Jaffe*); Carole Lombard (*Lily Garland*); Walter Connolly (*Oliver Webb*); Roscoe Karns (*Owen O'Malley*); Charles Levison [Charles Lane] (*Max Jacobs*); Etienne Girardot (*Matthew J. Clark*); Dale Fuller (*Sadie*); Ralph Forbes (*George Smith*); Billie Seward (*Anita*); Cliff Thompson (*Lockwood*); James P. Burtis (*Train Conductor*); Gigi Parrish (*Myrtle Schultz*); Edgar Kennedy (*Oscar McGonigle*); Fred "Snowflake" Toones (*Porter*); Herman Bing (*First Beard*); Lee Kohlmar (*Second Beard*); Pat Flaherty (*Flannigan*); James Burke (*Sheriff*); Mary Jo Matthews (*Emmy Lou*); Fred Kelsey and Ky Robinson (*Detectives*); Nick Copeland (*Treasurer*); Sherry Hall and Charles O'Malley (*Reporters*); Howard Hickman (*Dr. Johnson*); Arnold Gray (*Stage Actor*); George Reed (*Uncle Remus*); Anita Brown (*Stage Showgirl*); Irene Thompson (*Stage Actress*); Buddy Williams (*Stage Actor*); Clarence Geldert (*Southern Colonel*); Lillian West (*Charwoman*); Gaylord Pendleton (*Brother*); George Offerman, Jr. (*Page Boy*); Frank Marlowe (*Stage Carpenter*); Lynton Brent (*Train Secretary*); A.R. Haysel (*Pullman Conductor*); "Kid" Herman (*Waiter*); Harry Semels (*Artist*); Eddie Chandler (*Cameraman*); King Mojave (*McGonigle's Assistant*).

Carole Lombard's landmark breakthrough film didn't come to her directly. Producer-director Howard Hawks already had the great John Barrymore (on the verge of his celebrated decline) set for the leading role of Broadway impresario Oscar Jaffe. But the key female part of Lily Garland (so dubbed by Jaffe to conceal her origins as Mildred Plotka) was up for grabs. At 52, Barrymore was already celebrated as an inebriate, which may have discouraged some of the women being considered for the role. Gloria Swanson, Ruth Chatterton, Ann Harding, Constance Bennett and Kay Francis were all reportedly offered the part and declined. When Hawks expressed interest in the ever-elusive Miriam Hopkins, Columbia's Harry Cohn was immediately reminded of the 25-year-old Lombard, a suggestion to which Hawks was favorably disposed.

And so Carole was released from Paramount's cast of *Wharf Angel* and, with the knowledge that an important project like *Twentieth Century* could make her the kind of major star her home studio had not yet managed, she was amazed to find herself playing opposite a stage and screen legend. Was she prepared for the challenge? Perhaps more so than she initially realized.

Lowly Columbia Pictures was only beginning to gain respect: *It Happened One Night* was drawing the favorable attention of critics and audiences around the country, and was heading for an unprecedented

THE FILMS: *Twentieth Century*

clean-sweep Academy Awards for Best Picture, Best Director Frank Capra, Best Screenplay (Robert Riskin) and both of its stars, Claudette Colbert and Clark Gable. It was under this optimistic atmosphere that Lombard reported to Cohn's always-welcoming domain for the fourth time.

On the stage, *Twentieth Century* had confined its action aboard the train of that name during its journey from Chicago to New York, with one final scene in Grand Central Station. But for the movie, playwrights Hecht and MacArthur opened up the action from their original script, beginning its story three years earlier to establish the relationships of their leading characters *before* they boarded that train. Thus we witness the egomaniacal director as he meets and makes a star of the former showgirl Mildred Plotka. Their partnership, both on-stage and off-stage, leads to a triumphant succession of hit plays before she grows tired of his possessiveness, including having her tailed by private eye Edgar Kennedy. Consequently, Lombard walks out on Barrymore to accept a Hollywood contract. While she repeats her Broadway success in motion pictures, his stage productions without her are all flops.

Three years later, with his *Joan of Arc* a failure in Chicago, Barrymore is broke and forced to skip town in disguise. On the Twentieth Century Limited, he learns that also on board is "the important movie star Lily Garland." She's traveling with her current fiancé (Ralph Forbes), to whom Barrymore takes an instant dislike. Determined to lure her back to him, he campaigns to have her play Mary Magdalene in his upcoming production of *The Passion Play*. But his plans evaporate when it develops that a fellow passenger (Etienne Girardot), who had promised to invest his wealth in Barrymore's show, is actually a penniless fugitive from a lunatic asylum.

Lombard is about to sign with Barrymore rival Charles Lane when the great impresario feigns a mortal injury, managing to obtain her signature on a contract as her last gesture to a "dying man." Too late, she realizes his ruse and, at fadeout, the couple resumes their embattled relationship of old.

As anticipated, Barrymore was in his actor's element as the flamboyant Jaffe. It's a marvel to watch him as he runs the gamut of inspired thespian tricks, disguises, impersonations and ploys to have his way with one and all. Lombard was at first awed by both the role and her celebrated co-star, but director Hawks took care to draw from her the wonderful comedy performance that is now permanently preserved on film.

The fan magazines took note, with *Shadowplay*'s critic suitably impressed: "When you see her, you'll forget the rather restrained and somewhat stilted Lombard of old. You'll see a star blaze out of the scene and that scene, high spots Carole never dreamed of hitting." *Photoplay* cited "a fiery talent which few suspected she had."

As Barrymore later recalled: "How Carole Lombard ever managed to stand the pace is more than I can imagine. But she took it in her stride, giving a whirlwind performance day after day, and always fresh as a daisy. Her terrific industry frightened me."

In a 1938 *New York Post* interview, Lombard called *Twentieth Century* her greatest opportunity and said of Barrymore, "I learned more about acting from that man in the six weeks it took to make the picture than I ever had before. I listened to him for the entire six weeks, and got a real course in dramatics. That was the beginning of knowing something."

It was this picture that finally established the dramatically seasoned actress as the wonderful comedienne for which she is so well and justly remembered. Unfortunately, for all its madcap comedy scenes and the great intensity of its stars and solid supporting cast, *Twentieth Century* bears the limitations of its eccentric subject matter—the theater—which has never captured the imagination of the general public, especially outside of urban areas. It was also, perhaps, a bit too sophisticated for 1934's general audiences. And, as it was also the year of *It Happened One Night*, Cohn elected to have Columbia's publicists concentrate on that movie when it came time to campaign for honors. It's hard to believe but the now-classic *Twentieth Century* failed to receive even a single nomination.

In 1978, a successful musicalization of this work reached Broadway under the title *On the Twentieth Century*, with Madeline Kahn, John Cullum and Kevin Kline. But, thus far, no version has surpassed the indelible creation of Barrymore, Lombard and Hawks.

Now and Forever
Paramount, 1934

Credits: Director: Henry Hathaway. Producer: Louis D. Lighton. Screenwriters: Vincent Lawrence and Sylvia Thalberg, adapted from a story by Jack Kirkland and Melville Baker. Cinematographer: Harry Fischbeck. Song: "I Owe the World a Living" by Harry Revel and Mack Gordon. Art Directors: Hans Dreier and Robert Usher. Costumes:

The Films: *Now and Forever*

Lombard in *Now and Forever* with Gary Cooper and Shirley Temple.

Travis Banton. 80 minutes. Released August 31, 1934. DVD availability: Universal Studios Home Entertainment: "Shirley Temple Little Darling Pack."

Cast: Gary Cooper (*Jerry Day*); Carole Lombard (*Toni Carstairs*); Shirley Temple (*Penelope Day*); Sir Guy Standing (*Felix Evans*); Charlotte Granville (*Mrs. J.H.P. Crane*); Gilbert Emery (*James Higginson*); Henry Kolker (*Mr. Clark*); Tetsu Komai (*Mr. Ling*); Jameson Thomas (*Chris Carstairs*); Harry Stubbe (*Mr. O'Neill*); Egon Brecher (*Doctor*); André Cheron (*Inspector*); Agostino Borgato (*Fisherman*); Richard Loo (*Hotel Clerk*); Luke Chan (*Assistant Manager*).

It was Fox that had sensational little Shirley Temple under contract when Paramount borrowed her services for a two-picture deal. It commenced with *Little Miss Marker* (1934), a resounding hit. Coming off the heady highs of *Twentieth Century*, Lombard might have expected her home studio to have something better for her than the humdrum dramatics of *Now and Forever*. But she realized the advantages of being associated with a Temple picture, and there was nothing wrong with once again having Gary Cooper as her leading man.

This can hardly be considered a Temple vehicle: Despite her above-the-title billing, under Cooper and Lombard, she's really not on-screen that much. But the movie's plot revolves around her, and her adorable presence lends interest to a standard tale of romance and larceny.

The story opens in Shanghai, where Cooper and Lombard are a pair of jewel thieves who run out of luck and go their separate ways. He returns to America, planning to sell custody of his little daughter (Temple) to his wealthy brother-in-law (Gilbert Emery). But renewing acquaintance with the irresistible Temple changes his plans, and he takes her to Europe with him, after swindling colleague-in-crime Sir Guy Standing.

Together again, Cooper and Lombard establish a home for Temple. He tries to make an honest living as a realtor, but is later forced to resort to jewel thievery. The climax centers on Cooper's stealing a valuable necklace belonging to wealthy old Charlotte Granville, who's anxious to adopt Temple and give her the advantages that her father cannot. When Standing turns up to blackmail Cooper, there's an exchange of gunfire. Although wounded and facing punishment, Cooper foresees a brighter future with Lombard and Temple.

In *The New York Times*, Andre Sennwald dubbed *Now and Forever* "visually handsome and attractively played": "[I]t becomes, despite its violent assaults upon the spectator's credulity, a pleasant enough entertainment."

Lady by Choice
Columbia, 1934

Credits: Director: David Burton. Producer: Robert North. Screenwriter: Jo Swerling, based on a story by Dwight Taylor and suggested by characters created by Damon Runyon. Cinematographer: Ted Tetzlaff. Editor: Viola Lawrence. Assistant Director: Arthur Black. Sound: Glenn Rominger. 78 minutes. Released October 15, 1934. DVD availability: Sony Pictures Home Entertainment, Turner Classic Movies Vault Collection: "Carole Lombard in the Thirties."

Cast: Carole Lombard (*Georgia "Alabam" Lee*); May Robson (*Patricia "Patsy" Patterson*); Roger Pryor (*Johnny Mills*); Walter Connolly (*Judge Daly*); Arthur Hohl (*Kendall*); Raymond Walburn (*Front O'Malley*); James Burke (*Brannigan*); Mariska Aldrich (*Lucretia*); John T. Doyle (*Walsh*); Henry Kolker (*Opper*); Lillian Harmer (*Miss Kingsley*); Abe Denovitch (*Louie*); Fred "Snowflake" Toones (*Mose*); Kathleen Howard (*Mrs. Mills*); William Faversham (*Booth*); Akim Tamiroff (*Poupoulis*); Charles Coleman

THE FILMS: *Lady by Choice*

(*Butler*); Hector V. Sarno (*Florist*); Harry C. Bradley (*Clerk of Court*); Crauford Kent (*Brooke*); Christian J. Frank (*Proprietor*); Edith Conrad (*Mrs. Kingsley's Assistant*); Helene Barclay, Lorena Carr and Eleanor Johnston (*Secretaries*); Irene Thompson (*Chorus Girl*); Harold Berquist (*Bailiff*); Gino Corrado (*Head Waiter*); Kit Guard, Jack Stone, Jack Walters and Jack Lowe (*Waiters*); Adele Cutler Jerome (*Dancing Teacher/Dance Double for Carole Lombard*).

In *Lady by Choice* with May Robson.

Lombard returned to Columbia for the fifth and final time to team with scene-stealing character star May Robson in this obvious follow-up to the studio's 1933 Frank Capra hit *Lady for a Day*. But this one was directed by David Burton (who had also worked with Lombard on 1933's *Brief Moment*) instead of Capra, from a script by Jo Swerling instead of Robert Riskin, leaving only the wonderful Robson (aged 76) to recreate the Runyonesque atmosphere of *Lady*.

Robson plays an amiable old boozer who's arrested for disorderly conduct at the same time that fan-dancer Lombard's in court because of her risqué performance. Wealthy Roger Pryor persuades judge Walter Connolly to parole Robson to an old-ladies' home, where Lombard turns up to "adopt" her, both as a cynical publicity ploy and in observance of Mother's Day.

Subsequently, a warm mother-daughter relationship develops, with Robson not only hiring instructors to further the girl's career, but also promoting a romance with Pryor. When the dancer learns that he'll lose his inheritance if he weds her, she breaks their engagement and returns to her fans. Eventually, Robson plays Cupid and manipulates their reunion.

The Films: *The Gay Bride*

In the wake of Lombard's steady succession of prominent movies, coupled with Robson's notable presence in *Lady for a Day*, *Lady by Choice* did very well. Unlike the studio's more high-toned *Twentieth Century*, this one would effectively be promoted as "a picture that's just plain, ordinary swell."

Although the top-billed Lombard was essentially stooging for Robson, she did win the notice of some critics. *Variety* opined: "Carole Lombard does a lot for the picture. She is forceful, vibrant, and once or twice she shows far greater power than in her previous work."

Working titles for the movie were *Orchids and Onions* and *Part Time Lady*.

The Gay Bride
MGM, 1934

Credits: Director: Jack Conway. Executive Producer: Harry Rapf. Producer: John W. Considine, Jr. Screenwriters: Sam and Bella Spewack, based on the *Saturday Evening Post* story "Repeal" by Charles Francis Coe. Cinematographer: Ray June. Editor: Frank Sullivan. Art Director: Cedric Gibbons. Music: Jack Virgil. Sound: Douglas Shearer. 80 minutes. Released December 14, 1934.

Cast: Carole Lombard (*Mary*); Chester Morris ("*Office Boy*"); ZaSu Pitts (*Mirabelle*); Leo Carrillo (*Mickey*); Nat Pendleton (*Shoots Magiz*); Sam Hardy (*Dingle*); Walter Walker (*MacPherson*).

At first, Lombard was impressed that she was loaned out to prestigious MGM for this unpretentious dramedy opposite her *Sinners in the Sun* teammate, Chester Morris. But she was accorded more respectful guest-star treatment at lowly Columbia; and she later regarded this picture as her all-time worst!

Again, she's a chorus girl, this time marrying an underworld boss (Nat Pendleton) who's the producer of her current show. It's strictly a for-money arrangement, but complications ensue when he's wiped out by mobster Sam Hardy. Then Hardy is eliminated by sinister Leo Carrillo. Eventually she marries Morris, Pendleton's former bodyguard, whose only cast identification is "Office Boy."

As an underworld spoof, *The Gay Bride* ("gay" in the old-fashioned sense, of course) was considered passé. Lombard perhaps expected firmer directorial guidance from the usually reliable Jack Conway. Whatever charm her character displays can only be credited to Lombard's efforts to make something of very little.

THE FILMS: *Rumba*

As *Variety*'s critic put it, "Morris and Miss Lombard are handicapped by both parts and dialogue, while ZaSu Pitts and Leo Carrillo, among supporters, go nowhere." *The New York Times* observed, "Carole Lombard enacts the role with a comic gravity which is decidedly effective."

Following a one-week run at New York's Capitol Theatre, *The Gay Bride* was allowed to play out as the lower half of double-feature programming. Its working title, reflecting its source material, was *Repeal*.

Rumba

Paramount, 1935

Credits: Director: Marion Gering. Producer: William LeBaron. Screenwriters: Howard J. Green, Harry Ruskin and Frank Partos, based on a story by Guy Endore and Seena Owen. Cinematographer: Ted Tetzlaff. Songs "The Rhythm of the Rumba," "The Magic of You" and "I'm Yours for Tonight" by Ralph Rainger and Francois B. de Valdes. Music: Andrea Setaro, S.K. Wineland and Maurice Lawrence. Choreographers-Dance Doubles: Veloz and Yolanda. Editor: Hugh Bennett. Art Directors: Hans Dreier and Robert Usher. Costumes: Travis Banton and Lily Del Barrio. Sound: J.A. Goodrich. 77 minutes. Released February 8, 1935.

Cast: George Raft (*Joe Martin*); Carole Lombard (*Diana Harrison*); Lynne Overman (*Flash*); Margo (*Carmelita*); Monroe Owsley (*Hobart Fletcher*); Iris Adrian (*Goldie Allen*); Samuel S. Hinds (*Henry B. Harrison*); Virginia Hammond (*Mrs. Harrison*); Gail Patrick (*Patsy*); Jameson Thomas (*Solanger*); Soledad Jiminez (*Maria*); Paul Porcasi (*Carlos*); Raymond McKee (*Dance Director*); Akim Tamiroff (*Tony*); Eldred Tidbury (*Watkins*); Mack Gray (*Assistant Dance Director*); Hallene Hall (*Wardrobe Woman*); Dennis O'Keefe (*Man in Diana's Party*); Peggy Watts (*Girl in Diana's Party*); Bruce Warren (*Dean*); Hugh Enfield (*Bromley*); Rafael Corio (*Alfredo*); Charles Stevens (*Ticket Vendor*); Rafael Storm and Paul Logan (*Cashiers*); Victor Sabini (*Waiter*); Carli Taylor (*Steward on Yacht*); James Burke and James B. Burtis (*Reporters*); Dick Rush (*Policeman*); Bud Shaw (*Ticket Taker*); E.H. Calvert (*Police Captain*); Frank O'Connor (*Police Sergeant*); Alfred P. Jones (*Stage Doorman*); Hooper Atchley (*Doctor*); Mason Litson (*Stage Manager*); Paul Ellis (*Waiter at Café Elefante*).

This virtual clone of the previous year's *Bolero* was Paramount's very obvious attempt to repeat the success of the earlier teaming of

The Films: *Rumba*

On the set of *Rumba*, choreographer LeRoy Prinz instructs George Raft and Carole Lombard in the moves for one of the film's dance numbers.

Lombard and George Raft. Once again, they work well together under Marion Gering's workmanlike direction. But there's less substance to the plot of *Rumba* and its climactic dance number can't compare with the one in *Bolero*. We can well understand why there was no second encore of this pairing, perhaps entitled *Tango*!

Raft portrays a featured dancer in a Havana nightclub, where wealthy vacationer Lombard catches his act. This first encounter doesn't go well, but she later catches another performance and now finds him more attractive. After a misunderstanding leads to a brawl with her escort (Monroe Owsley), Raft is fired. Experiencing a native performance of the rumba, he's inspired to open his own club, where he appears opposite a new dance partner, Margo. Impressed with what she sees, Lombard offers to back his act in Manhattan.

Raft receives a mysterious note, threatening his life if he goes to New York. It's a warning he ignores. Just before they are to perform their rumba routine, Margo collapses from the tension, and guess who takes her place? Lombard's character apparently harbors hidden terpsichorean skills, which she displays with gusto in front of the night club audience, and without a single rehearsal! As to that threatening note, it turns out to have been the fabrication of Raft associate Lynne Overman, designed to publicize his American debut.

Rumba marked the first Paramount assignment for Ted Tetzlaff, Lombard's favorite cameraman, following his work on her Columbia features *Brief Moment* and *Lady by Choice*. At her insistence, he photographed her next five movies.

Hands Across the Table
Paramount, 1935

Credits: Director: Mitchell Leisen. Production Supervisor: Ernst Lubitsch. Producer: E. Lloyd Sheldon. Screenwriters: Norman Krasna, Vincent Lawrence and Herbert Fields, based on the story "Bracelets" by Viña Delmar. Cinematographer: Ted Tetzlaff. Editor: William Shea. Song "The Morning After" by Sam Coslow, Frederick Hollander, Mitchell Parish and Jean Delettre. Costumes: Travis Banton. Art Directors: Hans Dreier and Roland Anderson. Set Decorator: A.E. Freudeman. Sound: Harry Lindgren and Walter Oberst. Assistant Director: Edgar Anderson. 80 minutes. Released October 18, 1935. DVD availability: Universal Home Entertainment: "Carole Lombard: The Glamour Collection."

Cast: Carole Lombard (*Regi Allen*); Fred MacMurray (*Theodore Drew III*); Ralph Bellamy (*Allen Macklyn*); Astrid Allwyn (*Virginia Snowden*); Ruth Donnelly (*Laura*); Marie Prevost (*Nona*); Joseph Tozer (*Peter*); William Demarest (*Matty*); Edward Gargan (*Pinky Kelly*); Ferdinand Munier (*Miles—Butler*); Harold Minjir (*Couturier at Valentine's*); Marcelle Corday (*Celeste—French Maid*); Bess Flowers (*Diner*); Harold Miller (*Barber Customer*); Nell Craig and Alla Mentone (*Salesladies*); Jerry Mandy (*Headwaiter*); Phil Kramer (*Supper Club Waiter*); Murray Alper (*Cab Driver*); Nelson McDowell (*Man in Nightshirt*); Sam Ash (*Maitre d'Hotel*); Edward Peil Sr., Jerry Storm, Francis Sayles, Chauncey M. Drake, S.H. Young, Rafael Gavilan, Harry Williams and Sterling Campbell (*Barbers*); Mary MacLaren (*Chambermaid*); Rod Wilson (*Piano Player*); Albert Conti (*Maitre d'Hotel in Speakeasy*); John Buettner (*Shoe Clerk*); Pat Sweeney (*Manicurist*); Fred "Snowflake" Toones and James Adamson (*Porters*); Peter Allen (*Jewelry Clerk*); Ira Reed and Dutch Hendrian (*Taxi Drivers*).

THE FILMS: *Hands Across the Table*

Beautiful, popular and talented though she was, Carole Lombard had, by 1935, made only one motion picture (*Twentieth Century*) that matched her talent for comedy—until *Hands Across the Table*. Not only was this her first genuine starring vehicle, it was also the first film expressly written for her and produced under the guidance of Paramount's newly appointed comedy specialist Ernst Lubitsch. Viña Delmar's story "Bracelets" was the basis for the bright and witty screenplay whipped up by the team of Norman Krasna, Vincent Lawrence and Herbert Fields. It was at Lombard's request that her friend Mitchell Leisen was assigned to direct.

For her leading man, Leisen wanted Ray Milland, with whom he had just filmed *Four Hours to Kill*. But Milland, while admitting to his adoration of Carole, recalled the making of *We're Not Dressing*, in which he had supported her: "She was so highly strung she made me very nervous. I asked Mitch if he could possibly find somebody else." Which left the director to consider Fred MacMurray: "I was terribly worried, since it was only his third picture."

Claudette Colbert, whom MacMurray had recently supported in *The Gilded Lily*, had apparently helped the ex-saxophone player solidify the basics of his unique and charming bent for comic acting. At first, Lombard thought him stiff and sexless, so she went out of her way to help the young actor relax, drawing forth his natural abilities. As MacMurray recalled to David Chierichetti: "She worked with me on every scene. I owe so much of that performance and my subsequent career to her."

Hands Across the Table's humor springs from a situation of male-female role reversal. Lombard plays the aggressor here, a disillusioned hotel manicurist who doesn't believe in marrying for love. Instead, she plans to find a rich husband and improve her social lot. At first, her best prospect appears to be wealthy and attractive Ralph Bellamy, a former flier now confined to a wheelchair. But then she finds herself giving a manicure to the handsome and supposedly well-heeled MacMurray, whose family, she's later chagrined to learn, lost everything in the stock market crash.

It seems that Fred is little more than a charming wastrel who, like Carole, aspires to marry wealth—in this case, fiancée Astrid Allwyn. But he's as reluctantly attracted to Lombard as she is to him, and he impulsively treats her to a costly evening out with the money Allwyn's given him for a Bermuda vacation. At the evening's end, he's too intoxicated to get home, and spends the night (innocently, of course; this was

THE FILMS: *Love Before Breakfast*

the Code-restricted mid–1930s) and, eventually, the whole *week* at the manicurist's apartment.

This occasions one of the movie's best scenes, an inspired comedy turn in which, over the telephone, Lombard impersonates a nasal-voiced Bermuda operator, while MacMurray works to convince Allwyn that he's enjoying a week of rest on that British resort island. As Leisen described it: "When they finished the take, Carole and Fred collapsed on the floor in laughter until they couldn't laugh any more. It wasn't in the script, but I made sure the cameras kept turning, and I used it in the picture. It is so hard to make actors laugh naturally, I wasn't about to throw that bit out."

By the movie's end, Carole and Fred have reasoned that their former mercenary values be damned, they're meant for each other. They'll wed as soon as he finds a job, thus leaving the abandoned Bellamy and Allwyn to fend for themselves—or one another?

Hands Across the Table is much more than a typical '30s screwball comedy. The characters portrayed by Lombard and MacMurray, in particular, are far removed from cut-and-paste cardboard. Their complexities are as well suggested in Leisen's direction as they are in the serio-comic playing of the two stars, whose cinematic chemistry worked so well that Paramount re-teamed them in three subsequent pictures. None, however, equaled the remarkable quality of *Hands Across the Table*, one of 1935's surprise hits.

Love Before Breakfast
Universal, 1936

Credits: Director: Walter Lang and (uncredited) Phil Karlstein [Karlson]. Producer: Edmund Grainger. Screenwriters: Herbert Fields and Gertrude Purcell, based on the story "Spinster Dinner" by Faith Baldwin. Cinematographer: Ted Tetzlaff. Editor: Maurice Wright. Art Director: Albert S. D'Agostino. Costumes: Travis Banton (Carole Lombard's wardrobe) and Brymer. Music: Franz Waxman. Sound: Charles Carroll and Gilbert Kurland. Assistant Director: Phil Karlstein [Karlson]. 70 minutes. Released March 9, 1936. DVD availability: Universal Home Entertainment: "Carole Lombard: The Glamour Collection."

Cast: Carole Lombard (*Kay Colby*); Preston Foster (*Scott Miller*); Janet Beecher (*Mrs. Colby*); Cesar Romero (*Bill Wadsworth*); Betty Lawford (*Countess Campanella*); Douglas Blackley (*College Boy*); Don Briggs

THE FILMS: *Love Before Breakfast*

With Cesar Romero in *Love Before Breakfast*.

(*Stuart Farnum*); Bert Roach (*Fat Man*); Andre Beranger (*Charles*); Richard Carle (*Brinkerhoff*); Ed Barton (*Jerry*); Diana Gibson (*Secretary*); Joyce Compton (*Mary Lee Jackson*); John King (*Johnny*); E.E. Clive (*Captain*); Forrester Harvey (*Chief Steward*); Mia Ichioka (*Yuki*); John Rogers (*Dixon*); Pushface (*Junior*); Nan Grey (*Telephone Girl*).

Walter Lang had directed Lombard in Columbia's *No More Orchids*, and it was an association that they both enjoyed. Subsequently, they were friendly opponents on the tennis court, and he became a steady companion of (and eventual husband to) her best friend, Madalynne "Fieldsie" Fields. When Carole heard that he was set to direct Universal's *Love Before Breakfast*, and was seeking a glamorous leading lady with a light comic touch, she read the script, liked it and asked Paramount to loan her out. Her home base was willing, but insisted that she be accorded sole billing over the film's title, and in lettering twice as large as any co-stars. Carole was no prima donna, but she knew she had to ensure on-screen her movie-star appearance, which meant bringing her favorites, cameraman Ted Tetzlaff and designer Travis Banton, along with her to Universal. And she even secured work for her friend Dixie Pantages as her stand-in.

THE FILMS: *The Princess Comes Across*

Love Before Breakfast is a pleasantly foolish trifle about a young woman who has trouble deciding between rich oil man Preston Foster and his employee Cesar Romero. In an effort to break up their relationship, Foster dispatches Romero to the firm's Japan office for two years, then sets out to woo a totally unresponsive Lombard. In situation after situation, she tries to foil Foster's plan, only to eventually give in. And why not? He's charming, attractive and generous, whereas faraway Romero can't even bother to write a letter to her. The movie's Foster-Lombard denouement comes as no surprise.

But what could have been a tiresome and predictable 70 minutes instead comes off as pleasant entertainment, thanks to a good cast and expert direction by Lang, who makes it all seem better than it is by maintaining a snappy comic pace. Thirty-five years later, Lang recalled the pleasure of working with his visiting star: "She was always on time and knew her lines, and she was a great, great artist."

Love Before Breakfast, following in the wake of Paramount's Lombard hit *Hands Across the Table*, became Universal's biggest box office attraction for the spring of 1936.

The Princess Comes Across
Paramount, 1936

Credits: Director: William K. Howard. Producer: Arthur Hornblow, Jr. Screenwriters: Walter DeLeon, Francis Martin, Frank Butler and Don Hartman, based on the story adaptation by Philip MacDonald and the novel *A Halalkabin* by Louis Lucien Rogger. Cinematographer: Ted Tetzlaff. Special Effects: Farciot Edouart and Dewey Wrigley. Song: "My Concertina" by Phil Boutelje and Jack Scholl. Editor: Paul Weatherwax. Costumes: Travis Banton. Art Directors: Hans Dreier and Ernst Fegte. Set Decorator: A.E. Freudeman. Sound: Harold Lewis and Don Johnson. Assistant Director: Harry Scott. 76 minutes. Released May 22, 1936. DVD availability: Universal Home Entertainment: "Carole Lombard: The Glamour Collection."

Cast: Carole Lombard (*Princess Olga, aka Wanda Nash*); Fred MacMurray (*Joe King Mantell*); Douglass Dumbrille (*Detective Lorel*); Alison Skipworth (*Lady Gertrude Allwyn*); William Frawley (*Benton*); Porter Hall (*Robert M. Darcy*); George Barbier (*Captain Nicholls*); Lumsden Hare (*Cragg*); Sig Rumann (*Steindorf*); Mischa Auer (*Morevitch*); Tetsu Komai (*Kewati*); Bradley Page (*The Stranger*); Bennie Bartlett (*Ship's Bellhop*); Pat Flaherty (*Officer*); Christian Rub (*Gustavson*);

THE FILMS: *The Princess Comes Across*

Harry Hayden (*Master of Ceremonies*); George Chandler (*Film Man*); Edward Keane (*Chief Purser*); Gaston Glass (*Photographer*); Nanette Lafayette (*French Woman*); André Cheron (*French Man*); Gladden James (*Third Ship's Official*); Charles Fallon and Jean de Briac (*French Baggage Officials*); Phil Tead (*Jones—American Newsreel Man*); Milburn Stone (*American Reporter*); Tom Herbert and James T. Mack (*Cabin Stewards*); Chloe Douglas (*Girl*); Paul Kruger, Larry Steers and David Clyde (*Assistant Pursers*); Bernard Suss (*Steward*); Dick Elliott (*Ship's Surgeon*); Dink Templeton (*Purser*); Isabelle LaMal, Eva Dennison and Maybelle Palmer (*Gossips*); Keith Daniels, George Sorrell, Jack Raymond, Jacques Vanaire, Eddie Dunn and Jack Hatfield (*Reporters*); Creighton Hale (*Officer*).

Obviously a title with two likely interpretations, *The Princess Comes Across* offers no outward indication of its oddly entertaining blend of comedy, romance, music and murder-mystery, most of it transpiring amid a transatlantic crossing.

Sporting an amusing Garbo-esque Swedish accent, Lombard plays a Brooklyn-born actress named Wanda Nash who travels in the guise of glamorous, mysterious "Princess Olga," accompanied by drama coach Alison Skipworth, who's incognito herself as "Lady Gertrude Allwyn." Also aboard the New York–bound luxury liner are bandleader Fred MacMurray and friend William Frawley, unaware that the "royalty" charade is Lombard's roundabout bid for Hollywood stardom.

There's a mutual attraction evident between Carole and Fred, and he's only too glad to rally to her side when blackmailer Porter Hall threatens to blow her cover. Then Hall is found murdered in her stateroom. By chance, it seems that the passenger list also includes five international police detectives, who offer to solve the case—until one of *them* is killed.

MacMurray now determines to save Lombard from exposure by acting as decoy to track down the perpetrator, who's revealed as one of the police contingent. When the ship docks in New York, Lombard acknowledges her affection for MacMurray, but tells him that movie stardom is what's *most* important to her. After he leaves her, she faces the press to deliver a speech, but is unable to continue her impersonation, abandoning the Swedish accent and confessing her deception, all in the cause of love.

Variety's critic appeared pleased: "[W]ith William K. Howard's direction accounting for a slick piece of satire and whodunit merging, and Carole Lombard and Fred MacMurray given a set of story personalities that jell, *The Princess Comes Across* spells happy tidings around the

THE FILMS: *My Man Godfrey*

box office." In his 1976 book *Carole Lombard*, Leonard Maltin called her performance "one of [her] finest and subtlest."

My Man Godfrey
Universal, 1936

Credits: Director-Producer: Gregory La Cava. Executive Producer: Charles R. Rogers. Screenwriters: Gregory La Cava, Morrie Ryskind and Eric Hatch, based on a story by Eric Hatch. Cinematographer: Ted Tetzlaff. Editor: Ted Kent. Art Director: Charles D. Hall. Costumes: Travis Banton and Brymer. Music: Charles Previn. Assistant Director: Scott R. Beal. 95 minutes. Released September 6, 1936. DVD availability: Universal Pictures Home Entertainment, Universal Vault Series, Universal Classic Comedy Spotlight Collection, Criterion and Legend Films (black & white and colorized).

Cast: William Powell (*Godfrey Parke*); Carole Lombard (*Irene Bullock*); Alice Brady (*Angelica Bullock*); Eugene Pallette (*Alexander*

Lombard (seated) with Eugene Pallette (at left), Alice Brady and Mischa Auer in *My Man Godfrey*.

THE FILMS: *My Man Godfrey*

Bullock); Gail Patrick (*Cornelia Bullock*); Alan Mowbray (*Tommy Gray*); Jean Dixon (*Molly*); Mischa Auer (*Carlo*); Robert Light (*George*); Pat Flaherty (*Mike*); Robert Perry (*Hobo*); Franklin Pangborn (*Scorekeeper*); Selmer Jackson (*Blake*); Ernie Adams (*Forgotten Man*); Phyllis Crane (*Party Guest*); Grady Sutton (*Charlie Van Rumple*); Jack Chefe (*Headwaiter*); Eddie Featherston (*Process Server*); Edward Gargan and James Flavin (*Detectives*); Arthur Singley (*Chauffeur*); Reginald Mason (*Mayor*); Bess Flowers (*Mrs. Meriwether*); Jane Wyman (*Girl at Party*).

Between its opening credits and a traditional boy-gets-girl conclusion, this typically mid–'30s screwball comedy exposes, with sparkling verve and wit, the mindless artificiality of some Fifth Avenue socialites. The wit derives from a well-crafted screenplay by Morrie Ryskind, Eric Hatch and Gregory La Cava. The verve is easily attributed to the inspired guidance of comedy expert La Cava, a producer-director with a celebrated penchant for improvisation. And, in this whimsical tale of a well-born down-and-outer who's engaged as a butler for a family of wealthy loonies (whom he later rescues from financial ruin), the fun lies in the development of character as the Bullock clan's fortunes change for the worse and they learn a few hard lessons in humanity.

As in most such escapades, this wacky social farce relies on the comic expertise of its cast. In the title role, William Powell is completely at home with the character's wry humor and unflappable reactions to the chaos all around him. Lombard, as a heroine somewhat less colorful than in *Twentieth Century*, is as delightfully zany as she is beautiful, while Gail Patrick, as her calculating sister, frequently manages to steal the scenes they share and actually leaves the more indelible impression. As their mother, Alice Brady plays one of her trademarked characters, a fluttering, falsetto-voiced flibbertigibbet with scattered brains and inane dialogue ("If you're going to be rude to my daughter, you might as well at least take your hat off"). But because of a superior script, Brady never quite becomes the irritant she did in other films, such as *The Gay Divorcee*. Basement-toned Eugene Pallette, as the family's failing breadwinner, is inimitable, while Mischa Auer, as Brady's ape-mimicking protégé, almost makes the nuttiest of the Bullocks appear sane.

It all begins with a Park Avenue scavenger hunt during which empty-headed Lombard and her rich friends descend upon a "hobo jungle" searching for that Depression-era icon, "the forgotten man." Lombard is so impressed with derelict Powell and his disrespectful treatment of her snooty sister that she pays him his requested $5 to take him back as her trophy individual. Lombard also takes advantage of the situation to offer Powell employment as the family butler.

It's soon evident that this is a smart, intelligent man, determined to succeed at a job he could not otherwise have hoped to land. Nor is he about to be sidetracked by the spoiled Lombard, who harbors romantic notions about him. When the rehabilitated Powell announces plans to leave the family's employ to pursue his own aspirations, he's well in command of their problems. His clever investments have created a sound financial portfolio for Pallette, who finds the backbone to kick out his wife's sponging protégé, Auer. And the conniving Patrick's efforts to brand Powell a jewel thief are exposed and she is humiliated. Finally, the "forgotten man" realizes his dream, building a nightclub at the city dump to employ his fellow "forgottens." And, of course, Lombard finally lands her hero.

My Man Godfrey was immensely popular and racked up six Oscar nominations, among them a Best Actress nod for Lombard. But there was stiff competition from fellow nominees Irene Dunne (*Theodora Goes Wild*), Gladys George (*Valiant Is the Word for Carrie*), Norma Shearer (*Romeo and Juliet*) and Luise Rainer (who won for *The Good Earth*). *My Man Godfrey* failed to take home *any* awards, although it fostered inferior imitations like 1938's *Merrily We Live* and an uninspired 1957 remake with David Niven and June Allyson.

Swing High, Swing Low
Paramount, 1937

Credits: Director: Mitchell Leisen. Screenwriters: Virginia Van Upp and Oscar Hammerstein II, based on the play *Burlesque* by George Manker Watters and Arthur Hopkins. Cinematographer: Ted Tetzlaff. Editor: Edna Warren. Special Effects: Farciot Edouart. Musical Director: Boris Morros. Songs: "Swing High, Swing Low" by Burton Lane and Ralph Freed; "I Hear a Call to Arms" and "Panamania" by Al Siegel and Sam Coslow; "If It Isn't Pain, Then It Isn't Love" by Ralph Rainger and Leo Robin, and "Lonely Little Senorita" by Leo Robin and Julian Oliver. Art Directors: Hans Dreier and Ernst Fegte. Interior Decorator: A.E. Freudeman. Costumes: Travis Banton. Assistant Director: Edgar Anderson. Sound: Earl Hayman and Don Johnson. 96 minutes. Released March 12, 1937. DVD availability: public domain (various sources).

Cast: Carole Lombard (*Maggie King*); Fred MacMurray (*Skid*

THE FILMS: *Swing High, Swing Low*

Johnson); Charles Butterworth (*Harry*); Jean Dixon (*Ella*); Dorothy Lamour (*Anita Alvarez*); Harvey Stephens (*Harvey Howell*); Cecil Cunningham (*Murphy*); Charles Arnt (*Georgie*); Franklin Pangborn (*Henri*); Anthony Quinn (*The Don*); Bud Flanagan [Dennis O'Keefe] (*The Purser*); Charles Judels (*Tony*); Harry Semels (*Police Chief*); Ricardo Amendia (*Interpreter*); Enrique de Rosas (*Judge*); Chris Martin (*Servant*); Charles Stevens (*Man at Cockfight*); Ralph Remley (*Musselwhite*); George Jiminez (*Magistrate*); Al Morro (*Bouncer*); Martha Arcos (*Girl*).

Swing High, Swing Low derives from the old stage play *Burlesque*. That play first reached movie screens in 1929 as *The Dance of Life* with Nancy Carroll and Hal Skelly (who had created the role on Broadway opposite newcomer Barbara Stanwyck). A third adaptation of the story, 20th Century–Fox's *When My Baby Smiles at Me* (1948), was a vehicle for the team of Betty Grable and Dan Dailey; it appears to have tied up the rights. Over the years, critical evaluations of the Lombard-MacMurray picture have ranged from mixed notices at the time of its release to seesawing re-evaluations in later decades. Lombard biographer Robert Matzen termed *Swing High, Swing Low* "a

Lombard starred in *Swing High, Swing Low* with Fred MacMurray.

mean-spirited, weakly-scripted comedy-drama ... that seems far longer than its running time. ...[Lombard] adequately sings two songs."

Mitchell Leisen biographer David Chierichetti wrote that this picture "represents Lombard at her zenith, both as an actress and as a star. ...In every aspect [it's] a rich work. ...Ted Tetzlaff's photography of Lombard makes her screen image the most beautiful of all her films." Leonard Maltin simply calls her "exquisite."

The storyline centers on the backstage and marital ups and downs of an itinerant show business couple (Lombard and MacMurray) who meet on a ship bound for Panama, where he's got a cabaret gig as a trumpeter. Jobs are lost and won, and eventually they're both employed in a nightclub where she's a dancer and he's in the band. Their success swells MacMurray's head, and he's further distracted by conniving vocalist Dorothy Lamour. Eventually Lombard is moved to seek a divorce to marry handsome admirer Harvey Stephens.

After Lombard leaves him, MacMurray turns to drink and neglects his career. Although a friend sets him up for a radio comeback, he lacks the energy to perform—until Lombard arrives to give him moral support. It seems that they belong together.

Under Russ Columbo's tutelage, Lombard had delivered a couple of songs several years earlier in *White Woman*; she appears to have lost confidence here, especially in the company of real-life radio songstress Lamour. But director Leisen applied gentle persuasion:

> I insisted that Carole do her own singing. She didn't think she could do it, and she begged me to have somebody dub her numbers, but I said that nobody could have the same quality of voice and it would be unbelievable. So she did it [performing "I Hear a Call to Arms" and "If It Isn't Pain, Then It Isn't Love"] and it came out beautifully.

The New York Times' Frank S. Nugent credited *Swing High, Swing Low*'s two headliners with handling formulaic material "with their usual ease" and "raising a routine story to a routine-plus picture." In his Lombard biography *Screwball*, Larry Swindell singled this out as "Carole's picture": "It was not a radical departure for her, but she plumbed new dramatic depths in defining Maggie King as a gamy lowlife—smacking her chewing gum and calling everyone dearie, but nourishing a crucial reservoir of integrity and common sense." This remained a personal Lombard favorite of all her roles.

Regardless of its critical assessments, *Swing High, Swing Low* was the right picture at the right time for its public, becoming Paramount's top box office attraction of 1937.

THE FILMS: *Nothing Sacred*

Nothing Sacred

Selznick-International Pictures–United Artists, 1937

Credits: Director: William A. Wellman. Producer: David O. Selznick. Screenwriter: Ben Hecht, based on the *Saturday Evening Post* story by William Street. Technicolor Cinematographer: W. Howard Greene. Special Effects: Jack Cosgrove. Editor: James E. Newcom. Art Director: Lyle Wheeler. Costumes: Travis Banton and Walter Plunkett. Music: Oscar Levant and Raymond Scott. Assistant Director: Frederick A. Spencer. 75 minutes. Released November 26, 1937. DVD availability: Kino Lorber.

Cast: Carole Lombard (*Hazel Flagg*); Fredric March (*Wally Cook*); Charles Winninger (*Dr. Enoch Downer*); Walter Connolly (*Oliver Stone*); Sig Rumann (*Dr. Emil Eggelhoffer*); Frank Fay (*Master of Ceremonies*); Maxie Rosenbloom (*Max*); Alex Schoenberg (*Dr. Kerchinwisser*); Monty Woolley (*Dr. Vunch*); Alex Novinsky (*Dr. Marachuffsky*); Margaret Hamilton (*Drug Store Lady*); Troy Brown (*Ernest Walker*); Hattie McDaniel (*Mrs. Walker*); Katherine Sheldon (*Dr. Downer's Nurse*); Olin Howland (*Baggage Man*); Ben Morgan and Hans Steinke (*Wrestlers*); George Chandler (*Photographer*); Claire Du Brey (*Miss Rafferty*); Nora Cecil (*Schoolteacher*); Raymond Scott and His Quintet (*Orchestra*); Aileen Pringle (*Mrs. Bullock*); Dick Rich (*Moe*); A.W. Sweatt (*Office Boy*); Clarence Wilson *(Mr. Watson)*; Louise Clark (*Walker's Girl*); John Dilson (*City Editor*); Bob Perry and Art Lasky (*Mugs*); Charles Lane (*Rubenstein*); Edwin Maxwell (*Mr. Bullock*); Phillip Hurlie, Rudolph Chavers and Dolores Lilly (*Walker's Kids*); Ernest Whitman and Everett Brown (*Policemen*); Tenen Holtz (*Sad Waiter*); Alex Melesh (*D.S.C. Head*); Betty Douglas (*"Helen of Troy"*); Eleanor Troy (*"Katherine of Russia"*): Monica Bannister (*"Pocahontas"*): Jinx Falkenberg (*"Katinka"*): Margaret Lyman (*"Salome"*); Shirley Chambers (*"Godiva"*); Bill Dunn and Lee Phelps (*Electricians*); Hedda Hopper (*Dowager*); John Qualen (*Fireman*); Hilda Vaughn (*Mrs. Cartwright*); Walter Walker (*E.J. Southern*); Vera Lewis (*Miss Sedgwick*); Charles Richman (*Mayor*); Mickey McMasters (*Referee*); Bobby Tracy (*Announcer*); Ann Doran (*Telephone Girl*); Billy Barty (*Midget*); Helen Brown (*Secretary*).

Screenwriter Ben Hecht's cynical satire on ballyhoo and sensational journalism centers on a small-town Vermont girl (Lombard) diagnosed with a fatal case of radium poisoning and given six months to live. When her sad story reaches New York, reporter Fredric March sees it as a human-interest opportunity to improve his status with

THE FILMS: *Nothing Sacred*

Morning Star publisher Walter Connolly by increasing circulation, and he convinces his boss to fulfill Lombard's lifetime wish of visiting Manhattan.

Unaware that her doctor (Charles Winninger) has since reversed his diagnosis and declared her in perfect health, March oversees Lombard's big urban vacation, which includes various tributes, a key to the city and, of course, a great deal of bleeding-heart press coverage. Eventually, March and Connolly discover the truth, taking pains to keep it from public knowledge. By now, Lombard and March have fallen in love, and she agrees to stage a "suicide" to protect his job and reputation. Incognito, they sail away together, leaving behind her letter of farewell to New York.

This cursory description gives scant indication of the plot elements that make *Nothing Sacred* so enjoyable, such as Lombard's guilty attempt to fake an earlier suicide, her inebriated scene in a New York nightclub and her physical battles with March when he attempts an "illness" act to impress Connolly.

While saluting the "agreeable trouping of a perfect passel of clowns," *The New York Times* cited *Nothing Sacred* as "one of the merriest jests of the cinema year." *Life* magazine reported that it was "acted with finesse by an unbeatable pair of light comedy experts" (Lombard and March). The public obviously agreed, prolonging its New York City engagement by three weeks at the prestigious Radio City Music Hall.

Lombard's legendary reputation as a classic screwball comedienne rests mainly with this picture and *My Man Godfrey*, divergent styles of humor but two of her most popular movies. The fact that *Nothing Sacred* was photographed in the Technicolor process—the only chromatic feature of her career—only added cachet to the attraction of a new Lombard comedy. With "Wild Bill" Wellman as its director, *Nothing Sacred* remains a minor film classic, but one can only imagine how much more inventive it might have been in the hands of a true comedy genius such as Leo McCarey, Frank Capra or Ernst Lubitsch. Despite an excellent professional reputation, Wellman's expertise derived mainly from melodrama and not from farce. Nevertheless, the picture proved a great success for producer David O. Selznick, and it's still considered among the best comedies of the '30s. It was filmed at Selznick-International, which Carole had known as Pathé earlier in her career.

In 1954, Paramount remade *Nothing Sacred* as *Living It Up* with Dean Martin and, in the Lombard role, Jerry Lewis!

The Films: *True Confession*

True Confession
Paramount, 1937

Credits: Director: Wesley Ruggles. Producer: Albert Lewin. Screenwriter: Claude Binyon, based on the play *Mon Crime* by Louis Verneuil and Georges Berr. Cinematographer: Ted Tetzlaff. Editor: Paul Weatherwax. Music: Frederick Hollander. Song: "True Confession" by Frederick Hollander and Sam Coslow. Art Directors: Hans Dreier and Robert Usher. Interior Decorator: A.E. Freudeman. Costumes: Travis Banton and (uncredited) Edith Head. Sound: Earl Hayman and Don Johnson. 85 minutes. Released December 24, 1937. DVD availability: Universal Studios Home Entertainment: "Carole Lombard; The Glamour Collection."

Cast: Carole Lombard (*Helen Bartlett*); Fred MacMurray (*Kenneth Bartlett*); John Barrymore (*Charley Jasper*); Una Merkel (*Daisy McClure*); Porter Hall (*Prosecutor*); Edgar Kennedy (*Darsey*); Lynne Overman (*Bartender*); Fritz Feld (*Krayler's Butler*); Richard Carle (*Judge*); John T. Murray (*Otto Krayler*); Tom Dugan (*Typewriter Man*);

Lombard again paired with Fred MacMurray for *True Confession*.

The Films: *True Confession*

Garry Owen (*Tony Krauch*); Toby Wing (*Suzanne Baggart*); Hattie McDaniel (*Ella*); Bernard Suss (*Pedestrian*); Irving Bacon (*Coroner*); Eleanor Fisher (*Reporter*); Pat West, Herbert Ashley, Dudley Clements, Walter Soderling, Jim Toney, Gertrude Simpson, Chester Clute, Irving White, George Ovey, Elmer Jerome, Peggy Leon, Jane K. Loofbourrow and George B. French (*Jurors*); Anne Cornwall (*Alternate Juror*); Harry Fleischmann and Jack Daley (*Policemen*); Frank Austin (*Caretaker*); Jack Kennedy (*Jail Guard*); Cora Shumway (*Jail Matron*); Arthur Lake (*Attendant*); Frank DuFrane (*Maitre d'Hotel*); John Nasboro (*Doorman*); Charles Sherlock (*Chauffeur*); Joyce Matthews (*Girl in Cocktail Lounge*); Dorothy Howe (*Brunette Girl*); Peggy Montgomery, Bradley Metcalfe, Wesley Giraud, Billy O'Brien, Carmencita Johnson, Seesel Ann Johnson, Rosita Butler and Beaudine Anderson (*Autograph Hunters*); Byron Foulger (*Ballistic Expert*); Lew Kelly (*Court Captain*); Sharon Lewis (*Yvonne Bolero*); Franklin Parker (*Reporter*); Art Rowlands and Ned Glass (*Photographers*); Mark Strong (*Assistant Court Clerk*); Charlotte Dabney (*Newspaper Sketch Artist*).

Lombard completed her eight-year contractual obligation to Paramount with this disappointing effort at wacky comedy. And the key word here is *effort*, for it shows! Whereas her Irene Bullock of *My Man Godfrey* is delightfully zany, Lombard's Helen Bartlett of *True Confession* is pathetically scatterbrained and an inveterate liar. So foolish is this character that one is put in mind of Carole's former Paramount colleague Gracie Allen. It doesn't take much imagination to visualize Gracie taking over this role, with the ever-present George Burns stepping into the husband part played here by a mustachioed Fred MacMurray.

True Confession presents her as the restless wife of idealistic, struggling young attorney Fred, who forbids her to work. To help solve their financial problems, Carole secretly accepts a position as secretary to wealthy John T. Murray, only to find that her employer's intentions are purely lecherous. So fast does she quit that she leaves her hat and handbag behind. When friend Una Merkel accompanies her back to retrieve them, they find that Murray has been murdered, a crime for which they are arrested.

MacMurray takes on her case, entering a plea of justifiable homicide, in defense of her honor. Found not guilty, Lombard is pleased to witness her husband's revitalized career in the wake of her case's publicity, despite her having been totally innocent. But then their lives are complicated by the presence of John Barrymore, an eccentric, alcoholic opportunist who attended her trial and who now attempts to blackmail

Lombard, threatening to tell MacMurray what he knows and reveal the real killer: Barrymore's own brother-in-law, who has since died in an automobile accident. When Fred learns the truth, he prepares to walk out on Carole—until she reveals that they're about to become parents. When that revelation appears to be yet another Lombard lie, he re-evaluates their relationship and decides he can't live without her, leading to a mindless "happy ending."

The New York Times' Frank Nugent called Lombard "a tower of comic strength, and the pivotal point around which the picture spins." In *The Hollywood Citizen News*, James Francis Crow wrote: "Miss Lombard plunges headlong into her role, and comes through with a vigorous piece of trouping which will delight her fans and win her many new ones." And apparently it did, for the late–1937 holiday season was marked by two Carole Lombard hits, *True Confession* and *Nothing Sacred*.

In 1946, Paramount remade the picture as *Cross My Heart*, a mediocre vehicle for Betty Hutton.

Fools for Scandal
Warner Brothers, 1938

Credits: Director-Producer: Mervyn LeRoy. Screenwriters: Herbert Fields, Joseph Fields and Irving Beecher, based on the play *Return Engagement* by Nancy Hamilton, James Shute and Rosemary Casey. Cinematographer: Ted Tetzlaff. Editor: William Holmes. Art Director: Anton Grot. Costumes: Travis Banton (for Carole Lombard) and Milo Anderson. Music Director: Leo Forbstein. Songs: "There's a Boy in Harlem," "How Can You Forget?" and "Fools for Scandal" by Richard Rodgers and Lorenz Hart. "Le Petite Harlem" staged by Bobby Connolly. Sound: E.A. Brown and David Forrest. Assistant Director: Sherry Shourds. 81 minutes. Released April 16, 1938.

Cast: Carole Lombard (*Kay Winters*); Fernand Gravet (*Rene*); Ralph Bellamy (*Phillip Chester*); Allen Jenkins (*Dewey Gelson*); Isabel Jeans (*Lady Paula Malverton*); Marie Wilson (*Myrtle*); Marcia Ralston (*Jill*); Ottola Nesmith (*Agnes*); Heather Thatcher (*Lady Potter-Porter*); Jacques Lory (*Papa Joli-Coeur*); Tempe Pigott (*Bessie*); Michellette Burani (*Mme. Brioche*); Jeni Le Gon (*Specialty Performer*); Norma Varden (*Cicely*); Ara Gerald (*Mrs. Bullit*); Leland Hodgson (*Mr. Bullit*); Bruce Devon (*John Sutton*); Les Hite and His Orchestra.

Following her trio of popular 1937 pictures, Lombard's sole 1938 release—her only movie for Warner Brothers—was this unqualified dud.

The Films: *Fools for Scandal*

***Fools for Scandal* with Fernand Gravet.**

This one was developed in reverse order from the customary: Having worked at every other major studio, Lombard expressed interest in doing a Warners picture, for which she even lowered her asking price. That studio was then seeking a project for their Belgian import Fernand Gravet, and so screenwriter Julius J. Epstein was engaged by Jack L. Warner to produce a serviceable script. Warner wasn't sure what he wanted outside of some farcical scenes, stunning gowns for Carole and Continental romancing by Gravet. Producer-director Mervyn LeRoy proved equally vague, causing a discouraged Epstein to withdraw and leave the project to the writing team of Herbert and Joseph Fields, with some uncredited input from their sister Dorothy. The end result, based on a little-known play called *Return Engagement*, was an uneasy stew of screwball farce and sophisticated high comedy that totally failed to amuse.

While vacationing in Paris, an American movie star (Lombard) meets impoverished nobleman Gravet. With no knowledge of one another's identity, they enjoy a day together; they later become reacquainted in London where he crashes her Noah's Ark party. As a joke, she offers him employment as a servant, which he accepts, hampering her relationship with suitor Ralph Bellamy. Eventually, an unlikely pairing of film star and aristocrat is achieved.

Of minor redeeming value were the star's Travis Banton wardrobe and Ted Tetzlaff's flattering cinematography. But the dark wig sported by Lombard in her opening scenes was an unbecoming turn-off.

The film met with a deadly press reception. *Variety*'s critic called it as he saw it: "For a picture of its pretentions and talented personnel, this falls short of distinction and is in many respects pretty dull stuff. For Carole Lombard, it must be reckoned below her usual standard, and for the director-producer, it is not up to the Mervyn LeRoy par." Difficult-to-please *Time* magazine opined, "In spite of Actress Lombard's strident earthiness, the result is as unearthly as Actor Gravet's French-flavored, concave British inflection."

Not even fan-oriented *Photoplay* could muster kind words for *Fools for Scandal*: "[T]his is the straw that probably will break the back of that slapstick camel Carole Lombard's been riding for so long." The *New York Herald Tribune* called it "a witless, wearisome entertainment in which Carole Lombard works overtime to achieve a clowning mood."

No doubt crushed and chagrined by the film's reception, Lombard did not face the cameras again for ten months.

Made for Each Other

Selznick-International Pictures–United Artists, 1939

Credits: Director: John Cromwell. Producer: David O. Selznick. Screenwriter: Jo Swerling, based on a story by Rose Franklin. Cinematographer: Leon Shamroy. Special Effects: Jack Cosgrove. Editor: James E. Newcom. Production Designer: William Cameron Menzies. Art Director: Lyle Wheeler. Interior Decorator: Edward G. Boyle. Costumes: Travis Banton. Sound: Jack Noyes. Music: Lou Forbes. Assistant Director: Eric Stacey. 93 minutes. Released February 10, 1939. DVD availability: MGM Home Entertainment.

Cast: Carole Lombard (*Jane Mason*); James Stewart (*John Mason*); Charles Coburn (*Judge Doolittle*); Lucile Watson (*Mrs. Mason*); Eddie Quillan (*Conway*); Alma Kruger (*Sister Madeline*); Ruth Weston (*Eunice Doolittle*); Donald Briggs (*Carter*); Harry Davenport (*Dr. Healy*); Esther Dale (*First Cook*); Renee Orsell (*Second Cook*); Louise Beavers (*Lily*); Ward Bond (*Hatton*); Olin Howland (*Farmer*); Fern Emmet (*Farmer's Wife*); Bonnie Bell Barber (*John Mason, Jr., newborn*); Jackie Taylor

THE FILMS: *Made for Each Other*

Made for Each Other with Lombard and James Stewart.

(*John Mason, Jr., age one*); Mickey Rentschler (*Office Boy*); Ivan Simpson (*Simon*); Russell Hopton (*Collins*); Betty Farrington (*Hospital Cashier*); Wilhelmina Morris, Nella Walker, Marjorie Wood and Ethel Manical (*Nurses*); Harlan Briggs (*Judge*); Arthur Hoyt (*Jury Foreman*); Monte Collins, James McNamara and John Piccori (*Jurymen*); Ruth Gillette (*Blonde in Café*); Edgar Dearing (*Mounted Policeman*); Robert Elliott (*Airport Operations Manager*); Jack Mulhall (*Rock Springs Radio Operator*); Gary Owen (*Denver Radio Operator*); Carlyle Moore (*North Platte Radio Operator*); Russ Clark (*Omaha Radio Operator*); Arthur Gardner (*Iowa City Radio Operator*); Mike Killian (*Chicago Radio Operator*); John Austin (*Allentown Radio Operator*); Harry North (*New York Hospital Chemist*); J.M. Sullivan (*Johns Hopkins Chemist*); Raymond Bailey (*Salt Lake Hospital Chemist*); Mary Field (*Indianapolis Lab Assistant*); Lane Chandler and Tom London (*Rangers*); Betty Farrington (*Hospital Cashier*); Robert Emmet O'Connor (*Elevator Starter*); Robert Strange, Perry Ivins and Gladden James (*Doctors*); Edwin Maxwell (*Messerschmidt*); Harry Depp (*Hutch*); Fred Fuller (*Younger Doolittle*).

With her Hollywood image still firmly rooted in comedy and the passage of months beginning to dim sour memories of *Fools for*

Scandal, Lombard sought to establish herself as a character actress with this domestic comedy-drama that leaned more toward the serious.

Cast opposite fast-rising James Stewart, she worked for the first time under the direction of John Cromwell, whose acquaintance she'd made in her early Paramount days. Before filming was completed on *Made for Each Other*, he would loom high on her list of favorite directors.

Lombard and Stewart play newlyweds struggling to make a go of it against numerous odds. He's a young lawyer getting nowhere in Charles Coburn's law firm; she's a well-intentioned homemaker coping with fault-finding mother-in-law Lucile Watson and a stack of unpaid bills. Things grow steadily worse. When their baby contracts a serious illness, Coburn finally rallies to his employee's aid, and sees to it that a life-saving medication is flown across the country in time to prevent tragedy. That's the basic storyline, but it's the simple details in Jo Swerling's screenplay and Cromwell's painstaking direction that make this film special, leaving its audiences unaware that their emotions are being manipulated

In a year that would go down in Hollywood history for its number of outstanding films, *Made for Each Other* was hailed by *The New York Times* as one of 1939's ten best pictures. *Newsweek* declared Lombard's "the best performance of her career," and *Time* said, "[T]his mundane, domestic chronicle has more impact that all the hurricanes, sandstorms and earthquakes manufactured in Hollywood last season."

Made for Each Other made a respectable profit, but it wasn't the smash-hit anticipated, and perhaps that was due to its serious content. Lombard fans anticipating laughter couldn't find it here.

In Name Only
RKO, 1939

Credits: Director: John Cromwell. Producer: George Haight. Screenwriter: Richard Sherman, based on the novel *Memory of Love* by Bessie Breuer. Cinematographer: J. Roy Hunt. Editor: William Hamilton. Art Directors: Van Nest Polglase and Perry Ferguson. Set Decorator: Darrell Silvera. Costumes: Edward Stevenson and Irene (Carole Lombard's wardrobe); Sound: Hugh McDowell, Jr. Assistant Director: Dewey Starkey. Music: Roy Webb. 94 minutes. Released August 18, 1939. DVD Availability: Warner Brothers Home Entertainment Archive Collection.

THE FILMS: *In Name Only*

Cast: Carole Lombard (*Julie Eden*); Cary Grant (*Alec Walker*); Kay Francis (*Maida Walker*); Charles Coburn (*Mr. Walker*); Helen Vinson (*Suzanne*); Katherine Alexander (*Laura Morton*); Jonathan Hale (*Dr. Gateson*); Maurice Moscovitch (*Dr. Miller*); Nella Walker (*Mrs. Walker*); Peggy Ann Garner (*Ellen Eden*); Spencer Charters (*Gardner*); Harriet Matthews and Sandra Morgan (*Women on Boat*); Harold Miller and John Dilson (*Stewards*); Douglas Gordon, Tony Merlo and James Adamson (*Waiters*); Frank Puglia (*Manager*); Alex Pollard (*Butler*); Charles Coleman (*Archie Duross*); Florence Wix and Katherine Wilson (*Women at Party*); Clive Morgan and Major Sam Harris (*Men at Party*); Grady Sutton (*Escort*); Burt Moorhouse (*College Man*); Byron Foulger (*Owen*); Arthur Aylesworth (*Farmer on Truck*); Lloyd Ingraham (*Elevator Operator*); Gus Glassmire (*Hospital Attendant*); Mary MacLaren (*Nurse*); Robert Strange (*Hotel Manager*); Jack Chapin, Harold Hoff and Allen Wood (*Bellhops*); George Rosener (*Hotel Doctor*); Fern Emmett (*Chambermaid*); Edward Fligle (*Night Clerk*); John Laing (*Chauffeur*); Frank Mills (*Bartender*).

Lombard is flanked by Cary Grant and Kay Francis in a scene from *In Name Only*.

In Name Only must be considered a prime example of that long-obsolete genre, the "woman's picture," for it's pure soap opera, albeit of the highest quality in every respect—and beautifully acted.

Unhappily married Cary Grant meets and is immediately attracted to Lombard, a young widow with a little girl (Peggy Ann Garner). Once he and Lombard fall in love, he asks for a divorce from wife Kay Francis, who's only interested in his money and position. At first, she misleads him into believing she'll agree, but later reneges, vowing to sue Lombard for alienation of affection if he attempts to pursue the idea.

After her estranged husband takes seriously ill with pneumonia, Francis admits to Lombard that she only cares for his family fortune. Her remarks are overheard by his previously sympathetic parents. With Francis' true nature revealed, the future begins to brighten for Lombard and a recovering Grant.

Years later, director John Cromwell recalled Lombard as "just a joy, a wonderful, wonderful gal. She was enough of an actress to display her personality and her great charm, but I don't think she did any more than just fill the ordinary aspirations of somebody in that position. I think she was interested in other things in life besides being an actress."

Saluting her second successful 1939 foray into more serious territory, *The New York Times'* Bosley Crowther wrote that Lombard "plays her poignant role with all the fragile intensity and contained passion that have lifted her to dramatic eminence." And he called *In Name Only* "one of the most adult and enjoyable pictures of the season." In London's *Spectator*, Graham Greene observed, "Miss Lombard's wavering and melancholy voice, her bewildered eyes, which have in the past faltered so well among the rapid, confused events of crazy comedy, work just as satisfactorily here—wringing out tears instead of laughs."

So popular was *In Name Only* that it was held over for three weeks at New York's premiere movie showcase, Radio City Music Hall.

Vigil in the Night
RKO, 1940

Credits: Director-Producer: George Stevens. Executive Producer: Pandro S. Berman. Screenwriters: Fred Guiol, P.J. Wolfson and Rowland Leigh, based on the novel by A.J. Cronin. Cinematographer: Robert de Grasse. Editor: Henry Berman. Art Directors: Van Nest Polglase and L.P. Williams. Set Decorator: Darrell Silvera. Costumes: Walter Plunkett. Music: Alfred Newman. Assistant Director: Syd Fogel.

THE FILMS: *Vigil in the Night*

Sound: Richard Van Hessen. 96 minutes. Released February 9, 1940. DVD Availability: Warner Brothers Home Entertainment Archive Collection.

Cast: Carole Lombard (*Anne Lee*); Brian Aherne (*Dr. Prescott*); Anne Shirley (*Lucy Lee*); Julien Mitchell (*Matthew Bowley*); Robert Coote (*Dr. Caley*); Brenda Forbes (*Nora*); Rita Page (*Glennie*); Peter Cushing (*Joe Shand*); Ethel Griffies (*Matron East*); Doris Lloyd (*Mrs. Bowley*); Emily Fitzroy (*Sister Gilson*); May Beatty (*Mrs. Merchant*); John Bridges (*Jury Foreman*); James Carlisle (*Jury Member*); Wallis Clark (*Mr. Peterson*); Donnie Dunagan (*Tommy*); Edward Fielding (*Forest*); Jack Gargan (*Courtroom Spectator*); Helena Grant (*Nurse Gregg*); Charlie Hall (*Courtroom Spectator*); Winifred Harris (*First Matron*); Tiny Jones (*Distraught Mother*); Colin Kenny (*Court Bailiff*); Rafaela Ottiano (*Henrietta Sullivan*); Reginald Sheffield (*Judge Tyler*).

For the second picture under her RKO contract, Carole selected this adaptation of an A.J. Cronin novel, cognizant that his *The Citadel* had been a prestige 1938 offering from MGM. In fact, under the well-respected guidance of producer-director George Stevens, *Vigil in*

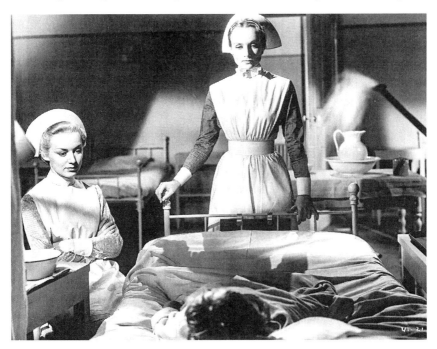

Vigil in the Night with Carole Lombard (standing) and Anne Shirley.

THE FILMS: *They Knew What They Wanted*

the Night was to be among RKO's major releases of 1940. With a wary eye to the failed comedies of her recent past, Lombard focused on this work for its strong dramatic possibilities, perhaps ignoring the increasingly evident fact that her fans longed to see her in more light-hearted pictures.

The setting is a hospital in the British city of Manchester, where sisters Lombard and Anne Shirley are nurses. When Shirley's negligence results in a child's death, her older sister assumes responsibility before leaving to work in another hospital. There she meets, and forms an emotional attachment to Dr. Brian Aherne. But her employment is compromised by the unwanted attentions of hospital VIP Julien Mitchell, and she's fired.

Lombard is temporarily re-hired when an epidemic strikes. She's joined by Shirley who, determined to redeem herself, bravely saves another youngster's life before succumbing herself. Mitchell, whose own son has perished in the plague, demonstrates his approval of their dedicated work by fully reinstating Lombard as Aherne's colleague, while allocating funds for an improved medical facility.

Vigil in the Night is reputedly among the most authentic hospital pictures ever made, rating closely alongside Britain's esteemed *White Corridors* (1951). *Motion Picture Herald* called it "grim from start to finish and often violently realistic," adding, "Carole Lombard gives a commanding portrayal of the austerely fervent nurse who shelters her sister and struggles on to exemplify the ideals of her profession."

Released in the first quarter of 1940, the much-underrated *Vigil in the Night* never found its audience, with negative word-of-mouth undoubtedly accounting for RKO's failure to wage a significant Oscar campaign for the excellent work of Anne Shirley and, especially, Carole Lombard, who had entertained high hopes of just such recognition.

They Knew What They Wanted
RKO, 1940

Credits: Director: Garson Kanin. Producer: Erich Pommer. Executive Producer: Harry E. Edington. Screenwriter: Robert Ardrey, based on the play by Sidney Howard. Cinematographer: Harry Stradling. Special Effects: Vernon L. Walker. Editor: John Sturges. Art Directors: Van Nest Polglase and Mark-Lee Kirk. Set Decorator: Darrell Silvera. Costumes: Edward Stevenson. Sound: John L. Cass. Assistant Director:

THE FILMS: *They Knew What They Wanted*

A shot from *They Knew What They Wanted* with Charles Laughton.

Ruby Rosenberg. Music: Alfred Newman. 96 minutes. Released October 25, 1940.

Cast: Carole Lombard (*Amy Peters*); Charles Laughton (*Tony Patucci*); William Gargan (*Joe*); Harry Carey (*Doctor*); Frank Fay (*Father McKee*); Joe Bernard (*The R.F.D.*); Janet Fox (*Mildred*); Lee Tung-Foo (*Ah Gee*); Karl Malden (*Red*); Victor Kilian (*Photographer*); Paul Lepere and Tom Ewell (*Hired Hands*); Marie Blake, Millicent Green and Patricia Oakley (*Waitresses*).

Sidney Howard's prize-winning stage play was filmed first as *The Secret Hour*, a 1928 silent with Pola Negri and Jean Hersholt, and again as a 1930 talkie, *A Lady to Love*, with Vilma Banky and Edward G. Robinson. But the moving story of an unattractive middle-aged Napa Valley rancher and his mail-order bride works best in this 1940 Erich Pommer production, directed by Broadway's Garson Kanin.

In its 1940 incarnation, *They Knew What They Wanted* presents Lombard as a hard-working San Francisco waitress who harbors dreams of a better life. Helping her realize that future is the marriage offer of a man she has never met—Charles Laughton's shy and homely

THE FILMS: *They Knew What They Wanted*

grape-grower, whose correspondence includes the misleading photo of his good-looking hired man, William Gargan. When Laughton's mail-order bride arrives, she's understandably shocked by her suitor's subterfuge.

On the eve of their wedding, amid a spirited local celebration, Laughton suffers an accident, breaking both his legs and delaying the ceremony, yet giving them both time to nurture their relationship. As a result, Lombard's original resentment of his deception turns to affection, despite the unwanted attentions of Gargan.

During Laughton's recuperation, she succumbs to the hired hand's advances and finds herself pregnant with the child of someone (Gargan) with no interest in marriage. After a fight with Gargan, Laughton forgives Lombard and looks forward to making a home for his new wife and her child.

Movie censorship restrictions of the era cloud some of the story's sexual aspects, rendering it difficult to understand Lombard's love-hate relationship with Gargan or make believable the intimacy that results in her pregnancy. Presumably, he caught her in a moment of weakness and wore down her resistance to his lothario charm. To her credit, Lombard never loses audience sympathy. In the words of her director, "I thought her a fine actress, one of the finest I had ever encountered."

In *Commonweal*, Philip T. Hartung wrote, "Garson Kanin's intelligent direction has resulted in a poignant, sincere adult film about three people who seem pathetically dumb and helpless, but who are real people who know what they want." In London's *Spectator*, Basil Wright opined, "[Lombard] proves a much more talented actress than one had supposed; both she and William Gargan stand up splendidly to Laughton's moving sincerity no less than to his enormous acting technique."

Assessing *They Knew What They Wanted* as "Laughton's film," Leonard Maltin (in his book *Carole Lombard*) nevertheless focuses admiringly on its leading lady: "Lombard is wonderful as Amy, the dreamy-eyed waitress who longs for an opportunity to hop off the treadmill and enjoy life. She doesn't need dialogue to convey her emotions; they flash across the screen through her marvelously expressive face and voice."

The film's Alfred Newman music score evokes uncanny pre-echoes of Frank Loesser's memorable songs for the tale's 1956 musical-theater adaptation, *The Most Happy Fella*.

Mr. & Mrs. Smith
RKO, 1941

Credits: Director: Alfred Hitchcock. Executive Producer: Harry E. Edington. Screenwriter: Norman Krasna. Cinematographer: Harry Stradling. Special Effects: Vernon L. Walker. Editor: William Hamilton. Art Directors: Van Nest Polglase and L.P. Williams. Set Decorator: Darrell Silvera. Music: Edward Ward. Costumes: Irene. Assistant Director: Dewey Starkey. Sound: John E. Tribby. 95 minutes. Released January 31, 1941.

Cast: Carole Lombard (*Ann Krausheimer Smith*); Robert Montgomery (*David Smith*); Gene Raymond (*Jeff Custer*); Jack Carson (*Chuck Benson*); Philip Merivale (*Ashley Custer*); Lucile Watson (*Mrs. Custer*); William Tracy (*Sammy*); Charles Halton (*Mr. Deever*); Esther Dale (*Mrs. Krausheimer*); Emma Dunn (*Martha*); William Edmunds (*Proprietor of Lucy's*); Betty Compson (*Gertie*); Patricia Farr (*Gloria*); Adele Pearce (*Lily*); Frank Mills (*Taxi Driver*); Alec Craig (*Thomas*); Francis Compton (*Mr. Flugle*); Robert Emmett Keane (*Section Manager*); Jack Gardner (*Elevator Boy*); Ralph Sanford (*Store Checker*); Murray Alper (*Harold*); Georgia Carroll (*Pretty Girl*); Ralph Dunn (*Policeman*); James Flavin (*Escort*); Ralph Brooks (*Waiter Captain*); Ronnie Rondell (*Waiter*); Jim Pierce (*Doorman*); Barbara Woodell (*David's Secretary*); Beatrice Maude (*Jeff's Secretary*); Allen Wood and Ernie Alexander (*Bellhops*); Emory Parnell (*Conway*); Stan Taylor (*Clerk*).

Lombard finally returned to the sort of wacky comedy for which she's best remembered with this pleasant but predictable farce about marital mix-ups. It was the last of her four contracted pictures for RKO, and she had enough clout also to serve as its uncredited producer. Thus, she was instrumental in selecting a director and cast, as well as its production crew. As a result, *Mr. & Mrs. Smith* came to be known as the least characteristic of all the American films directed by suspense specialist Alfred Hitchcock.

Lombard was already socially acquainted with the rotund and dry-witted Englishman (who harbored a well-known penchant for blonde leading ladies), and at a time when he was between assignments she approached him to inquire whether he might like to direct a screwball comedy. The prospect didn't hold much interest for him, but he did indicate that having her as the leading lady would increase his enthusiasm.

For Carole's co-star they initially sought the much-in-demand

THE FILMS: *Mr. & Mrs. Smith*

Mr. & Mrs. Smith **with Lombard and Robert Montgomery.**

Cary Grant, and learned that they'd have a two-year wait. At the time, Robert Montgomery was considered Grant's equal at light comedy, and he was cast. So successful was his teaming with Lombard that Hitchcock predicted their future as one of the great comedy teams.

Norman Krasna's screenplay casts Lombard and Montgomery as a combative New York couple whose one marital pledge is never to part company in the heat of a quarrel. Following one such incident, confining them to their bedroom for several days, she asks of her husband, "Darling, if you had to do it all over, would you marry me?" To which he teasingly responds, "Honestly, no."

Soon afterward, they're both shocked to discover that, through a technicality, their union isn't legal. With his bantering reply to her marital question in mind, Lombard hopes that they'll immediately legalize their situation. Instead, he makes a bumbling attempt to recreate their courting days, with disastrous results. Deciding that he's not really interested in making their relationship legal, she locks him out, goes back to her maiden name and encourages the attentions of his attractive business partner Gene Raymond.

Montgomery is set on winning Lombard back. Matters come to

a head when all three meet at a Lake Placid resort where, finally convinced of her "husband's" love, Lombard is happy to reconcile.

Atypical though it may be of Hitchcock's *oeuvre*, *Mr. & Mrs. Smith* nevertheless displays its moments of sly, characteristic visual touches. When Hitch made his customary cameo appearance, Carole took the director's chair and forced Hitchcock to repeat his brief scene with Montgomery over and over, as she kidded him mercilessly about his handling of actors.

Mr. & Mrs. Smith isn't in a class with Lombard screwball classics like *Twentieth Century* and *My Man Godfrey*, but it does offer 90 minutes of amusing diversion for undemanding audiences, and it restored movieland's goddess of comedy to the métier for which she was most widely appreciated. As *The Hollywood Reporter* stated, "It may be disappointing to many of the followers of Norman Krasna, Alfred Hitchcock and Carole Lombard who expected extreme brilliance from the trio, but there's enough fun in it to send you home happy with your entertainment."

For the record, the only similarity between this movie and the 2005 film teaming Brad Pitt and Angelina Jolie is its title.

To Be or Not to Be
United Artists, 1942

Credits: Director-Producer: Ernst Lubitsch. Executive Producer: Alexander Korda. Screenwriter: Edwin Justus Mayer, based on a story by Ernst Lubitsch and Melchior Lengyel. Cinematographer: Rudolph Maté. Special Effects: Lawrence Butler. Editor: Dorothy Spencer. Production Designer: Vincent Korda. Associate Art Director: MacMillan Johnson. Interior Decorator: Julia Heron. Costumes: Irene. Sound: Frank Maher. Music: Werner R. Heymann. Makeup: Gordon Bau. 99 minutes. Released February 15, 1942. DVD Availability: Warner Home Video.

Cast: Carole Lombard (*Maria Tura*); Jack Benny (*Joseph Tura*); Robert Stack (*Lt. Stanislav Sobinski*); Felix Bressart (*Greenberg*); Lionel Atwill (*Rawatch*); Stanley Ridges (*Prof. Siletsky*); Sig Rumann (*Col. Ehrhardt*); Tom Dugan (*Bronski*); Charles Halton (*Dobosh*); Henry Victor (*Capt. Schulz*); Maube Eburne (*Anna*); George Lynn (*Actor-Adjutant*); Halliwell Hobbes (*Gen. Armstrong*); Miles Mander (*Major Cunningham*); Armand Wright (*Makeup Man*); Erno Verebes (*Stage Manager*); Leslie Denison (*Captain*); Frank Reicher (*Polish*

The Films: *To Be or Not to Be*

Official); Peter Caldwell (*William Kunze*); Wolfgang Zilzer (*Man in Bookstore*); Olaf Hytten (*Polonius in Warsaw*); Charles Irwin, Leland Hodgson (*Reporters*); Alec Craig, James Finlayson (*Scottish Farmers*); Edgar Licho (*Prompter*); Robert O. Davis (*Gestapo Sergeant*); Roland Varno (*Pilot*); Helmut Dantine, Otto Reichow (*Co-Pilots*); Maurice Murphy, Gene Rizzi, Paul Barrett, John Kellogg (*Polish R.A.F. Fliers*).

Carole Lombard's last film, made in collaboration with the iconic producer-director Ernst Lubitsch—the man she had so wanted to work with, during her Paramount contract years—almost didn't happen for her. Originally, Lubitsch had envisioned her role for his long-time favorite Miriam Hopkins, who'd be cast opposite America's then-favorite radio comedian, Jack Benny. But there were problems, not only in financing this offbeat project, but also in convincing Hopkins to serve as "straight man" to Benny, about whom she apparently harbored private reservations. Also, Miriam wanted her role built up on a par with that of her co-star.

Lombard, who had then been away from movie production for a year, learned of this project and expressed her interest. To work with Lubitsch, she would happily accept a secondary role. After Hopkins

To Be or Not to Be with Robert Stack.

THE FILMS: *To Be or Not to Be*

finally rejected Lubitsch's offer, Lombard impressed him with her enthusiasm. And once she had signed on, there was no longer a problem securing the financing.

Written for the screen by Edwin Justus Mayer, this highly original mixture of World War II comedy and serious political drama presents Benny and Lombard as a husband-and-wife team of ham actors. When the Polish government cancels their Warsaw-based troupe's premiere of the anti–Nazi play *Gestapo* for fear of antagonizing Berlin, the acting company substitutes their repertory production of *Hamlet*.

At every performance, as Benny begins the celebrated "To be or not to be" soliloquy, a young man (Robert Stack) in the second row gets up and walks out. As it develops, the offender visits with Lombard backstage while her husband is busy reciting Shakespeare. It takes Benny a while to uncover this ploy.

With the German invasion of Poland, their theater is closed and Stack, a lieutenant in the Polish Air Force, flees to London. There he encounters Stanley Ridges, a Nazi posing as a Polish patriot, who claims he's heading for Warsaw on a secret mission, and who gathers the Polish addresses of friends and relatives of London refugees. Stack becomes suspicious and, after consulting British Intelligence, he is sent to Warsaw to intercept Ridges. Once there, Stack seeks out Lombard, whose arrest is ordered by Ridges.

Plot complications now involve the entire acting troupe in a Nazi masquerade, with Benny impersonating the murdered Ridges and company actor Tom Dugan posing as Hitler. Eventually, they escape by plane and find refuge in Britain. As this unlikely tale concludes, Benny begins the soliloquy during a London production of *Hamlet*, only to see a *new* Lombard admirer make his exit for a backstage rendezvous.

Released a month after Lombard's tragic death in a plane crash, *To Be or Not to Be* met with a decidedly mixed response from both critics and the public. First and foremost was the question of taste and the mining of humor from such serious subject manner. And, for many, there wasn't much pleasure to be derived from watching the posthumous comedy performance of the beloved and recently demised Lombard. Maintaining an unemotional perspective, *Photoplay* said, "The last picture made by Carole Lombard remains a fitting tribute to the vital, arresting beauty and personality of the star." *Variety*'s critic wrote, "It is characteristic of the roles which were most becoming to Miss Lombard, lovely with laughter, lush with entertainment, appropriate to the valedictory of a persuasive actress and a glowing personality."

THE FILMS: *To Be or Not to Be*

In *The National Board of Review Magazine*, James Shelley Hamilton lauded what may have been Lombard's greatest performance; "She shows better than ever before those rare qualities of a fine comedienne, an intelligent mind and a blithe spirit expressing themselves easily and gracefully through an assured technique of acting."

Time magazine focused on the film itself: "In *Ninotchka*, Director Ernst Lubitsch deliciously kidded the vagaries of the Soviets; in *To Be or Not to Be* he succeeds—as Hollywood had not yet done—in deftly ridiculing Hitler and the Nazis."

To those who accused Lubitsch of callous opportunism, the filmmaker responded: "What I have satirized in this picture are the Nazis and their ridiculous ideology. I have also satirized the attitude of actors who always remain actors regardless of how dangerous the situation might be...."

In 1983, humor-meister Mel Brooks directed himself and wife Anne Bancroft in a *To Be or Not to Be* remake that entertained a latter-day audience with the cynical perspective of hindsight history. Yet, for many, it failed to erase memories of a 1942 black-and-white comedy classic that's now widely considered a masterpiece.

Carole Lombard on Radio

My Man Godfrey
CBS—*Lux Radio Theatre*
Broadcast May 8, 1938
William Powell, Lombard and Gail Patrick repeated their original roles in an adaptation of the 1936 Universal movie. It also featured David Niven, who would star in Universal's 1957 remake.

The Circle
NBC discussion series
Broadcast January 15–February 5, 1939
Lombard took part in the first four episodes of this weekly Sunday night talk show, which featured an all-star cast of celebrities expounding on current events, philosophical ideas and the arts. The show continued for another five months and folded in July 1939.

Tailored by Toni
Gulf Screen Guild Show
Broadcast March 12, 1939
Lombard teamed with James Stewart, Spring Byington and Edward Everett Horton in this romantic comedy about a clothing designer and a struggling playwright.

In Name Only
CBS—*Lux Radio Theatre*
Broadcast December 11, 1939

Lombard, Cary Grant and Kay Francis recreated their film performances in an adaptation of their August film release.

Made for Each Other
CBS—*Lux Radio Theatre*
Broadcast February 19, 1940
Lombard and Fred MacMurray reunited three years after their last movie pairing for this adaptation of the film in which she'd played opposite James Stewart a year earlier.

The Awful Truth
Gulf Screen Guild Theater
Broadcast May 17, 1940
Ralph Bellamy repeated his role as the second male lead in this popular screwball comedy, with Lombard and Robert Young assuming the parts played in the 1937 hit film by Irene Dunne and Cary Grant.

The Moon's Our Home
CBS—*Lux Radio Theatre*
Broadcast February 10, 1941
Lombard and James Stewart once again proved a winning team in this adaptation of the 1936 comedy vehicle for Margaret Sullavan and Henry Fonda.

Mr. & Mrs. Smith
CBS—*Lux Radio Theatre*
Broadcast June 9, 1941
Lombard and Bob Hope (playing Robert Montgomery's movie part) made a promising comedy team in this adaptation of her January release. Jack Arnold and Bill Goodwin took on the roles originally portrayed by Gene Raymond and Jack Carson.

Bibliography

Alcott, Kate (Patricia O'Brien). *A Touch of Stardust*. New York: Doubleday, 2015.
Basinger, Jeanine. *Shirley Temple*. New York: Pyramid, 1975.
Behlmer, Rudy, editor. *Memo from David O. Selznick*. New York: Viking, 1972.
Bogdanovich, Peter. *Allan Dwan: The Last Pioneer*. New York: Praeger, 1971.
Bogdanovich, Peter. *Who the Devil Made It*. New York: Alfred A. Knopf, 1997.
Carr, Larry. *More Fabulous Faces*. Garden City, NY: Doubleday, 1979.
Chierichetti, David. *Hollywood Director: The Career of Mitchell Leisen*. New York: Curtis Books, 1973.
Crosby, Bing (as told to Pete Martin). *Call Me Lucky*. New York: Simon & Schuster, 1953.
Deschner, Donald. *The Films of Cary Grant*. Secaucus: Citadel, 1973.
Dickens, Homer. *The Films of Gary Cooper*. Secaucus: Citadel, 1970.
Eames, John Douglas. *The Paramount Story*. New York: Crown, 1985.
Essoe, Gabe. *The Films of Clark Gable*. Secaucus: Citadel, 1969.
Finch, Christopher, and Linda Rosenkrantz. *Gone Hollywood: The Movie Colony in the Golden Age*. Garden City, NY: Doubleday, 1979.
Fowler, Gene. *Good Night, Sweet Prince*. New York: Viking, 1944.
Francisco, Charles. *Gentleman: The William Powell Story*. New York: St. Martin's, 1985.
Gable, Kathleen. *Clark Gable: A Personal Portrait*. Englewood Cliffs, NJ: Prentice-Hall, 1961.
Garceau, Jean, with Inez Cocke. *Dear Mr. G*. Boston: Little, Brown, 1961.
Garceau, Jean, with Inez Cocke. *Gable: A Pictorial Biography*. New York: Grosset & Dunlap, 1977.
Gargan, William. *Why Me? An Autobiography*. Garden City, NY: Doubleday, 1969.
Hanson, Patricia King, executive editor. *The American Film Institute Catalog: Feature Films, 1931–1940*. Berkeley: University of California Press, 1993.
Hanson, Patricia King, executive editor. *The American Film Institute Catalog: Feature Films, 1941–1950*. Berkeley: University of California Press, 1999.
Harris, Warren G. *Gable and Lombard*. New York: Simon & Schuster, 1974.
Haver, Ronald. *David O. Selznick's Hollywood*. New York: Alfred A. Knopf, 1980.
Hayne, Donald, editor. *The Autobiography of Cecil B. DeMille*. Englewood Cliffs, NJ: Prentice-Hall, 1959.
Head, Edith, and Jane Kesner Ardmore. *The Dress Doctor*. Boston: Little, Brown, 1959.
Heimann, Jim. *Out with the Stars: Hollywood Nightlife in the Golden Era*. New York: Abbeville Press, 1985.
Hirschhorn, Clive. *The Columbia Story*. New York: Crown, 1990.
Hirschhorn, Clive. *The Universal Story*. New York: Crown, 1983.
Jordan, Rene. *Clark Gable*. New York: Pyramid Publications, 1976.
Kanin, Garson. *Hollywood*. New York: Viking, 1974.
Maltin, Leonard. *Carole Lombard*. New York: Pyramid Publications, 1976.
Mann, William J. *Wisecracker*. New York: Viking Penguin, 1998.
Matzen, Robert. *Fireball: Carole Lombard*

Bibliography

and the Mystery of Flight 3. Pittsburgh: Goodknight Books, 2014.
Matzen, Robert D. *Carole Lombard: A Bio-Bibliography*. Westport, CT: Greenwood Press, 1988.
McBride, Joseph, editor. *Focus on Howard Hawks*. Englewood Cliffs, NJ: Prentice-Hall, 1972.
Milland, Ray. *Wide-Eyed in Babylon*. New York: William Morrow, 1974.
Miller, Patsy Ruth. *My Hollywood: When Both of Us Were Young*. Brigantine, NJ: O'Raghailligh, 1988.
Morella, Joe, and Edward Z. Epstein. *Gable and Lombard and Powell and Harlow*. New York: Dell, 1976.
Munden, Kenneth W., executive editor. *The American Film Institute Catalog: Feature Films 1921–1930*. New York: R.R. Bowker, 1971.
Niven, David. *Bring on the Empty Horses*. New York: G.P. Putnam's Sons, 1975.
Ott, Frederick W. *The Films of Carole Lombard*. Secaucus: Citadel, 1972.
Parish, James Robert. *The Paramount Pretties*. New Rochelle, NY: Arlington House, 1972.
Parsons, Louella. *Tell It to Louella*. New York: G.P. Putnam's Sons, 1961.
Platt, Frank C., editor. *Great Stars of Hollywood's Golden Age*. New York: Signet, 1966.
Quinlan, David. *Quinlan's Film Stars* (5th edition). Washington, D.C.: Brassey's, 2000.
Quinn, Anthony. *The Original Sin*. Boston: Little, Brown, 1972.
Quirk, Lawrence J. *The Films of Fredric March*. New York: Citadel, 1971.
Ritchie, Donald. *George Stevens: An American Romantic*. New York: Museum of Modern Art, 1970.
Rubin, Benny. *Come Backstage with Me*. Bowling Green, OH: Bowling Green State University Popular Press, ca. 1972.
St. Johns, Adela Rogers. *The Honeycomb*. Garden City, New York: Doubleday and Co., 1969.
St. Johns, Adela Rogers. *Love, Laughter and Tears: My Hollywood Story*. New York: Doubleday, 1978.
Samuels, Charles. *The King: A Biography of Clark Gable*. New York: Coward-McCann, 1961.
Sarris, Andrew. *You Ain't Heard Nothin' Yet*. New York: Oxford University Press, 1998.
Sennett, Mack, and Cameron Shipp. *The King of Comedy*. Garden City, NY: Doubleday, 1954.
Stack, Robert, with Mark Evans. *Straight Shooting*. New York: Macmillan, 1980.
Stevens, George, Jr. *Conversations with the Great Moviemakers of Hollywood's Golden Age, at the American Film Institute*. New York: Vintage, 2007.
Swindell, Larry. *Screwball: The Life of Carole Lombard*. New York: William Morrow, 1975.
Thomas, Bob. *Selznick*. Garden City, NY: Doubleday, 1970.
Thompson, Charles. *Bing: An Authorized Biography*. New York: David McKay, 1975.
Thomson, David. *The New Biographical Dictionary of Film*. New York: Alfred A. Knopf, 2004.
Tornabene, Lyn. *Long Live the King*. New York: G.P. Putnam's Sons, 1976.
Truffaut, François. *Hitchcock*. New York: Simon & Schuster, 1967.
Turconi, David. *Mack Sennett*. Paris: Editions Seghers, 1966.
Turner, Lana. *Lana: The Lady, the Legend and the Truth*. New York: E.P. Dutton, 1982.
Wayne, Jane Ellen. *Clark Gable: Portrait of a Misfit*. New York: St. Martin's, 1993.
Wayne, Jane Ellen. *Gable's Women*. New York: Prentice-Hall, 1987.
Weinberg, Herman G. *The Lubitsch Touch*. New York: E.P. Dutton, 1968.
Wilkerson, Tichi, and Marcia Borie. *The Hollywood Reporter*. New York: Arlington House, 1984.
Yablonsky, Lewis. *George Raft*. New York: McGraw-Hill, 1974.

Index

Numbers in **_bold italics_** indicate pages with illustrations

Abel, David 85, 87, 91
Accent on Youth (1935 film) 43
Admirable Crichton (1957 film) 123
Admirable Crichton (play) 122
Adrian 91
Adrian, Iris 131
Agnew, Robert 70
Aherne, Brian 155, 156
Alexander, Katherine 153
Alice Adams (1935 film) 44
Allen, Gracie 25, 33, 34, 122, 147
Allwyn, Astrid 133, 134
Allyson, June 141
Alper, Murray 159
An American Tragedy (1932 film) 24
Ames, Adrienne 30, 104, 105, 111
Anderson, Doris 20
Annapolis Farewell (1935 film) 46
Arizona Kid (1930 film) 19, 92–93
Arlen, Richard 25
Armstrong, Robert 18, 86, 87, 89, **_90_**, 91
Arnold, Jack 166
Arnt, Charles 142
Arthur, Jean 21
Astor, Mary 18
Atwill, Lionel 161
Auer, Mischa 137, **_139_**, 140
August, Joseph 29, 73, 108, 123
The Awful Truth (radio, 1940) 166

Bacon, Irving 76, 77, 78, 82, 84, 86, 88, 103, 147
Ball of Fire (1941 film) 68
Bancroft, Anne 164
Bancroft, George 25
Bankhead, Tallulah 21, 35, 50
Banton, Travis 24, 30, 31, 33, 35, 37, 44, 47, 52, 99, 100, 102, 104, 105, 109, 111, 112, 114, 118, 119, 122, 127, 133, 135, 139, 141, 144, 146, 148, 150
Barbier, George 103, 109
Barnes, Anita 77, 84, 86
Barraud, George 15, 87
Barrie, James M. 33, 122
Barriscale, Bessie **_14_**, 86

Barry, Philip 15, 18
Barrymore, John 11, 35, 36, 52, **_123_**, 124, 125, 146
Barthelmess, Richard **_42_**
Barty, Billy 144
Basquette, Lina 15, 86
Baxter, Warner 19, 35, 92, **_93_**, 93
Beach Club (1928 film) 13, 77
Beatty, May 155
Beavers, Louise 94, 150
Bedtime Story (1941 film) 68
Beecher, Janet 135
Behrman, S.N. 19, 31, 116
Bellamy, Ralph 133, 148, 150, 166
Belmore, Lionel 77
Bennett, Alma 75, 78, 84
Bennett, Constance 18, 124
Bennett, Joan 14, 41, 83, 86
Benny, Jack 63, 64, 67, 161, 162, 163
Berman, Pandro S. 154
Bernds, Edward 36, 106, 108, 123
The Best Man (1928 film) 78
The Best People (1925 film) 20
The Best People (play) 94
Bevan, Billy 13, 75, **_76_**, 77, 78, 79, **_80_**, 82, 84, 86, 89
Bickford, Charles 18, 91, 118, 119
Bicycle Flirt (1928 film) 13, 79
The Big Broadcast (1932 film) 25, 26
Big News (1929 film) 18, 80, 89–90, 92
Bing, Herman 124
Binyon, Claude 52, 146
Blackmer, Sidney 30, **_111_**, 111
Blackton, J. Stuart 8
Blandick, Clara 101
Blane, Sally 5, 9, 39
Blue, Monte 70
Bluebeard's Eighth Wife (1938 film) 52
Blystone, John G. 70
Bogdanovich, Peter 6
Bolero (1934 film) 32, 33, 35, 38, 40, 52, 119–121, 132
Bond, Ward 106, 150
Boom Town (1940 film) 61
Borzage, Frank 11

169

Index

Boswell Sisters 25
Boteler, Wade 72, 90
Bow, Clara 21
Bowers, John 12
Boyd, William 17, 83, **88**, 88
Bradley, Grace 41
Brady, Alice **139**, 139, 140
Brecher, Egon 127
Bressart, Felix 161
The Bride Comes Home (1935 film) 43, 44
Brief Moment (1933) 31, 32, 38, 62, 116–117, 133
Brooks, Louise 97
Brooks, Mel 164
Brown, Lansing 39
Bruce, Virginia 94
Burke, Johnny 77, 84, 87, 88
Burlesque (play) 49, 141, 142
Burns, George 25, 33, 122, 147
Burton, David 38, 116, 128
Butterworth, Charles 142
Buzzell, Edward 27, 106, 107
Byington, Spring 165
Byron, Walter 104

Cagney, James 24, 25
The Campus Carmen (1928 film) 86–87
The Campus Vamp (1928 film) 13, 83, 84
Capra, Frank 38, 78, 124, 129, 145
Cardinale, Claudia 75
Carey, Harry 157
Carillo, Leo 130
Carr, Trem 80
Carroll, Nancy 21, 25, 28, 49, 142
Carson, Jack 159, 166
Cecil, Nora 144
Chandler, George 97, 138, 144
Chaplin, Charlie 8, 57
Charters, Spencer 153
Chase, Ilka 95
Chatterton, Ruth 21, 124
Chevalier, Maurice 22, 25, 31
Chierichetti, David 44, 115, 134
Churchill, Burton 111
The Circle (radio, 1939) 165
The Citadel (1938 film) 155
Claire, Ina 35
Clausen, Carl 69
Cline, Edward 76
Clyde, Andy 13, 75, 76, 77, 78, 82, 88, 89
Coburn, Charles 150, 152, 153
Coghlan, Junior 97
Cohen, Emanuel "Manny" 25, 36, 41
Cohn, Harry 26, 27, 28, 33, 35, 36, 38, 43, 63, 107, 108, 116, 124
Colbert, Claudette 21, 25, 33, 40, 43, 44, 45, 52, 61, 124, 134
Collier, Buster 67

Collyer, June 84
Columbo, Russ 32, 39, 40, **41**, 43, 92, 143
Compson, Betty 159
Compton, Joyce 28, 101, 108, 136
Compton, Juliette 103
Comrade X (1940 film) 61
Conan Doyle, Arthur 74
Connolly, Walter 39, 108, 124, 128, 145, 145
Conway, Jack 130
Cook, Donald 116
Cooper, Gary 14, 25, 28, 38, 52, 74, 79, 80, 101, **102**, 102, 108, **127**, 127, 128
Cooper, Harry 11
Coote, Robert 155
Corrigan, Lloyd 103
Cortez, Ricardo 24, 103, 104
Cosgrove, Jack 150
Cosgrove, Luke 73, 104
Coslow, Sam 146
The Cowboy and the Lady (1938 film) 102
Cowen, William J. 87
Cradle Song (1933 film) 44
Crawford, Joan 9, 10, 28, 68
Crawford, Kathryn 19, 94
Crisp, Donald 74
Cromwell, John 57, 60, 150, 152, 152
Cronin, A.J. 154, 155
Crosby, Bing 25, 33, 34, 39, 42, 122
Cross My Heart (1946 film) 148
Crowther, Bosley 154
Cukor, George 58, 59
Cullum, John 126
Cummings, Irving 74
Cunningham, Cecil 111, 142
Cushing, Peter 155

D'Agostino, Albert S. 135
Dailey, Dan 142
Dale, Esther 150, 159
The Dance of Life (1929 film) 49
Dantine, Helmut 162
Dare, Diana 77
Datig, Fred 19
Davenport, Harry 150
Davey, Allen 72, 73
Davidson, Max 74
Davidson, William 73
Davies, Marion 110
Davis, Bette 50
Death Takes a Holiday (1934 film) 44
De Brulier, Nigel 80, 85
Dee, Frances 21, 24
De Grasse, Robert 154
De Grasse, Sam 75
De Leon, Walter 89, 137
Dell, Dorothy 35, 38
Delmar, Vina 133
Demarest, William 133

170

Index

DeMille, Cecil B. 16, 18, 31, 75, 91, 119, 123
DeMille, William C. 104
Dent, Vernon 13, 77, 78, 79, *80*, 82, 84, 86, 87
Design for Scandal (1941 film) 63
De Silva, Fred 73
Dick Turpin (1924 film) 9, 70
Dietrich, Marlene 21, 25, 31, 40, *42*
Dinehart, Alan 112, *113*, 114
The Divine Sinner (1928 film) 13, 14, 80–81
Dix, Beulah Marie 87
Dix, Marion 19, 94
Dixon, Jean 140, 142
Donnelly, Ruth 133
Don't Get Jealous (1929) 16, 89
Doran, Ann 144
Doran, Mary 80
Douglas, Melvyn 43, 64
Drake, Frances 117, 120
Dreier, Hans 119, 126, 131, 137, 141, 146
Drew, Pat 46
Drew, Roland 18, 91
Dugan, Tom 146
Dumbrille, Douglas 137
Dunn, Emma 159
Dunn, Josephine 94
Dunne, Irene 141, 166
Durand of the Bad Lands (1925 film) 10, 73
Dvorak, Ann 31
Dwan, Allan 6, 69
Dynamite (1929 film) 18, 91–92

The Eagle and the Hawk (1933 film) 30, 114–116
Early to Wed (1925 film) 11, 12
Eburne, Maude 161
Edeson, Arthur 84
Edwards, Harry 75, 77, 78, 79, 81, 82, 84, 86, 87
Eight Girls in a Boat (1933 film) 35
Eilers, Sally 13, 16, 84, 87, 88
Ellis, Diane, 16, 17, 18, *88*, 89
Emery, Gilbert 99, 127
Emmett, Fern 150, 153
Epstein, Julius J. 149
Errol, Leon 33, 122
Erwin, Stuart 26, *100*, 100
Exclusive (1937 film) 51

Fair, Elinor 71
Fairbanks, Douglas 6
Falkenberg, Jinx 144
Farley, Dot 13, 76, 79, *80*, 82, 86
Farnum, William 113
Farrell, Charles 97, 116
Fast and Loose (1930 film) 20, 94–96
Fay, Frank 144, 157
Faye, Julia 75, 91

Feld, Fritz 146
Fellowes, Rockliffe 73
Fellows, Robert 83
Fenton, Leslie 73
Fields, Madalynne "Fieldsie" 13, 27, 54, 76, *81*, 81, 82, 87
Fields, W.C. 25
Fighting Eagle (1927) 74
Fischbeck, Harry 114, 118, 126
Fitzgerald, Cissie 78
Fitzroy, Emily 155
Fleming, Victor *59*, 60
Flowers, Bess 133, 140
Flynn, Errol 67
Fonda, Henry 166
Fools for Scandal (1938 film) 54, 148–150, 151
Forbes, Brenda 155
Forbes, Ralph 124
Ford, John 9
Foster, Norman 21, 22, 96, 101
Foster, Preston 45, 135
Foulger, Byron 153
Four Hours to Kill (1935 film) 44, 134
Francis, Kay 21, 22, 29, 60, 99, 124, *153*, 153, 154, 166
Frawley, William 120, 137, 138
French, William 68
From Hell to Heaven (1933 film) 30, 111–112, 121
Fuller, Dale 124

Gable, Clark 1, 27, 28, 33, 40, 46, 48, 53, 54, 55, 56, 57, *58*, *59*, 62, 63, 64, 67, 74, *109*, 109, 110
Gallagher, Skeets 96, *100*, 100
Garceau, Jean 55
Gargan, Edward 133
Gargan, William 157, 158
Garner, Peggy Ann 153, 154
Garnett, Tay 83
The Gay Bride (1934 film) 39, 130–131
The Gay Divorcee (1934 film) 140
Gaynor, Janet 54, 74, 97
George, Gladys 141
Geraghty, Carmelita 82, 84, 86, 87, 89
Gering, Marion 101, 131
Gerrard, Henry 94
Gibbons, Cedric 91
Gibson, Diana 136
Gibson, Wynne 21, 28, 97, 98
Gilbert, Billy 13, 75, 77, 86
Gilbert, Florence 74
The Gilded Lily (1935 film) 44, 134
Girardot, Etienne 124
The Girl from Everywhere (1927 film) 76
The Girl from Nowhere (1928 film) 81
Glass, Gaston 138

Index

Glazer, Benjamin 109, 119, 122
Gleason, James, 88
Goddard, Paulette 57
Going Hollywood (1933) 110
Gold and the Girl (1924 film) 9, 71
The Gold Digger of Weepah (1927 film) 13, 75
Gold Heels (1924 film) 70
The Gold Rush (1925 film) 8
Goldwyn, Samuel 12
Gone with the Wind (1939 film) 49, 54, 55, 58, 59, 60
Goodrich, Frances 100
Goodwin, Bill 166
Gordon, Mack 31, 34
Gordon, Maude Turner 99
Goulding, Alf 77, 78, 86
Goulding, Edmund 109
Grable, Betty 142
Grand Hotel (1932 film) 30, 112
Granstedt, Greta 86
Grant, Cary 25, 27, 30, 37, 40, *42*, 44, 60, 62, 104, 114, *153*, 153, 154, 160, 166
Grant, Lawrence 94, 97
Granville, Charlotte 127
Gravet, Fernand 53, 54, 148, *149*, 149
Gray, Mack 131
The Great Ziegfeld (1936 film) 48
Greene, Graham 154
Greene, W. Howard 144
Grey, Nan 136
Grey, Shirley 106, 111
Grey, Virginia 56
Griffies, Ethel 118, 155
Griffith, Corinne 21
Griffith, Edward H. 16
Grot, Anton 148

Hackett, Albert 100
Hale, Alan 70, 83
Hale, Jonathan 153
Hale, Louise Closser 108
Half a Bride (1928 film) 14, 18, 19, 79
Hall, Alexander 104
Hall, Gladys 56
Hall, Mordaunt 19, 28, 101, 105, 112, 114, 123
Hall, Porter 47, 137, 146
Halperin, Victor 30, 112
Halton, Charles 159, 161
Hamilton, Margaret 144
Hammerstein, Oscar II 141
Hammond, Virginia 131
Hands Across the Table (1935 film) 43, 44, 45, 46, 133–135, 137
Harding, Ann 18, 124
Hardy, Sam 89, 130
Hare, Lumsden 137

Harlow, Jean 17, 28, 68
Harris, Winifred 91, 95, 155
Hart, Sunshine 75, 78, 84
Harvey, Forrester 114, 136
Hatch, Eric 47, 139
Hathaway, Henry 126
Haver, Phyllis 75
Hawks, Howard 11, 35, 36, 73, 123
Head, Edith 24, 52, 146
Hearst, Jack 7
Hearts and Spurs (1925 film) 10, 72
Hecht, Ben 36, 50, 60, 123, 144
Heisler, Stuart 122
Hell's Angels (1930 film) 16, 17
Hepburn, Katharine 44, 50, 60
Hiatt, Ruth 78, 82
Higgin, Howard 17, 18, 83, 88, 91
High Voltage (1929 film) 17, 88–89
Hillie, Verna 111
Hinds, Samuel S. 131
His Unlucky Night (1928 film) 82
Hitchcock, Alfred 62, 159
Hobbes, Halliwell 161
Hohl, Arthur 116, 128
Holiday (1930 film) 18
Hollander, Frederick 146
Holloway, Sterling 76, 81
Holmes, Phillips 24, 106
Honky Tonk (1941 film) 63
Hope, Bob 62, 101, 166
Hopkins, Arthur 141
Hopkins, Harry 64
Hopkins, Miriam 20, 21, 22, 25, 27, 32, 33, 34, 36, 38, 50, 63, 95, 116, 162
Hopper, Hedda 91, 144
Hopwood, Avery 20, 94
Horn, Camilla 12
Hornblow, Arthur, Jr. 137
Horton, Edward Everett 165
Hot Saturday (1932 film) 27
The House That Shadows Built (1931 film) 103
Howard, Kathleen 128
Howard, Sidney 15, 60, 87, 156, 157
Howard, William K. 47, 137, 149
Howland, Olin 144, 150
Hubby's Weekend Trip (1928 film) 86
Hughes, Howard 16
Hughes, Rupert 99, 103
Hunt, J. Roy 152
Hurlock, Madaline 76, 77
Hurst, Paul 91
Hutton, Betty 148

I Take this Woman (1931 film) 24, 101–103
Idiot's Delight (1939 film) 55
If I Had a Million (1932 film) 28, 108
In Name Only (1939 film) 60, 106, 152–154

172

Index

In Name Only (radio, 1939) 165
Ince, Bill 7
Irene 152, 159, 161
Island of Lost Men (1939 film) 119
It Happened One Night (1934 film) 32, 41, 43, 60, 124, 126
It Pays to Advertise (1931 film) 21, 96–97

Jaffe, Sam 19
Jazz Singer (1927 film) 16
Jeans, Isabel 148
Jenkins, Allen 148
Johnson, Kay 91
Johnson, Noble 118
The Johnstown Flood (1926 film) 74
Jolie, Angelina 161
Jolson, Al 16
Jones, Buck 9, 10, 71, **72**, 73
June, Ray 104, 130
The Jungle Princess (1936 film) 49

Kahn, Madeline 126
Kanin, Garson 61, 156
Karlson, Phil 135
Karns, Roscoe 94, 124
Kemp, Matty 75, 84, 87, 88
Kennedy, Edgar 124, 146
Kennedy, Joseph P. 14, 16, 18
Kennedy, Tom 89, 97
Kent, Crauford 86, 114
Kenton, Erle C. 111
Kenyon, Charles 70
Keystone Cops 13
Kibbee, Guy 97, 98
Kilbride, Percy 118
Kilian, Victor 157
The King and the Chorus Girl (1937 film) 53
Kiss and Make Up (1934 film) 37
Kline, Kevin 126
Kohler, Fred 70
Korda, Alexander 161
Korda, Vincent 161
Krasna, Norman 62, 133, 159, 160
Kruger, Alma 150

La Cava, Gregory 18, 43, 47, 80, 89, 139, 140
Ladies' Man (1931 film) 22, 99–100
Lady By Choice (1934 film) 38, 128–130, 133
Lady for a Day (1933 film) 38, 129, 130
The Lady from Cheyenne (1941 film) 68
Lamarr, Hedy 61
LaMotte, Jean 73
Lamour, Dorothy 49, 142, 143
Landau, David 102
Landi, Elissa 31, 35, 118
Lane, Charles 125, 144

Lang, Charles 103, 104, 122
Lang, Walter 29, 54, 108, 135, 136
Langham, Ria 28, 46, 48, 54, 57, 58
La Rocque, Rod 75
La Roy, Rita 92, 104, 112
La Rue, Jack 106
The Last Command (1928 film) 24
The Last Train from Madrid (1937 film) 51
Laughton, Charles 25, 31, **32**, 61, **118**, 118, **157**, 157, 158
Lawford, Betty 135
Lawrence, Florence 74
Lawrence, Gertrude 116
Lawrence, Marc 118
Lawson, John Howard 91
LeBaron, William 51, 131
Leigh, Vivien 58, **59**
Leisen, Mitchell 43, 49, 74, 83, 85, 91, 114, 115, 119, 133, 141, 143
Leontovich, Eugenie 35
LeRoy, Mervyn 148, 149
Levant, Oscar 144
Lewin, Albert 146
Lewis, Jerry 145
Lewis, Vera 144
Lichtman, Al 8
Lightnin' (1925 film) 9
Lights of New York (1928 film) 16
Limehouse Blues (1934 film) 39
Little Annie Rooney (1925 film) 8
Littlefield, Lucien 70, 71, 97
Living it Up (1954 film) 145
Lloyd, Doris 155
Loder, John 91
Loff, Jeanette 91
Logan, Jacqueline 70, 83
Lombard, Carole: birth 3; death 66–68; divorce from William Powell 30; marriage to Clark Gable 58; marriage to William Powell 22; romance with Clark Gable 46; use of profane language 10–11, 47
London, Jack 19
Long, Walter 45
Lord, Robert 74
Love Before Breakfast (1936 film) 45, 135–137
Lowe, Edmund 10, **71**, 72
Loy, Myrna 47
Lubitsch, Ernst 20, 26, 41, 43, 45, 51, 63, 64, 133, 134, 145, 161, 164
Lucas, Wilfred 92
Lugosi, Bela 30
Lukas, Paul 24, **103**, 103, 104
Lux Radio Theatre 62, 165, 166

MacArthur, Charles 36, 123
MacDonald, J. Farrell 109
MacDonald, Jeanette 25

173

Index

Mackaill, Dorothy 109
MacMurray, Fred 44, 45, 47, 49, 52, 133, 134, 137, 138, 141, *142*, 143, *146*, 146, 147, 166
Macpherson, Jeanie 91
MacWilliams, Glen 92
Made for Each Other (1939 film) 57, 150–152
Made for Each Other (radio, 1940) 166
Malden, Karl 158
Male and Female (1919 film) 123
Maltin, Leonard 67, 139, 158
Mamoulian, Rouben 20
Man of the World (1931 film) 22, 97–99
Mander, Miles 161
Mankiewicz, Herman J. 97, 99
Mann, Hank 92
Manners, David 111
Mannix, Eddie 67
March, Fredric 25, 30, 50, 114, *115*, 144
Margo 131
Marion, Frances 122
Marion, George, Jr. 122
Maris, Mona 19, 92, *93*, 93
Marley, Peverell 83, 85, 91
Marriage in Transit (1925 film) 10, 71
Martin, Dean 145
Martinelli, Arthur 112
Matchmaking Mamas (1929 film) 16, 87–88
Mate, Rudolph 161
Mayberry, Mary 78, 82
Mayer, Edwin Justus 87, 161, 163
Mayer, Louis B. 33
McAvoy, May 73
McCarey, Leo 145
McCrea, Joel 18, 92
McCullough, Philo 70
McDaniel, Hattie 144, 147
McElwaine, Dan 16
McEnery, Peter 75
McIntosh, Burr 84
McKee, Raymond 78, 82
Me, Gangster (1928 film) 14, 84–85
Mendes, Lothar 99
Menzies, William Cameron 150
Mercer, Beryl 112
Merivale, Philip 159
Merkel, Una 146, 147
Merman, Ethel 122
Merrily We Live (1938 film) 141
Mescall, John 88
Methot, Mayo 106
Michael, Gertrude 120
Middleton, Charles B. 118
Milland, Ray 33, 44, 120, 122, 134
Miller, Arthur 74, 89
Miller, Patsy Ruth 67
Miller, Seton I. 114

Mills, Howard D. *66*
The Mills Brothers 25
Milner, Victor 97, 99, 101
Minter, Mary Miles 5
Mr. and Mrs. Smith (1941 film) 61, 62, 159–161
Mr. and Mrs. Smith (radio, 1941) 166
Mitchell, Geneva 94
Mitchell, Grant 109
Mitchell, Julien 155
Mix, Tom 9, 70
Mong, William V. 108
Montana, Bull 71
Montgomery, Robert 32, 33, 62, 159, *160*, 166
The Moon's Our Home (radio, 1941)
Moore, Owen 17, 89
Morgan, Frank 35, *95*, 95
Morris, Chester 39, 104, *105*, 105, 130
Morris, Margaret 95
Mortimer, Edmund 71
Moscovitch, Maurice 153
The Most Happy Fella (play) 158
Motorboat Mamas (1928 film) 84
Mowbray, Alan 140
Mulhall, Jack 151
Muni, Paul 48
Muse, Clarence 112
My American Wife (1936 film) 41
My Man Godfrey (1936 film) 47, 48, 52, 60, 80, 139–141, 145, 147, 161
My Man Godfrey (radio, 1938) 165
Myers, Kathleen 70, 71

Nagel, Conrad 18, 91
Naish, J. Carrol 119
Ned McCobb's Daughter (1928 film) 15, 87
Neill, Roy William 71
Newman, Alfred 154, 157, 158
Newmeyer, Fred 94
Ninotchka (1939 film) 164
Nissen, Greta 16
Niven, David 46, 141, 165
Nixon, Marion 73
No Man of Her Own (1932 film) 28, 52, 109–111
No More Orchids (1932 film) 28, 45, 108–109, 110
No One Man (1932 film) 24, 103–104
Nolan, Lloyd 44
Nothing Sacred (1937 film) 50, 51, 144–145, 148
Now and Forever (1934 film) 38, 126–128
Nugent, Edward J. 101
Nugent, Frank S. 143, 148

Oakie, Jack 25, 28, 30, 108, 111, 114
O'Brien, George 74

174

Index

O'Brien, Pat 27, *106*, 106, 107
O'Keefe, Dennis 131
One Way Passage (1932 film) 29
Osborne, Vivienne 112, 114
Ottiano, Rafaela 155
Overman, Lynne 131, 146
Owen, Seena 131
Owsley, Monroe 116, 131

Page, Bradley 111, 137
Page, Rita 155
Pallette, Eugene 96, *139*, 139
Pangborn, Franklin 140
Pantages, Dixie 7, 9, 12
Panzer, Paul 74
Paris Bound (1929 film) 16
Parnell (1937 film) 54
Parsons, Louella 8
Patrick, Gail 131, 140, 165
Patterson, Elizabeth 109
Pembroke, Scott 13, 80
Pendleton, Nat 39, 130
A Perfect Crime (1921 film) 7, 69
Perry, Kathryn 12
Peters, Elizabeth Knight "Bess" (mother of Carole Lombard) 3, 43, 65, 66
Peters, Frederick (father of Carole Lombard) 3, 4, 43
Peters, Frederick, Jr. "Fritz" 3, 4, 6, 7, 21
Peters, Jane Alice (see Lombard, Carole)
Peters, Stuart 3, 4, 6, 21, *26*
Peterson, Carol 7
Pickford, Mary 8
Pidgeon, Walter 63
Pigott, Tempe 148
Pitt, Brad 161
Pitts, Zasu 130, 131
Plunkett, Walter 144, 154
Polglase, Van Nest 152, 154, 156, 159
Pollard, Daphne 13, 76, 77, 78, *81*, 81, 82, 84, 87, 88
Pommer, Erich 156
Porcasi, Paul 131
Powell, William 22, *23*, 23, 24, 25, 27, 28, 29, 31, 47, 48, 97, *98*, 98, 99, 109, 110, 139, 165
Power (1928 film) 14, 83
Previn, Charles 139
Prevost, Marie 133
The Princess Comes Across (1936 film) 45, 47, 137–139
Pringle, Aileen 144
Prinz, LeRoy 120, *132*
The Private Life of Henry VIII (1933 film) 31, 119
Pryor, Roger 39, 128, 129
Purcell, Gertrude 108, 135

Qualen, John 144
Quillan, Eddie *14*, 15, *85*, 86, 150

The Racketeer (1929 film) 91, 92
Radwin, Marcella 55
Raft, George 25, 32, 33, 38, 39, 40, 47, 55, *120*, 120, 131, *132*, 132
Raine, Norman Reilly 118
Rainer, Luise 48, 141
Ralston, Esther 20, 79
Ralston, Marcia 148
Rand, Sally 120
Rapf, Harry 130
Ravel, Maurice 119
Raymond, Gene 44, 62, 116, 117, 159, 160, 166
Rebecca (1940 film) 62
Reeve, Arch 19
Reeves, Alfred 8
Remember the Night (1940 film) 52
Reynolds, Lynn 73
Reynolds, Vera 80, 81
Rich, Irene 87
Ridges, Stanley 161, 163
Rinehart, Mary Roberts 101
Riskin, Robert 27, 32, 33, 38, 40, 106, 107, 124
Roach, Bert 136
Road to Glory (1926 film) 11, 73
Roberts, Theodore 87
Robertson, Willard 106, 113
Robin Hood (1921 film) 6
Robson, May 38, 39, 128, *129*, 129
Rogers, Charles "Buddy" 19, 25, 94
Romero, Cesar 45, 46, 135, *136*, 137
Roosevelt, Pres. Franklin D. 67
Rosenbloom, Maxie 144
Ross, Shirley 101
Rub, Christian 137
Ruggles, Wesley 28, 43, 52, 109, 110, 110, 146
Rumann, Sig 137, 144, 161
Rumba (1935 film) 38, 39, 40, 41, 131–133
Run, Girl, Run (1928 film) 77
Runyon, Damon 128
Russell, Rosalind 63
Ryskind, Morrie 47, 139

Safety in Numbers (1930 film) 19, 20, 94
Sailor Beware 42
St. Johns, Adela Rogers 68
Salter, Thelma 86
Santell, Alfred 19, 92
Sarris, Andrew 37
Saunders, John Monk 114
Schertzinger, Victor 19, 94
Schildkraut, Joseph 35
Schulberg, B.P. 19, 25

175

Index

Scott, Randolph 25, 30, 40, 112, *113*
The Sea Wolf (1930 film) 19
Sebastian, Dorothy 9, 12
Selznick, David O. 19, 49, 54, 55, 57, 58, *59*, 59, 62, 144, 150
Selznick, Myron 24, 26, 46,49, 53, 58, 59, 62
Sennett, Mack 13, 16, 75, 76, 77, 78, 79, 81, 82, 84, 86, 87, 89
Seward, Billie 124
Shamroy, Leon 150
Sharp, Henry 111
Shaw, Peggy 70
She Married Her Boss (1935 film) 43
Shea, Gloria 120
Shearer, Douglas 91
Shearer, Norma 28, 45, 46, 55, 141
Sheehan, Winfield 8, 9, 19, 29
Sherman, Richard 152
Shirley, Anne 61, *155*, 155, 156
Show Folks (1928 film) 15, 85–86
Sidney, Sylvia 21, 25, 31, 43
The Sign of the Cross (1932 film) 119
Sinners in the Sun (1932 film) 25, 39, 104–106
Sisters Under the Skin (1934 film) 35
Skelly, Hal 142
Skipworth, Alison 104, 137
Smiling Lieutenant (1931 film) 22
Smith, C. Aubrey 108
Smith, Kate 25
Smith's Army Life (1928 film) 77
Smith's Pony (1927 film) 13, 75
Smith's Restaurant (1928 film) 82
Somewhere I'll Find You (1942 film) 64, 66
Sothern, Ann 42
Spewack, Bella 130
Spewack, Sam 130
Stack, Robert 161, *162*, 163
Standing, Guy 114, 127
Stanwyck, Barbara 49, 52, 57, 68, 111, 142
Starrett, Charles 95
Stein, Paul 15, 85
Steiner, William 95
Stephens, Harvey 49, 142
Sterling, Ford 73
Stevens, George 60, 154
Stevens, Ruthelma 108
Stewart, James 57, 150, *151*, 152, 165, 166
Stolen Harmony (1935 film) 41
Stone, John 72
Stone, Milburn 138
The Story of Louis Pasteur (1936 film) 48
Stout, Archie J. 96
Stradling, Harry 156, 159
Strickling, Howard 60
Struss, Karl 100
Sturges, John 156

Sturges, Preston 20, 52, 94, 100
Sullavan, Margaret 166
Supernatural (1933 film) 30, 112–114, 121
Sutherland, A. Edward 100
Sutton, Grady 140
Swain, Mack 76, 81
Swanson, Gloria 123, 124
Swerling, Jo 38, 128, 150
The Swim Princess (1928 film) 13, 78
Swindell, Larry 7, 10, 51, 92, 110, 143
Swing High, Swing Low (1937 film) 49, 141–143
Sylvia Scarlett (1935 film) 44

Tailored by Toni (radio, 1939) 165
Talbot, Lyle 108
Tallichet, Margaret 47
Talmadge, Constance 5
Tamiroff, Akim 131
Tashman, Lilyan 21, *100*, 100
Taurog, Norman 122
Taxi! (1932 film) 24, 25
Taylor, Dwight 128
Taylor, Kent 118
Taylor, Robert 57
Tell, Olive 99
Tempest (1928 film) 11,12, 36
Temple, Shirley 38, *127*, 127, 128
Tennant, Barbara 84
Terry, Don 84
Tetzlaff, Ted 31, 44, 47, 116, 117, 128, 131, 133, 135, 136, 137, 139, 141, 146, 148, 150
Thalberg, Irving 16, 45, 55
Thalberg, Sylvia 126
Thanks for the Memory (1938 film) 101
Thatcher, Heather 148
Thew, Harvey 112
They All Kissed the Bride (1942 film) 63, 64, 68
They Knew What They Wanted (1940 film) 61, 156–158
Thin Man (1934 film) 47
To Be or Not to Be (1942 film) 63, 64, 67, 161–164
To Be or Not to Be (1983 film) 164
Todd, Arthur 70
Tone, Franchot 44
Too Hot to Handle (1938 film) 55
Tover, Leo 33, 109, 119
Tracy, Spencer 61, 67
Tracy, William 159
Trowbridge, Charles 101
True Confession (1937 film) 52, 146–148
Truffaut, François 62
Tucker, Richard 94
Turner, Lana 63–64, 66
Tuttle, Frank 96
Twelvetrees, Helen 9

176

Index

Twentieth Century (1934 film) 1, 35, 36, 37, 38, 41, 47, 52, 123–126, 140, 161

Unger, Gladys 91
Union Depot (1932 film) 112
Up Pops the Devil (1931 film) 22, 100–101

Vail, Lester 101
Van Dyke, W.S. 70, 72
Van Upp, Virginia 141
Varden, Norma 148
Vaughn, Hilda 101
Vigil in the Night (1940 film) 60, 154–156
Vincent, Allen 108
Vinson, Helen 153
Virtue (1932 film) 27, 28, 106–108
Von Eltz, Theodore 92, 93, 101
Von Seyffertitz, Gustav 84
Von Sternberg, Josef 24

Wadsworth, Henry 95, 96
Wake Up and Dream (1934 film) 39
Walburn, Raymond 128
Walker, Joseph 106
Walker, Nella 153
Walker, Stuart 31, 114, 117
Wallace, Richard 97
Walsh, Raoul 57, 84, 85
Ware, Helen 101
Ware, Irene 101, 116
Warner, H.B. 112, 114
Warner, Jack L. 53, 149
Washburn, Bryant 21, 97
Watson, Lucile 150, 159
Watts, Richard, Jr. 39
Waxman, Franz 135
The Way to Love (1933 film) 31
Wedding Present (1936 film) 41
Wellman, William A. 144

We're Not Dressing (1934 film) 33, 34, 122–123
West, Mae 25
Westman, Nydia 111
Westmore, Wally 49
Wharf Angel (1934 film) 35, 36, 38, 124
Wheeler, Lyle 144, 150
White, Pearl 3
White Corridors (1951 film) 156
White Woman (1933 film) 31, 32, 61, 117–119, 143
White Zombie (1932 film) 30, 113
Whitman, Phil 82, 84, 89
Whitney, John Hay 46
Wilkerson, Billy 23
Wilkerson, Edith **23**
Williams, Kathlyn 3
Wilson, Carey 119
Wilson, Dorothy 35
Wilson, Lois 21, 97
Wilson, Marie 148
Wing, Toby 147
Winkler, Otto 60, 64, 65
Winninger, Charles 144, 145
Wolff, Nat 62, 63
Wong, Anna May 119
Woolley, Monty 144
Worthington, William 79, 108
Wray, Fay 35
Wyman, Jane 140

Yost, Dorothy 71
Young, Loretta 5, 25, 68
Young, Polly Ann 5, 9
Young, Robert 166
The Young in Heart (1938 film) 54

Zukor, Adolph 41